Hornets
over
Kuwait

HORNETS

OVER
KUWAIT

JAY A. STOUT

Naval Institute Press
Annapolis, Maryland

The views expressed are those of the author and do not reflect
the official policy or position of the Department of Defense,
the Department of the Navy, or the United States Marine Corps.

Library of Congress Cataloging-in-Publication Data
Stout, Jay A., 1959–
    Hornets over Kuwait / Jay A. Stout.
        p.   cm.
    ISBN 1-55750-835-6 (alk. paper)
    1. Persian Gulf War, 1991—Personal narratives, American.
    2. Persian Gulf War, 1991—Aerial operations, American.
    3. Stout, Jay A., 1959–   . I. Title.
    DS79.74.S76   1997
    956.7044'248—DC21   96-49844

Printed in the United States of America on acid-free paper ∞
04 03 02 01 00 99 98   9 8 7 6 5 4 3 2

For my beautiful wife, Monica. Her unfailing love, sacrifice, and support are an unceasing source of wonderment to me. And for my daughters, Kristen and Katherine. Their unquestioning love in the face of my shortcomings is a selfless gift of which I am not worthy. My family is my life raft.

Contents

Author's Note

This is not a story about heroic deeds in the face of daunting odds. There weren't a whole lot of those in the Gulf War. Indeed, there were very few occasions that even called for the type of courage that characterized the battles of the world wars, Korea, and Vietnam. Though he possessed the means, the enemy did not possess the will or the determination to seriously challenge the threat arrayed against him. And so there was relatively little loss of life on our side. However, the pain and grief of those who did lose loved ones is neither forgotten nor belittled because of this.

Instead, this is my record of participation as a Marine Corps aviator, from just before the initial movement of coalition forces to a month or so after the cease-fire. It has been told without embellishment, just as events occurred, recorded while the events were still fresh in my mind. Where memory failed, or details became blurred,

I referred to a journal I kept through the entire period. Rather than dwell on grand strategy (something I had only a general knowledge of then—and even now), I have concentrated on the individual pilot's point of view. How I got there, what I ate, what the missions were *really like*. Because the experiences related are typical for marine Hornet pilots involved in the conflict, perhaps this book will not only be useful as a historical document but also make interesting reading.

Additionally, I want to highlight marine aviation's part in the war. Many people have no idea that the Marine Corps even flies jets. Yet during the conflict, except for the U.S. Air Force (which was executing its primary mission, its reason for being), the marines flew more strike missions than any other service—indeed, any other nation!

Finally, I am still on active duty in the U.S. Marine Corps as I write this, as are many of the people mentioned. Overwhelmingly, the people I have known and worked with have been among the finest this nation produces. It is a fact of life, however, that every organization, whether it builds cars, sells insurance, or makes war, has in its ranks people who are best described as boobs, or goofs. I've tried to make life a little less hard for the boobs by not using their names. The goofs too. I must also remind the reader that many of my views are a matter of opinion. The way I describe events or people (true as that description might be) may differ from the manner in which others might describe them.

Chapter One
First Mission Southern Iraq

Fumbling anxiously around the cockpit, trying to figure out what, if anything, should be done next, I swallowed and suddenly became firsthand familiar with the phrase. *The Taste of Fear.* All at once acid, bitter, metallic, and distracting. And it was being caused by nothing more mysterious or complex than an upset stomach. Stomach bile. From a very nervous, bordering on terrified, stomach. My stomach.

Now I knew. Some variation or twist of the phrase had been in use from the time of Hercules all the way up to today's techno-adventures. The secret was mine. I knew what they were talking about because it was happening right that very moment to someone no more gallant than a very frightened Yours Truly. The Taste of Fear, indeed. It was nothing that couldn't be remedied by a trip to Grandma's medicine cabinet. Here, have an Alka-Seltzer, Mr. Indiana Jones.

At any rate, I felt my digestive system had plenty to be nervous about. Right along with the rest of my systems: respiratory, circulatory, and reproductive. It was night. Dark. And despite what all the glossy aviation editions in the bookstores say, it doesn't matter whether you're in an F/A-18 Hornet with all the latest in advanced targeting systems or a Cessna with a flashlight. When you look out the window, you can't see anything. And what you can't see can get you. And if it doesn't want to get you, then you can run into it. Simply put, my way of thinking was, and still is, there's no sense flying at night because you can't see anything. It was hard enough when there was no one shooting at you, and my nervous stomach knew that there was indeed someone shooting at me. Lots of someones.

Crossing the coast into Iraq, it seemed that targeting my, and everyone else's, fearful stomach, in the fifty or so aircraft in the strike, was about every sort of weapon the Iraqis could send skyward. . . .

Chapter Two

Marine Corps Air Station
Beaufort, South Carolina

August 1990 found me assigned to the finest fighter squadron in the Marine Corps. The Warlords of VMFA-451 (VMFA stands for Fixed-wing Marine Fighter Attack) were one of six F/A-18 squadrons based at the Marine Corps Air Station (MCAS) in the marshy low country of Beaufort, South Carolina.

As a four-year captain, at thirty years of age, I had been in the Marine Corps for nine years. Previous stints included a tour flying F-4 Phantoms in Beaufort and a three-year tour as an intermediate jet instructor in Beeville, Texas. I had just completed transition training to the F/A-18 Hornet in March 1990, and so was relatively new to the Hornet, despite solid experience in other airframes.

The billet, or job, I had been assigned was that of the S-4, or logistics officer. What that really meant was that I was held accountable for everything from toilet paper acquisition to the movement of unit personnel and equipment when it came time to deploy. If it had any-thing remotely to do with a supply or logistical matter, I was respon-sible for it. To say that this was not a sought-after job would be an understatement. Fighter pilots don't care about pencils, paper clips, or urinal cleanliness. Fighter pilots like to supervise lots of marines in the maintenance of their mounts. Or schedule and execute fighter sweeps against aircraft from other services or nations. But fighter pilots *do not,* in any fashion or form, enjoy bothering about facility maintenance or the location of the CO's (commanding officer's) parking spot.

Unfortunately, when I checked aboard the squadron, the current S-4 officer had orders elsewhere and I was a perfect fit. When I got wind of the impending assignment, my first impulse as a true profes-sional, an officer of marines, duty-bound and brimming with integrity, was to hide out and wait until some other poor sucker checked in. But it was too late, and besides, there is nowhere to hide in Beaufort.

Actually, "supply" in the Marine Corps is something of a misnomer. To supply your own squadron, you generally wait until a neighbor-ing unit is out of town, then use a "master key" (bolt cutter) to gain access to that unit's spaces and whatever was left behind. Using proper channels to get supplies is akin to ordering a new car in Russia. I have no doubt that supplies I ordered in 1990 are just now arriving at the Warlord Logistics Shop.

The other major responsibility associated with my billet, the expe-ditious, orderly, and safe embarkation of all squadron personnel and equipment, was one I was soon going to exercise in a real-world, crisis scenario.

Chapter Three

No, I'm Sure We're Not Going Anywhere

Well, it was true. I *was* sure. We really hadn't been involved in much of anything since Vietnam. At first glance, developments in the Persian Gulf didn't seem much different than any of a number of others that had occurred in the last fifteen years.

For at least a couple of weeks, the Iraqis had been allowing as to how the rich oil fields both it and Kuwait shared really belonged in their entirety to Iraq. To reinforce their way of thinking, and perhaps readjust the Kuwaiti perspective, they had moved men, material, and equipment close to their common border. All of this had been reported in newspapers and magazines throughout the United States, where from my point of view, it didn't seem to create much concern.

And then, incredibly, they invaded Kuwait. I can remember standing in front of the TV in the squadron ready room, watching the initial

reports and footage of Iraqi armor and helicopters in downtown
Kuwait City. The reports described the confusion and the desperate
(and ultimately hopeless) defense being put up at the palace. Most
of all though, I recall remarking to a fellow pilot that the whole thing
seemed amazingly simple-minded and crude. And that Saddam
would almost certainly get away with it. He gave a kind of half-smile
and nodded. Like most of the rest of us, he probably didn't even
know where Kuwait was, and at that time didn't care.

After all, since our last late, great, adventure in Southeast Asia, we
hadn't been very eager to involve ourselves too deeply in other
nations' conflicts. Though we had supplied rebels with some limited
arms support in Afghanistan, we certainly had not aided them by
directly confronting the Soviet Union. Again in our own hemisphere,
arms support and some training in El Salvador and Nicaragua, but
not much more. Earlier we had fumbled and bumbled a rescue
attempt of hostages in Iran with disastrous effects to our national
prestige and confidence. The tragedy in Beirut was much worse.
Granada and Panama had indeed involved U.S. troops in direct
combat, but nothing on the scale of what would be required to drive
Hussein's army out of Kuwait. An ironic fact was that, only a couple
of years earlier, we had been quasi-allied with Iraq against Iran in
our efforts to keep shipping routes in the Persian Gulf open and safe.

The weekend following the invasion found me with my wife,
Monica, en route to Indiana to retrieve our children from a visit with
our families. When you've spent a lot of time in the military, moving over and over again, sixteen-hundred-mile weekend road trips
don't seem to be such a big deal. I explained to my wife that even
though I personally felt that U.S. intervention was warranted, there
was no way we would do much about it militarily. Again, while
home, I pooh-poohed the idea raised by many of my relatives that I
would soon find myself en route to the Middle East. There was, however, as reported in the news, a very stiff stance being taken by the
president, as well as by the United Nations. This surprised me.

I had a bigger surprise waiting for me when I returned to work
the following week. The skipper (slang for commanding officer) had

called a meeting of the squadron's department heads. One consolation of being the S-4 officer was that I was a department head, thus one of the first to know when something was afoot. And something was.

Aside from the invasion itself, there were other things Hussein was doing which were not endearing him to the world community. There was the proclamation that Kuwait was now a part of Iraq. There was the taking of Western hostages, as well as atrocities against both the military and the civilian populace of Kuwait. And very notable, perhaps most important of all, there was the threat to Saudi Arabia (a major source of the West's imported oil). There were alarming reports of troops and equipment being massed along the border with Saudi Arabia, perhaps poised for a strike straight through the Arabian Peninsula.

Our commanding officer had just returned from a meeting with the group commanding officer (in the Marine Corps a group is composed of several squadrons) and the other squadron skippers throughout the group. If the United States was going to get involved in the crisis in Kuwait, there was no doubt that the marines were going to be major players. If marines were going to be deployed anywhere on the ground in significant numbers, they were going to have marine air support. Marine air support meant F/A-18s.

At that moment there was no concrete plan for how many or which units from Beaufort would deploy, if, indeed, the marines deployed any aviation elements at all. But that morning it was tentatively decided that if the balloon went up, two other squadrons would deploy. Our unit, VMFA-451, was to be a backup.

Following another meeting later that morning, it was decided that perhaps our squadron would fill a contingency role aboard an aircraft carrier if the navy requested help. Our unit had been deployed aboard the USS *Coral Sea* for a Mediterranean cruise the previous year and still had some carrier-experienced personnel. Finally, following another meeting in the afternoon, it was decided that the Warlords of VMFA-451 would be one of the two primary squadrons that the group (or MAG, marine aircraft group) in Beaufort would send if the call went out.

Why, and how, the final decision was made was probably based on a number of factors, including personnel strength, aircraft maintenance, experience of squadron personnel, and, not least, personality. Good or bad, our commanding officer, Lieutenant Colonel Andrew S. "Scotty" Dudley, had personality. A *strong* personality. He had taken command of the squadron about the same time I had arrived five months previous, and came with a wealth of experience.

As a first lieutenant while carrier-deployed off the coast of North Vietnam, he was wingman to the legendary "Bear" Lassiter when the latter had scored the only marine air-to-air kill in Vietnam (from a marine aircraft; at least one marine on exchange with the air force had also bagged a MIG). In fact, Scotty had fired a missile during the same engagement at a separate MIG and there was speculation that this aircraft had also been downed, but there was never any confirmation. At any rate, the engagement was rated a mixed success as both Lassiter's and Scotty's jets (F-4 Phantoms), targeted by surface fire and low on gas, were lost.

Scotty's hallmark while commanding officer of VMFA-451 was concern for his troops, and mission accomplishment. If this meant stepping on some toes, then there were going to be some sore feet. My personal hunch with regard to our unit's selection for deployment to the Middle East was that Scotty jumped up and down, and screamed and yelled, until the group skipper relented and gave our squadron the nod. This may not have been the case, but if I told that story to anyone who knew Scotty it would be accepted with little hesitation.

At any rate, President Bush having drawn his "line in the sand," I watched television a few days later as U.S. Air Force F-15s departed for Saudi Arabia, and realized that, just maybe, I would be a participant in this thing, whatever it might develop into.

Chapter Four

Getting Ready to Go

Getting ready to go to war is something rarely shown in the movies. Usually Johnny America hits the beach "guns a' blazin'," engages the enemy in a number of skirmishes (in which he loses a buddy or two), and then, in one last great encounter, glowing handsomely in a masterfully applied Hollywood patina of blood, sweat, and battlefield grunge, prevails over the wicked and evil enemy.

What the movies don't show is how Johnny got to the beach. Or who issued him his ammo and uniform. Or Johnny getting three dozen inoculations. (He would be flirting with the nurses, unintimidated by the needle. Not like real people. I faint.) How 'bout Johnny's last will and testament and power of attorney? Who gets Johnny's stereo and checking account when he gets caught in that unscripted barrage of friendly artillery fire?

In the real world we had a lot to do. First, the jets themselves. You just don't grab a set of keys, jump inside, and go. A marine fighter squadron is assigned twelve jets. Typically, one or two of those jets will be out of the squadron undergoing modification or depot-level repair. Another one or two will be nonflyable because of lack of parts or engines. And perhaps another will be under some sort of scheduled maintenance, not unlike warranty work you might have done on your car. A normal marine fighter squadron will usually have six to eight "racers" ready to fly on any given day.

But a squadron goes to war with twelve. To make that happen involved a great deal of work and sacrifice on the part of everyone in all six Hornet squadrons of Marine Aircraft Group 31, and the rest of MCAS Beaufort.

The jets that were away on a modification line were replaced "out of hide" from units that were not scheduled to deploy in the first wave. To say that this hurt some feelings would only be scratching the surface ("Not only am I *not* going, but I have to give up *my jets* so *they* can go!"). Additionally, parts that were in short supply and keeping some jets down appeared seemingly out of nowhere. Personnel from all squadrons pitched in to ensure that the deploying jets were as mechanically sound and well prepared as possible.

The actual preparation of the aircraft was quite involved. First, just for the trip over, each jet had to be fitted with three external 330-gallon fuel tanks. After loading the tanks, the jets had to be flown and refueled airborne to ensure that the entire fuel system was working correctly. As it was unknown what the situation would be when the squadron arrived in theater, it was decided to fly over armed with missiles and loaded guns. Drawing the ammo from a peacetime base was, in itself, no small evolution. This, along with the tweaking of weapons systems, and the actual loading, kept our ordnance folks plenty occupied.

Mechanically, the aircraft were given a thorough going-over. Engines were checked for remaining flight hours and high-time components. Electrical and hydraulic systems were checked and fine tuned. The airframe itself was groomed for missing fasteners, loose panels, and corrosion.

Aircraft never deploy far from a ready parts supply. Where we were going there was none, so it was to be embarked with us. Again, the parts seemed to mysteriously appear from nowhere. This was startling, as even in the best of times parts are always in short supply. The magic "goody locker"? Some guys had their money on the "parts fairy." Actually, there seemed to be little contingency packages loaded with essential items squirreled away for just this sort of event.

Augmentation of the squadron with additional personnel also quickly got under way. A marine fighter squadron is designed to have a certain number of personnel assigned to complete its mission in wartime. This is called the table of organization, or TO. In real life, because of budget constraints and the demands of other activities (the lifeguard staff comes to mind), the squadrons are never manned at TO. A unit manned at 80 percent of TO would be considered "fat." Filling the rosters of the deploying squadrons was done, again, at the expense of those units remaining behind. That they maintained their humor so well is to their credit.

Then there was the endless list of small details. Updating of personnel and medical records. Immunizations. Locating and issuing clothing and equipment appropriate to the location. Preparation of orders and embarkation lists. And on and on.

Personal gear. Where does America shop before it marches off to war? In Beaufort's case it was Wal-Mart. The place was packed. Every Marine Corps haircut within fifty miles was in the place, buying everything from snuff to socks. Myself, I bought some reading material, shaving supplies, and two hundred rounds of nine-millimeter pistol ammunition. For some stupid reason I felt that the standard issue of thirty rounds was going to be insufficient to hold off the enemy if I was shot down and had to defend myself with my pistol (I would be lucky if I didn't shoot myself).

And finally, the movement itself. My supposed specialty. Except for the CO, who was busy handling details at the elephant level, none of us had ever been to a war before. What do you take, and what do you not take? How exactly were we and our stuff going to get there? And very important, where exactly were we going?

To make it sound like we were not used to deploying would be untruthful. In fact, marine squadrons typically deploy three or four times a year. It's the name of their game. Quick reaction. A potent force ready to go in a moment's notice. But in practice we usually had at least a couple of months' notice. This gave us time to plan what we were going to do, what we needed, and, of course, where we were going.

In fact, at the time we had been putting on the final touches for a huge multiservice deployment to Puerto Rico. In a way this helped ease preparations for the deployment to the desert. If nothing else, we weren't starting from scratch.

But now! And for real! I had bales of razor wire showing up on my doorstep packaged and ready to go. The stuff was great for breaking up a massed frontal assault by troops on foot, but I wasn't sure we even had anyone who knew how to lay it out. And did we need it? Whenever we deployed to Zoomie Air Force Base, in Anystate, U.S.A., we didn't take all this goofy stuff. Two hundred water cans? I wasn't sure I had enough space for all my aircraft parts, much less this.

Fortunately, I wasn't alone in the S-4 shop. I had working for me First Lieutenant Kevin "Wolf-Boy" Iiams. Wolfy—tall, skinny, and a whole lot smarter than me—was from the New Orleans area and was officially my embarkation officer. This didn't mean that he was trained or knew anything about the job. All it meant was that when he checked into the unit, the billet was open. The Marine Corps doesn't necessarily believe in formal training when adequate experience and performance can be gained by making very costly mistakes.

Additionally, and probably most importantly, we were blessed with two trained logisticians. Corporal Cunningham and Lance Corporal Davis fortunately were sharp enough to persuade their officer in charge (Yours Truly) to make the right decisions when it was absolutely crucial, as well as dynamic enough to provide the leadership and motivation to get the squadron properly prepared for embarkation. What couldn't be accomplished through normal channels, these men could do through hook and crook. If not, then they could persuade someone else to do it for them. Great marines.

And finally, I had Gunnery Sergeant Rosenberg as my ace in the hole. New to the squadron, he volunteered to help the S-4 shop get the squadron moving in the right direction as we began to gear up for the operation. He quickly made himself indispensable, giving my corporals horsepower and direction as required, and drawing upon his years of experience to find a way around seemingly impossible obstacles. Funny how it worked out, but somehow there seemed to be just enough going on logistically that I was able to justify hanging on to Gunny Rosenberg until we made it back to the States. He was an aircraft electrician by trade.

So, how exactly were we getting there? A long, long, time ago, when the various branches of the military were defining their turf, the U.S. Air Force and the Marine Corps, with I'm sure lots of prodding from someone's subcommittee, or its equivalent, reached an agreement. The gist of it was that the marines would not get into the big jet transport aircraft business, leaving that pot of money to the air force. In return, when it came time to move marines in large numbers, the air force would provide the means. This freed the marines from the burden of buying and maintaining an expensive fleet of large transports and made more assets and cash available to the air force and their heavy lift capability. Anyway, that's the story I heard.

Well, just about everybody in the world who had an association of some sort with the U.S. military was on alert for possible deployment. Consequently, the air force was busy. *Real* busy. A target date for departure was set, and planning for the airlift was begun.

He who plans early, plans twice. The dates changed. The type of lift available changed. The amount of lift available changed. My feelings for the air force and professional logisticians changed. The squadron packed, unpacked, repacked, and backtracked, over a period of about a week. Finally, as patience grew in short supply and tempers began to show, a halt was called until final, definitive, double-secret, absolutely conclusive word was received.

It was, and two days later transports were being loaded as the squadron prepared to leave.

Chapter Five
Saying Good-Bye

S ometimes the movies show Johnny leaving for war. Usually it's a great "torn from the arms of a lover" scene at the pier, in a train station, or riding out of Fort Apache. And sometimes it probably really is like that. But not usually.

They usually don't show Johnny's wife nervously throwing up in the toilet prior to his departure. Or Johnny's mother screaming and crying into the phone with long-distance pleas for him not to go. And Johnny usually doesn't have any children to wonder, terrified, if Daddy's ever going to come back.

In my own family, though there was an unsettled, anxious feeling in the house, there was no tremendous fear yet. After all, we weren't actually at war. And most people felt we would probably not go to war, at least not unless directly attacked. I felt we would probably sit at the sidelines wringing our hands while our diplomats engaged in fruitless negotiations. Then, finally, we'd give up, make up some excuses, and go home. Having not really committed to winning anything since World War II, this scenario seemed entirely plausible, if not probable.

Monica did well. While she was understandably anxious, she was realistic and did nothing to make leaving any harder on me than it already was. While we discussed all the possibilities, we didn't dwell on the prospect of me being hurt or killed. She was very respectful of my sensitivities and didn't ponder aloud how she would lead a merry widow's life on the considerable insurance settlement. What a gal! Though, now that I think about it, I distinctly recall that she was whistling happily as she helped me pack my bags. And what about all those slick travel brochures and expensive clothing catalogs?

The kids were okay. Being eight and six, I'm not sure they really understood everything that was going on. I'd been leaving on various deployments all their lives, so my leaving was nothing new to them. But they did understand that this time I was going to leave for a long time, and that we weren't sure when I was going to come home. Additionally, watching Daddy pack a helmet, flak jacket, and other war-fighting gear was, if not as disturbing to them as to their mother, certainly strange.

My parents handled it in different ways. Dealing with my mother (I love her dearly) was awful. She shrieked, screamed, cried, begged, and pleaded for me not to go. I dreaded hearing the phone ring, fearing it might be her again. So rock sure was she of my demise that it left me nervous and wondering about a mother's intuition. Looking back now, it's tempting to make light of her concern, though I realize I shouldn't. Lots of mothers, on both sides, lost their baby boys. To watch your son march off to perhaps kill, or be killed, must be one of the most wretched experiences on earth.

Dad's response was classic. Of the "I know you've got a job to do, and I'm sure you'll make us proud" genre, there was concern and worry in his voice, but he was determined not to make things hard for me. It made me think of all the ball games, hunting and fishing trips, and other "man" things we had done together, and I felt very close to him.

As for the rest of the squadron, I'm sure reactions were wide and varied. I'm sure that among the young enlisted marines in the barracks there was more of a sense of adventure than among those of us who had families. And in the other families, there were no doubt, when compared to my household, both stronger and milder reactions to the deployment.

Chapter Six
Getting There

We were scheduled to leave at about midnight on 20 August 1990. It was early evening when I pulled into the squadron parking lot with my family and unloaded my gear. We said good-bye then and there, rather than hanging around in the ready room or elsewhere, where my attention would be drawn from them and the pain of parting would drag on. Watching my wife and young girls as they drove off was very upsetting. I dragged my sleeve across my face a couple times before I joined the rest of the pilots in the ready room.

The atmosphere inside was only a little shy of chaotic. There were marines with their families, armorers handing out weapons, all manner of baggage, and people trying to take care of last minute details. I was thankful that I had said my good-byes outside.

Outside, troops were being marshaled and cargo was being loaded.

Our gear was traveling on a mix of about everything the air force had to offer: C-5s, C-141s, and KC-10s. (The C-5 and C-141 are cargo aircraft; the KC-10 is a converted DC-10 designed for aerial refueling but also capable of carrying passengers and cargo.) Our people would be traveling primarily on the KC-10s. On the flight line, the jets were being given final looks in preparation for the upcoming Atlantic-spanning flight.

Finally, inside, all nonessential personnel were shooed out and the preflight briefing was given. Most of the pilots had not done an Atlantic crossing before and the newness lent an edge to the upcoming flight. Airspeeds, altitudes, and divert bases (the latter in case of accidents or other problems) were briefed, as well as appropriate weather information. Of critical importance, aerial refueling procedures, the tanker rendezvous, and the refueling plan were thoroughly covered. With the briefing finally over, there wasn't a whole lot left to do other than to get suited up, get in the jets, and go. Not quite as simple as it sounds.

Flight gear for a jet aviator consists of about forty-five pounds of straps, buckles, helmet, life preserver, survival gear, and other assorted equipment, packaged in a fashion that would bring a smile of satisfaction to even the most hardened sadist. It is uncomfortable. But at least it's difficult to put on. And no matter how many trips to the rest room are made, ten minutes after becoming airborne, Mr. Bladder always transmits that familiar little twinge. A small and gentle reminder of what's to come an hour or two later into a ten-hour hop.

That night was very hot and humid. Before we even finished wrestling ourselves into our flight gear, we were drenched in sweat. After preflighting, loading our personal gear, and strapping ourselves into our jets, we were exhausted. At least it was bedtime and we only had a ten-hour flight ahead of us.

The night was very dark, and because the aircraft were loaded with live ordnance, they were parked in a special area, far removed from our own familiar flight line. This added a bit to the confusion as we started and checked our aircraft and began to taxi to the runway for takeoff. We were to get airborne in two seven-ship flights separated by half an hour. One aircraft in each flight was a designated airborne spare from another squadron, but flown by a pilot from our unit. In the event that one of our squadron jets was unable to get airborne, or experienced mechanical difficulties after taking off, the airborne spare would take its place. If things went well, the spare would return to base soon after takeoff. Each flight would be accompanied by an air force KC-10, which carried the fuel we would need for the ocean crossing, as well as cargo and many of the squadron personnel.

Tonight there was going to be a delay. As our flight, with Scotty in the lead, approached the runway, ground control told us that there was a problem with the KC-10s. They were overloaded. Way overloaded.

Fog of war and all that. Somehow a mistake had been made and the big airframes needed to be lightened. From what I learned later, the air force crews tried everything except the old "boiling oil" ruse to keep our marines and cargo from climbing on board. Actually, they were more professional than that, and after some calculating decided that they could download some fuel and still get airborne with enough to get the Hornets across "the pond."

While the fuel was being downloaded, the fighter crews, who had parked and shut down, crawled out for some nervous chitchat, and perhaps to relieve themselves under an aircraft wing. Finally, downloading complete, cargo and passengers ready, the KC-10s were ready. The F/A-18s of VMFA-451 were manned and started again, then launched into the darkness in preparation for the rendezvous with the tanker aircraft.

After launching, the Hornets joined on Scotty's ship, three on each side, as he flew a wide circle. Joined finally, and about five miles from the airfield, pointed down the runway, Scotty gave the signal for the KC-10 to start its takeoff roll, and the flight executed a perfect rendezvous as the big tanker lifted from the runway. Talking to Wolfy (who had been a passenger on the tanker) a few days later, I learned that the KC-10 crew chief had turned to him after the aircraft had lifted, using every bit of the thirteen-thousand-foot runway, and with a face as white as a sheet had exclaimed, "That was the God-damndest, longest-assed, takeoff roll" he'd ever experienced.

That was the sort of effort the airlift professionals from the air force were producing day in and day out, for the duration. Flying their aircraft right on the margins of airframe limitations, they performed tremendously. Truly, without the work done by these folks, the entire campaign would not have been possible.

Joined with the tanker, the fighter aircrews settled in and checked their aircraft as the entire flight climbed through scattered layers of weather. The trip ahead would be made at an altitude somewhere around twenty-three thousand feet and would involve seven to nine midair refuelings, depending on winds and weather encountered during the trip.

Midair refueling. Depending on the situation, it can be a "piece of cake" or a gut-twisting evolution that might mean the difference between life and death. The marines and navy use the "probe and drogue" system of aerial refueling. In simple terms, a transferring aircraft (the tanker) trails a length of hose with a basket attached to the end. The receiving aircraft (generally fighter or attack types) maneuver to a position behind the tanker from where they can fly forward and insert their refueling probe into the basket. Once contact has been made, the basket couples with the probe and fuel is transferred.

For an experienced pilot, daytime aerial refueling in smooth air is a walk in the park. Throw in some turbulence and the exercise can get a bit interesting. Make it dark and now interesting becomes frustrating. Throw in an aircraft emergency on top of all that. Over frigid North Atlantic water where no man can survive. And put five of your closest friends in line behind you, desperately wishing your probe into the basket so that you can finish and they can refill their fuel-hungry jets (that is, if *they* don't have any problems). Add for more tension an impending war. The pressure can range from none at all to enough to literally drive a man to tears.

But there wasn't going to be any pressure for "Guinness" (me) tonight. My trip was going to end real soon. Checking my fuel, I noted that I was carrying a lot less than I should have been, and it was disappearing faster than it should have been.

"Anyone else got 11.9 on the gas?" I said over the back, or second, radio, which our flight had set up on a "chitchat" frequency.

"Nope. Hey Guinness, that jet's been venting lately. Try switching to 'stop transfer.'"

What this meant was that the fuel system on my jet had been over-pressurizing and dumping fuel overboard from vents located in the vertical stabilators. Because it was dark, no one, including myself, had noticed. And I hadn't been quick enough to catch it on my gauges.

"Guess what, Guinness." That was Scotty.

"Yeah, I know sir."

Because my jet was lower on fuel, and had a problem which could be critical on a long oceanic crossing, I would have to return to Beau-fort and my place would be taken by our flight's airborne spare. That spare was being flown by John "Hatch" Borneman, augmented to us from VMFA-122 just for this contingency. Hatch, noisy, smart, and well liked, proved not only to be handy in this instance but would become invaluable as our flight schedule officer and all-around great pilot.

"See ya, Guinness." Hatch was not making the slightest effort to hide his pleasure. As the airborne spare, he had been scheduled to return to Beaufort if all the airplanes had been in good shape. From there he would board a marine KC-130 Hercules (a tanker and cargo aircraft), which carried our trail maintenance personnel and gear. That KC-130 would be making a long, uncomfortable, multistop trip as it trailed our aircraft into theater. Instead of Hatch being on it, though, now it was going to be me.

"Yeah. See ya." Me. Not happy.

I picked up a separate clearance from Air Traffic Control and returned to base. En route, I had to wait for an F/A-18 from the other deploying Hornet unit, VMFA-333. This ship had a true emergency, as it had suffered a broken fuel connection and was in danger of flaming out before it could land. Fortunately it landed safely, and I touched down soon after.

In the scramble not to get left behind, I borrowed a car and dashed home to get a bag for the flight gear I had been wearing and would now have to lug halfway 'round the world. I gave my surprised wife (no boyfriends yet) a quick kiss as we hurriedly said another good-bye and made my way back to base and the waiting KC-130.

At the transport they were ready and waiting for me, but amazingly, they were also still waiting for the squadron's trail maintenance personnel. They were late and the aircraft was not going to wait much longer. I extracted a promise from them to wait another twenty minutes and went off to find the errant marines.

I found them. Supervised by our young maintenance material control officer, a hard-charging first lieutenant. They were in our hangar sweeping the deck, emptying trash cans, and otherwise squaring the place away.

I was ready to strangle them.

"Well, I was told to make sure we left this place cleaned up, and it's still trashed," the first lieutenant said.

"I'll tell you what," I said. "Saddam's not going to win just because we left a couple of full trash cans behind. Now get your boys together and let's get our asses over to that airplane."

Our young hard-charger always did what he thought was right. And he was hard to derail once he had set his objective. Finally I had him convinced that if he didn't hurry, other folks were going to be winning a war while he was left behind dusting furniture. We got the men together, manifested aboard the KC-130, and soon after droned airborne, headed for the desert.

Chapter Seven
Arrival in Theater

After a stop in the Azores for refueling, we touched down at Naval Air Station (NAS) Rota, in Spain, about twenty hours later. Rota was a madhouse. It served as the major stopping point for a great many of the aviation units en route to the Middle East and so was overwhelmed as it struggled to accommodate the masses of troops and aircraft of all services that were passing through.

And accommodate it did. Though the base was overrun, everyone was provided a place to sleep and plenty of chow. Booze was in no short supply either. Our marines appeared to be taking advantage of this fact even more so than usual, perhaps because of the prebriefed strict prohibitions against alcohol at our destination.

Our destination. Even at this point in our transit, our destination was far from certain. Prior to our departure we were given a number of possibilities. The obvious country to operate out of was Saudi

Arabia. Two other countries mentioned were the United Arab Emirates (UAE) and the Emirate of Bahrain. Because of some back-channel murmurings, Bahrain was the heavy favorite.

I hooked up with some of our squadron aircrew prior to their departure from Rota and found that except for some weather early on, the Atlantic crossing had gone fairly smoothly and the jets were in good shape. I also took some good-natured abuse for ending up as "baggage" aboard a KC-130 Hercules, instead of flying a jet out. As for our ultimate destination, they had still not received definitive word. They had been given some photocopied data on potential destinations and were told to be flexible in-flight. The data they had weren't illuminating. Airfield locations and diagrams, but not much in the way of frequencies or instrument flying procedures. A setup for an aerial carnival at best, if they encountered weather at their destination.

Still fearful of missing out on something, and anxious to get to our ultimate home base, I snooped around until I was able to find another KC-130 that would be departing about ten hours prior to our previous ride. So, after less than a day of rest, and having buried one or two bottles of booze deep in my personal gear, I grabbed a couple of young lieutenant pilots from our squadron and we were on our way again.

This KC-130, I believe, was carrying the trail maintenance effort for a Harrier unit. It had a hodgepodge of Harrier pilots, maintenance marines, their gear, and me and my lieutenants. With me were First Lieutenants Pete "Fattie" Depatie and John "Kato" Marion. Both were new, our squadron being their first operational unit. They were great. Exactly what lieutenants were supposed to be. Fearless, loud, aggressive, and young and ignorant enough that they weren't held particularly accountable when they screwed up. Which really wasn't too often. They would prove to be top-notch as developments unfolded. Fattie, though sturdy, wasn't fat and got his nickname, or call sign, because it rhymed with his last name. Kato, though not oriental, reminded us of the character of the same name from the Pink Panther movies.

Individuals get tagged with call signs for a number of different reasons. Last names account for many of them. I was dubbed Guinness because my last name, Stout, is also a type of beer, of which

Guinness is one of the more popular brands. Personality traits also account for some of our cute little monikers. "Grumpy" would be a good example. Or a particularly auspicious, or inauspicious, event in a person's career might earn him a call sign. "Puker" comes to mind. Call signs themselves often evolve into new call signs. By the time Fattie left the unit after the war, he was more often called "Fatman" than Fattie, for no particular reason whatsoever.

Between the Marine Corps and the navy, the traditions and reasoning behind call signs are pretty much the same. Some air force units, it seems to me, tend toward "hot-shot" or "he-man" type call signs and shy away from anything that might seem demeaning or emasculating to its bearer (though there are exceptions). I once was in an air combat training flight against the air force in which we were fielding "Dizzy," "Skeeter," and "Binky" against our Boys in Blue: "Venom," "Hammer," and "Hornet." The guys with the goofy names won.

This Hercules ride was like all the others. Too hot, too cold, cramped, very dry, and loud. No matter how far you're going, the ride seems to take forever. Usually the saving grace from a passenger's standpoint is the crew. Always accommodating, the crews generally have a fairly liberal interpretation of regulations, and once safely airborne, allow the passengers to sprawl about the cabin however they desire in order to "nest up" for the trip.

Whatever its shortcomings in passenger comfort, the Marine Corps would find it very difficult to operate without this aerial workhorse. Cargo mover, troop transport, and aerial refueler, this airframe is in constant demand. The Marine Corps could have three times the number of KC-130s that it does and still keep them all busy. In service since the 1950s, this great aircraft will be front-line deployed at least a couple of decades into the next century. Blasphemous as it may sound, the C-130 will probably eclipse even the dear old C-47/DC-3 as the hardest working cargo aircraft of all time. Indeed, the C-130 has been in continuous production for over forty years. The C-47/DC-3 was in production for twelve.

Following a late-night stop for fuel at Sigonella Naval Air Station, in Sicily, we took off, made our way across the rest of the Mediterranean,

Egypt, the Red Sea, and into the skies over Saudi Arabia. I knew that
Saudi Arabia was mostly desert, and I had a pretty good idea of what
desert was. But this was different than any I had trained over in the
southwestern United States. This was *real* desert. Bare and desolate.
Devoid of any of the scrub, or cactus, or even geographic relief familiar in training areas we worked in the States. Being airborne above
it made it seem even more forbidding, as it stretched from horizon
to horizon without a break. Only occasionally would we fly over an
encampment or town, usually sited at a spot that, from our perspective, offered no advantage over any of the surrounding geography. This was the view for hundreds of miles until, as we approached
the eastern coast, great circles of bright green vegetation gave lie to
irrigation-dependent farming. Additionally, oil drilling and refining
sites became more common the closer we came to the Persian Gulf.

Bahrain was our briefed destination when we left Rota, and oddly
enough, Bahrain was where we ended up. Upon reaching the Saudi
coastline we proceeded south for just a bit, then crossed the fifteen
miles or so of water that separate the Kingdom of Saudi Arabia and
the Emirate of Bahrain.

Situated just off the eastern coast of Saudi Arabia and just northwest of Qatar, Bahrain is a tiny island nation measuring approximately thirty miles on a line from north to south, and about eight
to ten miles from east to west. Formerly a British protectorate, the
island gained full autonomy in the early 1970s and is governed by a
ruling family, headed by an Emir. Its economy, once based largely on
oil, has shifted and is now centered on banking and commerce, earn-
ing it a reputation as somewhat of a Middle Eastern Switzerland.
Additionally, though overwhelmingly Islamic, the religious tolerance
of its government and people is a bit more relaxed than some of
the surrounding nations. Alcohol is not forbidden, and (somewhat
because of that) the island attracts a good deal of tourism from neigh-
boring countries.

The main attraction for us, besides the relatively laid-back attitude
toward Mr. Booze, was a then-secret air base at the southern end of
the island. Under construction long before there was any hint of

conflict with Iraq, the runway at Shaikh Isa Air Base had been finished only a few weeks when our jets touched down on 22 August. Roughly two and a half miles in length, the runway was paralleled by a taxiway that could be used for takeoffs and landings if necessary. Scattered around the airfield were a number of enclosed, armored, and reinforced hangars in which the Bahraini air force housed their F-16s and F-5s. About midfield was the main parking ramp and two hangars, which would be the home of our aircraft maintenance effort for the next seven or eight months.

The rest of the base consisted of various operations and maintenance buildings, living quarters for the enlisted men, a mosque, and dining facilities. All the structures were brand new, and some of them literally had not even been moved into yet. We felt almost as if the base had been custom made, completed just in time for our arrival.

But there were problems. The base was intended to support the Bahraini F-16s and F-5s, which numbered under fifty and were maintained by well under a thousand personnel. At the height of the war the United States would have nearly two hundred aircraft and five thousand personnel aboard the base. The Bahrainis were very gracious as they made room, and willingly gave over their showpiece facilities, for the newly arrived American forces.

Looking out the porthole-sized window of the Hercules, I was taking in the new surroundings as the big aircraft touched down and taxied to the main ramp to unload. It was hot already. Very hot. The heat grew much worse as the ramp was lowered and we grabbed our bags and started out. It was obvious to me, having been around aircraft for nearly ten years, that we had parked directly in the jet exhaust of another aircraft. I stepped out and looked for the offending aircraft. But it wasn't there. The stifling heat was caused by nothing other than season and geography. August in the Middle East.

Chapter Eight

Chain Saw Chicken

Beaufort had been a madhouse when we left. Shaikh Isa was even more chaotic. The troops had all arrived in the previous day or so and were still pouring in. They had slept wherever they could make room, inside and out. Several squadrons had been sleeping outside under a huge aircraft washrack. It was covered and up out of the sand. The earlier arrivals were sprawled on the hangar decks along with aircraft maintenance equipment. And a luckier few were crammed into the handful of air-conditioned maintenance shops.

Hygiene was quickly becoming a problem. There were just a few sinks, toilets, and showers, and these were being given a workout that I'm sure the designers never envisioned. Many of the toilet facilities were not what boys from Indiana had been raised with. Dubbed "porcelain slit trenches," they weren't much more than a recessed

VMFA-451 F/A-18A over Shaikh Isa, October 1990. Note the crowded, unprotected parking ramp. Troop tents are located at the upper right-hand part of the complex. *[Photo by author]*

porcelain receptacle set in the floor. No seat. One had to develop a straddle technique to use them, which I'm sure comes as second nature after years of practice. We'd had no practice, and I know that more than a couple of our nation's finest accidentally ended up relieving themselves into their dropped trousers rather than the intended target. Join the marines. See the world. Shit yourself.

The marines at this time had moved a number of squadrons onto the field. VMFAs 333 and 451 from MCAS Beaufort, South Carolina, VMFA-314 from MCAS El Toro, California, and VMFA-235 from MCAS Kaneohe Bay, Hawaii, all flew F/A-18s. VMA-224 (Fixed-wing Marine Attack) brought a complement of the tried and true A-6E Intruders from MCAS Cherry Point in North Carolina. Our electronic warfare capability was being provided by a detachment of EA-6Bs (tactical electronic warfare aircraft) from VMAQ-2 (VMAQ stands for Fixed-wing Marine Attack Electronic Warfare) out of Cherry Point as well. Also, at this time there were two Harrier squadrons out of Cherry Point, though they would soon be moved north into Saudi Arabia. With their limited range they weren't very useful based so far south.

VMFA-451 officers at Shaikh Isa, Bahrain, November 1990. *(Photo by author)*

We marines weren't the only U.S. service represented at the base. The air force had deployed a number of F-4G Wild Weasel aircraft from Germany. Though initially numbering only a dozen or so, by the time the war was in full swing, there would be close to fifty Wild Weasels operating out of Shaikh Isa. The air force's aircraft didn't magically maintain themselves either, and so along with the jets came a great many personnel. Because the F-4 is older and not so easily maintained as the newer jets, and because the air force has a different philosophy when it comes to deploying for war, there would eventually be more air force personnel on the base than marines, though they would own only about one-third of the jets.

The jets were crowded even more than the men. The parking ramp was literally stuffed with aircraft, so much so that the overflow aircraft were parked on the taxiway—unheard of in normal operations. We were parked so close that we had to fold our wings to get in and out of the line. Acceptable perhaps on an aircraft carrier, but awkward, if not dangerous, without specially trained and experienced taxi directors. There was a very real danger that we might become our own worst enemies and attrite our assets through taxiing and parking mishaps.

The parking situation posed another dilemma that was even more disturbing. So many aircraft in such a small area presented an incredibly enticing, and easy, target. From the air or the ground. We used to joke that a terrorist in a bad mood with a book of matches could have taken out half the assets on the base. I have no doubt that a handful of trained commando types, such as our navy SEALs (*sea, air, land*—the navy's special operations forces), could have easily mounted a raid and destroyed a significant number of our aircraft. It was a disaster of monumental proportions waiting to happen. But fortunately, it never did.

Early on we were vulnerable from the air as well. Had they the will or the wits to do it (*we* could have done it with *their* equipment), the Iraqis could have mounted an air strike that would have done horrible damage. A coup such as this, early on in Desert Shield, could have influenced American opinion away from deep involvement. But maybe not. Remember Pearl Harbor.

As it turned out, other than the occasional Scud lobbed our way during the war, there was never any enemy action taken directly against the base (that we ever knew about). We were very, very, fortunate.

Anyway, back to that hot-ass parking ramp. Kato, Fattie, and I were met by a couple of other pilots and hustled off to where the officers would be settled in. For us, the Bahrainis had set aside three or four brand new barracks buildings. Our unit had grabbed three large rooms in the building which we had been assigned. The rooms measured about twenty by thirty feet. When I arrived, the rest of the guys were in a frenzy, sweeping and clearing debris out of our rooms. The reason for the rush was twofold. First, we were anxious to get settled in, drop our gear, and set up a routine. Having said that to try to legitimize our hustle and bustle, the real reason involved more selfish motives. Furniture, in the form of bunk beds, twin beds, lockers, desks, and tables, much of it still in boxes, was scattered throughout the barracks compound. The quicker we could clear a place for it, the quicker we could collect and lay claim to the best of what was around. With the rest of the squadrons doing the same thing, the good stuff was disappearing fast. I pitched in without missing a step.

After all, we had just finished the "me" decade, and I could be just as selfish as the best of them.

When it was all finished, we had made out quite well. Nine of us had crammed into the room with a nice mix of bunk beds and twins, full sets of linen, a pair of desks, and a wall locker for just about everyone. In fact, we had done so well that we had stuff stashed, which we surrendered up to the less fortunate (less *conniving*) as they poked around the next few days, looking for beds and other necessaries.

The best part of our room was the environmental control system. Or air conditioning. We had two wall units that could have kept the place at fifty degrees Fahrenheit all year long had we wanted. Primitive, yet effective. In fact, with both of them going (cost of electricity be damned), walking back into the room barefoot from the shower, on the cold terrazzo floor, was almost painful. Having been raised on shortages and hardship in the Marine Corps, and well aware of the Marine Corps's ability to repair them should they wear out (zero), we decided to run only one at a time. This kept the room more than comfortable, and we stayed that way for the duration.

We dubbed ourselves "the Bunkhouse Boys," for no real reason, and settled in. I shared a set of bunk beds with John "Z-Man" Zuppan. Also known as "Z-Poon" and "Poon-Boy." I don't know why. He was a first tour pilot who had flown with the squadron during their Mediterranean cruise on board the Coral Sea the year before. He had thus gained a lot of experience and was a valuable player. "Z-Butt," as he was also known (his back end stuck out a bit), could also sleep better and longer than anyone I had ever known. More of a hibernation than sleep. We joked that he only spent about half the time deployed as the rest of us because he spent twice as much time asleep. And he could squirrel away more candy, goodies, and other "pogey bait" than a drugstore checkout stand. The man was incredible. We had a tremendous time together and shared a lot of laughs. His best trick, much to my annoyance, was to pull my blankets down on top of him in the middle of the night instead of getting up and turning down the air conditioner. I'd wake up cold, shivering, and miserable, groping around in the dark for my covers.

At the time, early in Operation Desert Shield, we had no idea how fortunate we were with respect to our housing. Our rotary wing brethren in Saudi Arabia were in the dirt in tents, and would stay there until after war's end. We thought it was a hardship to walk down the hall and have to shower and shave with everyone else on the floor. The poor helo "bubbas" were on water rationing, and shower hours, and were lucky to get a shower when they wanted.

The grunts, our marine infantrymen, and other ground types had it the worst. They often were quite literally in the sand, spending the nights wrapped up in poncho liners on the ground. These poor guys had to take care of showers and other hygiene needs when and where they could. It was quite a while before they were able to get gear, to include tents and cots, and get themselves up out of the dirt. Later, as the infantry and other types made their way to Shaikh Isa, they were stunned by our relatively palatial living arrangements. To say that there was a bit of jealousy would be a gross understatement. Many went more than out of their way to finagle a couple days with us at the air base, for nothing more than to get a good hot shower and some decent chow.

Chow. Food for the officers, just like the living arrangements, was a bit nicer than it was for the troops. Arabs in general seem to be more conscious of the distinction between officers and enlisted men—and all the perks and privileges that officers rate—than we are. We were provided access to the Bahraini officers' dining facility. A new, nicely furbished building (with real shitters in the rest rooms!), it was staffed by what appeared to be mostly Pakistanis and Bangladeshis. We were served on real china, with silver plate, on finely linened tables. The atmosphere was very relaxing, and after a time we even installed a large screen TV and a VCR in the lobby.

The food itself was a bit different than what we were used to. Lots of vegetables and rice, which was fine. Mutton too, which was down-right tasty depending on how it was prepared. Occasionally, we had a certain main course which was not particularly familiar. We called it "camel knuckles," but I think in the end we decided it was pigeon or some other smaller fowl. The chicken was the most oddly prepared dish. Generally it was baked or stewed, but the distressing thing about it was the way it was cut. With neither rhyme nor reason. It was almost as if the butcher was blindfolded with a whole chicken laid out before him and simply whacked away at it for a couple of minutes with an axe. The cut that ended up on your plate might be half of a thigh with a piece of the back and neck attached to it. With bone splinters throughout for good measure. We always maintained that behind every chicken dinner produced at that chow hall, there was a surly Pakistani with a blood-and-feather-covered chain saw. For that particular dish, no name was more appropriate than "chain saw chicken."

During this initial "settling in" period, I spent a lot of time with the troops in both their living and working spaces. One of the first orders of business was ensuring that they had enough material and equipment to accomplish their mission. Upon touchdown in Bahrain, every piece of theater-specific gear that I had signed for back in South Carolina was taken immediately from the transport aircraft and put into a new common pool. This was the work of the logisticians from the newly formed expeditionary MAG (MAG-70). In reality this was a good idea. It ensured an even distribution of assets throughout the group. Personally, it made me mad as hell. I knew what I had brought, had carefully planned it, and knew that I had enough tents, cots, water equipment, and other gear to adequately house my men. Besides that, I had personally signed for all of it, tens of thousands of dollars worth, and now it was going to be distributed to hell and gone and back, with no way for me to track it (the Marine Corps after the war, in an uncommon display of common sense, relieved me and all others like me of any responsibility for gear that was brought in and redistributed on the initial lift).

At any rate, our troops were starting to get settled in as well. They had been issued, and were setting up, general purpose (GP) canvas tents. These were rectangular in shape, with no type of flooring, and normally housed fifteen to twenty troops. The tents they used for living quarters were erected in a large open area a couple of hundred yards from the maintenance spaces. Anywhere else, a large open area would be called a field. But a field normally intimates landscape covered with grass or brush. This place just had rocks, dirt, and sand.

As time went by, and more troops poured in, the tents were rearranged, reinforced, and erected over concrete pads. A huge field kitchen was also erected for use when the more distant inside facility was too far or off limits for some reason. Showers and outdoor privies were soon built as well. Separate facilities for men and women.

This was the first time the Marine Corps had deployed for war with a significant number of women. Not many. I'm guessing less than 5 percent. With females deployed in theater, there arose just about every problem that the critics had said would occur.

A female officer was sent home for having sex with a younger enlisted male. Women got pregnant. Male officers had sex with enlisted females. Some females weren't physically or emotionally capable of performing their duties (to be fair, that happened with men as well, albeit less frequently). There were women who couldn't perform during their menstrual cycle. Fights occurred over women. Time and attention was wasted by males in pursuit of females. Prostitution was suspected. Rumors got back to families in the States, which caused tremendous heartache.

Also based with us was an army medical unit which had a large number of female officer nurses. As officers they shared the same dining facilities as the aircrew, and so it was easy and pleasant to make liaisons with these ladies. That adultery resulted, there is little question.

We weren't the only ones who had problems. Other units, and other services elsewhere in the region, had problems to the point that their ability to perform their mission was questioned. That all of this occurred wasn't completely the fault of the men. Nor of the women. The majority of them performed their duties credibly, in a professional fashion. It was simply the nature of the beast. To quote one of our pilots (who had a rich southern accent, which seemed to add a certain earthy wisdom to the statement): "It's just mother nature. If you put men and women together, sooner or later, I don't care who they are, they're gonna start fuckin'." As one who has been there, I

dare anyone to argue. Bottom line, regardless of the politically driven positive rhetoric that emerged concerning women in the Gulf
War, I don't think it was worth all the problems it created. Most who
were there, I believe, would agree (my wife, and the Marine Corps,
will cream me for saying this).

But let me tighten my noose a bit more. After Tailhook, and under
President Clinton, the services had women fighter pilots jammed
down their throats. These women, five years after the war, are just
newly arrived to operational fighter squadrons. I think that, with a
few exceptions, they are below average performers.

As a jet instructor in the Naval Aviation Training Command for
over three years, I had the opportunity to see and instruct a number of women (including Kara Hultgreen, who later died in an F-14
crash, which generated a huge amount of controversy). At the time,
these women were being trained to fly jets in noncombat roles. To a
woman, they were unaggressive to the point of timidity, weak in aerobatics (yes, I know about Patty Wagstaff, the great sport aerobatics
champion: there are always exceptions), and glaringly lacking in
fighting spirit and esprit de corps. They were, to their credit, as good
as the males at instrument flying, which involves flying in simulated
bad weather in a flight simulator or under a hood. This demands
smooth and precise flying. Very regimented, smooth, and gentle. But
they were markedly inferior to the men in aggressive flying such as
that demanded in the air-to-air gunnery pattern. As a whole, I am certain that they were not as good as the men. And as evenhanded as
all the instructors tried to be (even me!), I think that they were graded
easier because they were women. It's the way we were raised. I know
for a fact that they were given more chances to make up for unsatis-
factory performances. There were quotas to meet.

Women as fighter pilots? Many times after an air-to-air engagement I am physically beat. Out of breath. Not too different from the
way one feels after a wrestling match. Most women can't outwres-
tle the average man. By and large, they don't possess the physical
strength and stamina required, nor the aggressive spirit. I'm not saying that this is good or bad in a woman, and I don't know if the fault

lies in genetics or our culture. But I do know that the lack of these qualities will cripple a fighter pilot. And who wants anything less than the very best defending this nation?

How about the social and cultural implications with the squadron? What about when Captain Bob and Lieutenant Tina go on a cross-country mission for several days? How's Captain Bob's wife going to like that? Shouldn't matter, right? Right. But it will. And worse, what if Commanding Officer Tom takes a shine to Lieutenant Tina? She's awful pretty. She also handles her administrative tasks much better than her peer, Lieutenant Pete. But Pete doesn't know about that. All he sees is the attraction between Commanding Officer Tom and Tina ("The only reason the CO is rating that bitch ahead of me is because he's sleeping with her!"). Situations like that will happen, and it will tear units apart. A squadron commanding officer in the Marine Corps has already been relieved for similar improprieties. Mark my words, the potential for trouble is endless.

"But, we're all adults here," you say. "Professionally educated and intensely disciplined. We can overcome this hormonal threat to our implementation of these progressive and worthy goals!"

Good luck.

Here, someone bring me a stool and help me off this high horse. . . . Thank God this story has nothing to do with Tailhook. I'm exhausted.

Back to Bahrain. For working spaces the troops erected more general purpose tents alongside the hangars. As time went on they became very ingenious and customized their tents with various features, including weight rooms, offices, and nap chambers. At any rate, in short order the marines were established on base, ready, able, and willing to wage, and win, a campaign of any degree or duration.

Chapter Nine

Desert Shield The Big Sleep

Quite literally, we had arrived in theater armed and ready for combat. Despite the living and working conditions, as soon as aircraft had landed, they were fueled, turned around, and launched to man a CAP (combat air patrol) station. These aircraft "on the CAP" were in position to intercept and destroy any enemy aircraft which might attempt to launch an attack. The situation relative to Saddam's forces and intentions was very unclear, and the last thing we in the Marine Corps wanted to happen was to get caught with our pants down and get blind-sided. No one wanted a repeat of the debacle that occurred in Beirut, Lebanon, in 1983, when a marine barracks was destroyed by a suicide bomber driving an explosives-laden truck. The cost in lives and credibility of the Corps was catastrophic.

The purpose of the CAP was to protect coalition forces in general, and marines in particular. There were marines and their gear being off-loaded at various points in Saudi Arabia. Meriting special attention and protection was the port and facilities at Jubail, on the east coast, where a number of the Maritime Pre-Positioned Force (MPF) ships were off-loaded and where the Third Marine Aircraft Wing Headquarters was eventually located. Additionally, there were a number of helo fields, and the Harriers at King Abdul Aziz Air Base, which were vulnerable to air attack.

In the beginning, we put a number of aircraft on CAPs just south of the Saudi Arabian border with Kuwait, over the water. As things settled down and it appeared that an attack was not necessarily imminent, we (the MAG) put two aircraft on CAP, two on fifteen-minute alert, and two on half-hour alert. However, the Marine Corps was not the only game in town by a long shot. The air force was manning CAPs over Saudi Arabia, as were the Royal Air Force (RAF), the French, and the Saudis. The Bahraini air force maintained a presence over their own island, and the U.S. Navy eventually sent jets from well south in the Persian Gulf. More on the CAP later.

A story featuring the Hornet should discuss the Hornet. In the 1970s, those with the naval aviation purse strings realized that the F-14 Tomcat was turning out to be more expensive than originally thought. It needed to be augmented by a less costly aircraft. Furthermore, it was known that sooner or later a replacement would have to be found for the A-7 Corsair II. The navy was directed to find an aircraft to replace the A-7 in the attack role and augment the F-14 in the fighter and intercept role.

The aircraft the navy settled on was a derivative of the Northrop YF-17, an aircraft that had lost the lightweight fighter competition to the YF-16 when the air force was looking for an inexpensive fighter to augment its F-15 Eagle fleet. In raw performance it was inferior in most respects to the YF-16. But it came out the loser, in part, for a couple of reasons that had nothing to do with performance. Because it was two-engined, and bigger, it was more expensive. The YF-16 was a single-engine craft—normally a detriment—but that single engine was essentially the same one used by the F-15. This meant that procurement, maintenance, and supply of the engine would be much more inexpensive, as it was already a tried and true product, in the supply system, and there were already people trained to work on it. Besides, it had tremendous performance as well as growth potential.

The navy liked the YF-17 *because* it had two engines. When operating far from land, it makes obvious sense, and gives the pilot some measure of comfort, to have two engines: if one engine develops problems, the other will bring the aircraft safely home. Also, the navy was going to install an advanced and very capable radar, the APG-65, which would be able to use the AIM-7 Sparrow (AIM stands for air intercept missile) (and later the AMRAAM—the advanced medium-range air-to-air missile) to destroy hostile aircraft beyond visual range. For a long time after its introduction, the F-16 did not have this capability and was limited to visual employment of its weapons. It wasn't that the F-16 wasn't capable of doing so (it now carries the AMRAAM, and one version carries the AIM-7), it's just that the air force leadership did not want the F-16 to threaten the F-15. Congressmen have a way of asking hard questions: "General, if the F-16 can do about everything the F-15 can, and at about half the price, why do we need the F-15?" Now that the air force has essentially finished buying the F-15, the smaller fighter is no longer a competitor for procurement funds. But even as late as the Gulf War there were no F-16s in theater which had BVR (beyond visual range) capability.

Back to the YF-17. Most important, it appeared to be an aircraft that would lend itself well to redesign and production for use aboard ship, a very stressful and demanding environment.

At the time all of this was happening, the Marine Corps was in the process of training aircrew and maintenance troops for the introduction of the F-14. It was felt that there was a real need to replace the F-4 Phantoms the Corps was operating, and the Tomcat appeared to be the only viable replacement. But the Tomcat was going to be expensive. And difficult to maintain. Just in the nick of time, someone (I'm not sure who he, she, or they are, but God bless him, her, or them) ordered a halt to the transition. It was decided that the Marine Corps would modernize its aging Phantoms and wait for something better.

Today, with the benefit of hindsight, and the clear knowledge that the F/A-18 is far superior to the F-14 in almost every respect, it would seem that the decision not to press ahead with the Tomcat transition would have been easy. I'm sure that it was not. It's never easy to change horses midstream, particularly when those horses are multi-billion-dollar military programs already under way. There is no doubt that this was one of the most important decisions concerning Marine Corps aviation during this half-century.

What the navy and Marine Corps ended up with was a jet that exceeded their highest expectations. At fifty-six feet in length, and with a wing span of thirty-eight feet, the Hornet is smaller than both the Phantom and the Tomcat. Its two General Electric F-404 engines produce in excess of thirty-two thousand pounds of thrust, which means that with an air-to-air combat load and about half internal fuel, its thrust-to-weight ratio is greater than one to one. This means that the thrust produced by the engines exceeds the entire weight of the jet, which translates into superior performance. Again, this is a quantum improvement over the earlier two aircraft.

With a multiredundant flight control system (lots of computers) and a "live" wing (all control surfaces move complementary to each other in response to the pilot's inputs), the F/A-18 has slow-speed maneuverability second to none and is easy to fly and to control. The cockpit, with its "hands on throttle and stick" (HOTAS) system, is a masterpiece of ergonomics and makes employment of its state-of-the-art weapons systems very user friendly. Those weapons make the Hornet an extremely lethal aircraft in both fighter and attack roles. Day or night.

When the F/A-18 was introduced to navy and marine squadrons, it was received with unguarded enthusiasm. It was easy and fun to fly. The attention to ease of maintenance that went into the design was obvious, and paid immediate dividends in terms of mission capability rates and reliability. The Hornet introduction went on to become the most safe and successful debut of any fighter ever.

Like all aircraft, though, it did, and does, have shortcomings. Initially, there were problems with engines coming apart that nearly grounded the fleet for a time. Also, there was a problem with cracks in the airframe structure, particularly the twin vertical stabilators. Those problems have been fixed. Though it flirts with the one-to-one class in terms of thrust to weight, it could use more power (the variants produced in the last three years or so have uprated engines which vastly improve performance) relative to the F-16, F-15, and the latest generation of Russian fighters (the F-15, F-16, F/A-18, and the latest Russian fighters are commonly called "fourth-generation" aircraft). It also has a relatively slow top-end speed compared to most modern fighters. However, its incredible maneuverability at very slow airspeeds, where most dogfights degenerate to, makes up for some of that.

Here you go: an honest comparison of how the aircraft performs relative to some of the other stuff that's out there. The F-15 carries the same air-to-air weapons as the F/A-18, but has a better radar and associated systems that allow it to be more discriminatory about who and how it's targeting at long range. Within visual range, similarly configured, the Hornet is more maneuverable and a better dogfighter. From a visual neutral start, similarly configured, I have never lost a "knife" fight with an Eagle.

Also, the F-15 is not configured for air-to-ground operations. I can shoot down MIGs before and after I support my marine brethren on the ground. The F-15*E* is designed for the air-to-ground strike role, and it does outperform the Hornet in this role. However, the F-15E is *very* expensive and there are relatively few of them.

At beyond visual range the F/A-18 is comparably equipped to the F-16, which is *now* (post Gulf War) capable of launching a radar missile. Within visual range I consider a well-flown Falcon (or Viper, as it is also called) to be a more formidable foe than the F-15. The Hornet's slow-speed capabilities are still superior. Again, from a visual neutral start, similarly configured, I have never lost a knife fight with an F-16. Like the F-15, and just about everything else, the F-16 is faster than the F/A-18 and can run it down in a pinch.

I've gotten engaged visually with a Mirage 2000 just once. I was carrying two external tanks, he was carrying none, and I beat him. The AV-8B Harrier doesn't stand a chance against the F/A-18, or any of the other fourth-generation fighters. The Air Defense Variant (ADV) of the

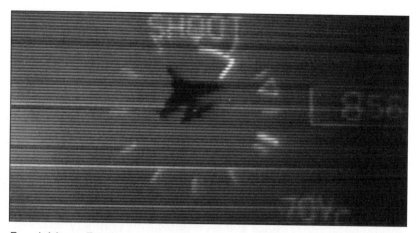

French Mirage F-1 shown under F/A-18 gun symbology. Training with coalition allies was common during Desert Shield, and training with the F-1s was particularly useful as the aircraft type was operated extensively by the Iraqi air force. *(Photo by author)*

Tornado is no match for the Hornet. The F-14 and F-4, likewise, are older and much less capable than the F/A-18. It is my opinion also that the Hornet can handle any Russian fighter currently fielded in any arena.

I don't mean to imply that Hornets don't get beaten in dogfights by other aircraft. They do. The performance figures of most fourth-generation fighters are very close. My personal contention is that an F/A-18, with an experienced pilot, in the visual arena against any similarly configured aircraft, is very difficult if not impossible to beat, depending on the other aircraft type and pilot. If you break out performance charts and start crunching numbers, you'll find that several fourth-generation fighters have a certain envelope or regime within which they are superior to another given fighter. But, in a slow-speed fight (where most fights end up), the Hornet is tops.

Having said all that, let me say that I think that the F-16/F-15/Mirage 2000 are beautiful and tremendous jets. I would love to have an exchange tour flying one or more of them. I'm sure those pilots feel the same about the Hornet. No doubt Porsche drivers look at Ferraris, and vice versa.

In the air-to-ground role the Hornet has few rivals. Capable of carrying a wide variety of air-to-ground ordnance, with the latest technology for accurate delivery, the Hornet is well suited to support that all important marine rifleman. And don't forget that this is in truth a naval aircraft. The Marine Corps regularly augments navy carrier air groups with squadrons of marine Hornets. This enhances marine aviation's ability to be "on the spot" when marines hit the beach. The navalization of the aircraft, particularly the arresting hook system, also makes it possible for the Hornet to operate from short expeditionary airfields.

To sum it up, the F/A-18 is the perfect aircraft at the perfect time for the U.S. Marine Corps. Extremely capable in both the air-to-ground and air-to-air roles, it is well suited for its primary task: supporting the marine rifleman on the ground, either through air superiority or ground attack.

Our role as Desert Shield unfolded was the aerial defense of coalition forces, primarily through CAPs but also with the capability to respond as required, offensively or defensively, in the air-to-ground role. To support these operations required a tremendous amount of equipment and supplies. Aside from the gear we had flown in with us, much of the equipment that was to sustain our operations long term was to be brought in on the MPF vessels.

There was a plan for the distribution of equipment from the MPF. I'm sure there was. The problem was that from what we could tell, the plan didn't seem to include VMFA-451, or even the marine aircraft group at Shaikh Isa. Normally the gear would have been off-loaded and received at the highest organizational level, then distributed down the chain to the end users. At the time, early on, we were swinging down at the end of the chain with nothing to use.

Deciding that we really had nothing to lose, I dispatched my S-4 troops up to the port at Jubail to take a look around and see what they could pick up in the way of information or, if we were very fortunate, in the way of supplies. What they found was what had become typical for any kind of operation during the early period. Massive confusion. The port was the scene of a tremendous free-for-all. Equipment was being picked up and taken away as fast as it could be signed for. Or as was very often the case, not signed for, or accounted for in any way whatsoever. HMMWVs (high-mobility multi-wheeled vehicle; pronounced "humvee") and trucks—indeed, vehicles of every form and fashion—were being loaded, taken, stolen, restolen, unloaded, and driven off at a frenetic pace. Gear was being unloaded, loaded, signed for, bartered for, or stolen at every turn. The poor logisticians were being overwhelmed, outranked, connived, cheated, lied to, and worn down. There must have been some method to the madness, but it escaped the casual observer. I'm sure that long after the fact, millions of dollars of equipment was written off as unaccounted for.

But it did get down to the users. Not necessarily in the intended manner, but it got there. My men, who really had no business being there in the first place, were able to pick up a couple of truck loads of gear that we were able to put to good use. The idea was not really to pick up only the equipment that you needed (it might not be there), but load up on whatever was available, and lots of it, and use it for bartering once it was safely in your possession. Possession being nine-tenths of the law. I'm sure that this attitude drives professional supply types nuts, but it was often the only way to get things done.

There were all manner of items at Shaikh Isa which were in short supply. As the ranking logistician, I was VMFA-451's point man in the rectification of supply deficits.

Modern warfare cannot be conducted without computers or photocopiers. These beauties run on electricity. The outlets about everywhere in the world operate off of a different flavor of electricity than that used in the United States. The plugs don't fit either. We had brought with us a number of power conversion units, but there were never enough. We were constantly stealing these from each other, as well as browbeating those units that were capable into manufacturing more. This was a constant problem.

I had embarked into theater our unit's only operable copier machine, which technically was not supposed to leave garrison. When we unpacked, the machine worked fine, but all the toner and other supplies to keep it operating had been lost. The sweetest supply coup of my life came when I picked up the local yellow pages and was able to cut a deal with an office supply dealer in Manama, Bahrain, to keep me supplied with everything I needed. I was a hero. That machine was the only operable one the MAG had for some time.

As Desert Shield began to become more established, we began to venture out and explore our surroundings. Once you ventured off of the base there wasn't much to explore except the capital city of Manama at the northern end of the island. With lots of Arabic charm, and way too many infuriating traffic circles (damned British), the city held plenty in the way of diversions. There were carpet dealers, a gold market, and a number of places for refreshment. The Londoner, the Rugby Club, the Sheraton, and the Diplomat Hotel all come to mind. Additionally, the navy had a small installation they ran as a support unit inside the city. Here, one could retreat into a little bit of America and use the recreational facilities, have a beer and a burger, and do some laundry. Relative to our counterparts in Saudi Arabia, we were in seventh heaven.

Technically, we were stretching our tethers a bit when we went into town to partake of anything that was even remotely enjoyable. If you really wanted to press the point, we were probably disobeying orders. Generally, we were only supposed to be in town on official business. "Well, officers should probably have their clothes professionally cleaned and pressed whenever possible. . . ." The only place to do that was out in town. "Since we're out in town anyway, we may as well have a beer. . . ." "Because we've probably had too many beers to safely drive, it's only smart and safe that we check into a hotel and stay until morning. . . ." "Gee, before we leave this morning, I'm going to duck into the gold market real quick and see if I can pick something up for Mom. . . ." You can see that it was very tempting to pass off a boondoggle into town as a "laundry run."

A real treat was to go into Manama and "make liaison" with the British Jaguar pilots. These guys flew out of Manama International Airport and had it made. They were living in the Diplomat Hotel and were receiving large per diem checks, as well as having meals, and a stocked bar, provided. On top of that, they were being rotated home every couple of months or so. They were tremendous fun and suffered our intrusions on their good fortune with very good humor.

In reality, as officers we probably made these trips into town only once or twice a month. We were too busy, and transportation (one or two vehicles per squadron) was too scarce. The poor troops got out even more infrequently.

The policy, official and unofficial, toward alcohol was clouded. The Emirate of Bahrain did not forbid alcohol, and it was sold out of liquor stores just as it is in the States. The navy sold it at stateside prices at their installation. The air force drank it freely and eventually erected a huge recreation center on base where it was served (NO MARINES ALLOWED!). However, the Marine Corps's stance was a bit different. As the bulk of our forces were based in Saudi Arabia, they legally could not drink, as alcohol was forbidden in the kingdom. The commander of marines in theater decided that since most of the marines deployed were not able to drink, then none of them would be able to drink. This was directed at those of us deployed to Bahrain. We were forbidden to drink alcohol and would bear this burden as a team.

Well, we sensed that our brethren in Saudi Arabia did not want us to suffer just because they were suffering. After all, if one of us was audited by the IRS, the rest of us didn't march right in to the local tax office and volunteer for an audit as well. So pretty much from the upper echelons of command on down, the "no booze" directive was ignored in Bahrain. Though discreetly.

Actually, it would have been very difficult to stop the flow of booze. Nearly everyone had relatives at home who were aware of our supposed deprivation and were determined to get the demon alcohol through to us at whatever cost. It arrived in all manner of containers, including water bottles, shampoo containers (gin and Head and Shoulders is not a good combination), plastic bags, and the original bottles. I had a bigger liquor cabinet in Bahrain than I have ever had stateside. I know that our boys in Saudi Arabia were receiving the same deliveries.

Aside from the liquor, mail and moral support from the folks back home was incredible. The amount of mail addressed to "Any Serviceman" was so prodigious that it was almost embarrassing. There was no way that all of it could have been answered. Many of the men would paw through huge boxes of mail and look for letters with obviously feminine handwriting. If after opening it they liked what they'd read, they would answer it. Otherwise, back into the stack. We became very spoiled.

I maintained several correspondences with different children, families, and classrooms. Not to mention my own family and friends. The strong feelings of support and well wishing were tremendous. Many sent pictures and packages. I received from one family in North Carolina a box of all the hottest items from their toy and hobby shop. My mother wrote every day. We received so much food that a lot of it spoiled before it could be eaten. Particularly around the holidays, we had so much food in our rooms that we had to worry about vermin.

The mail, aside from giving us a tremendous morale boost, kept us from getting too bored. After flying and eating, there wasn't much to keep us busy. One of our pilots did have a first-rate diversion. John "Vector" Hartke was an air force captain who had been assigned as an exchange pilot to the Warlords of VMFA-451 at about the same time Saddam invaded Kuwait. Though he had over a thousand hours in the F-16, he was fresh out of F/A-18 training and the initial line of thought was that he would be too inexperienced to deploy with us. After some thinking, however, it was decided that he would come along, as the air force would most certainly be running the air side of this war, and his ability to speak "air force-ese" might come in handy. It was an excellent decision. Not because we got much use out of his knowledge of air force doctrine, but simply because he was a great officer and pilot. Skinny, and so pale you could see clear through him in good light, he had a great sense of humor and a manner of speech that reminded you of Elmer Fudd on Valium.

His diversion also wore air force blue. Kim was a nurse who had been deployed with her unit to Saudi Arabia. They had become engaged a few months prior, and now found themselves tantalizingly close but separated by a gulf of red tape (as well as by a portion of the Persian Gulf). Vector viewed the matter of red tape and political boundaries as nothing more than a challenge. He simply went about "finding" all the required documents to make the trip across the causeway to her base. True love prevails. When the availability of vehicles threatened the frequency of his visits, he quite possibly became the only military man on the island to buy a car out of the local economy. When it came to scheming and conniving, Vector was more marine than most marines.

After a couple of months the two love birds were able to work out matching weekend leave periods and were married at a local church in Manama. Kim is a beautiful woman, and as she was the only female at her wedding, she was doubly certain of being the prettiest gal there (though some of us were getting desperate, and there was serious talk of putting Wolfy into a tight skirt and a pair of high heels).

The rest of us had no such diversions. For the most part Desert Shield was a big sleeper. Politically, from our standpoint, there seemed to be as much a chance that we would pick up and leave, or simply maintain the status quo, as there was a chance that we would try to force the Iraqis out of Kuwait. Frustration began to set in. We wanted nothing more than to strike out as soon as possible, eject Saddam from Kuwait, and go home. But we waited, and waited, and waited. We realized that during this time the coalition was strengthening its position as well as making diplomatic moves, but we felt (in hindsight, probably correctly) that we already had the forces we needed to do the job.

As pilots, most of our attention was dedicated to around-the-clock manning of the CAP. Normally we would brief up to three hours prior, suit up, and go start our jets, running them through all their preflight checks. Then we would shut down and sit around the maintenance spaces fulfilling the thirty-minute and fifteen-minute alert criteria. There were no ace-deuce or card games like in the movies. Usually we'd just sit around and jaw with the troops, or read a newspaper or magazine. When it came time to launch we would walk back out to the line and start up, then taxi out to the arming points, where all of our weapons would be checked and readied. Finally, about twenty to thirty minutes prior to our assigned CAP time, we would launch. All of this was accomplished using as little radio communication as possible.

Our configuration while on the combat air patrol was a fairly sturdy one. We carried two external fuel tanks, one under each wing, three or four AIM-7M Sparrow missiles, and four AIM-9M Sidewinder missiles, along with a full load of approximately 550 twenty-millimeter rounds for the M61 cannon.

Our CAP station was roughly two hundred miles north, just south of the Saudi-Kuwait border, and offset over the water. When we reached our point, the previous section of jets would depart and we would take up station. Generally we would split and set up in an opposing racetrack pattern with legs about twenty miles long, so that we always had a radar from one of our jets looking north into Kuwait and Iraq. Normally we would be controlled by navy ships (Red Crown), with occasional control provided by a marine air control squadron or an air force AWACS (airborne warning and control systems) aircraft. If the equipment was working, which was surprisingly often, all radio comm would be transmitted in an encrypted mode.

In a perfect world our tactics called for us to operate at an indicated airspeed of about 350 to 400 knots, at medium altitude. We weren't operating in a perfect world. If we had tried to operate at the desired airspeed, we would have run ourselves out of fuel much too quickly. We didn't have the fighter or tanker assets to afford that. Because of the fuel restrictions, we were driven up to thirty thousand feet and operated at airspeeds as slow as 250 knots. We concentrated our radar scans to the lower altitudes. The radar coverage of our controlling units was not as good at low altitude as ours was. Essentially we were betting that with our own radars and those of our controlling units, and the capabilities of our electronic eavesdropping aircraft, we would have enough warning to reach a favorable airspeed and altitude, reconstitute as a formation, and engage the enemy in plenty of time. This was not unrealistic, and we became comfortable with the limitations.

We were normally required to be on station anywhere from an hour and a half to three hours. After several months of the same thing day after day, with little or no variation, manning the CAP was sheer boredom. We often would engage the autopilot, go to an autotrack mode on the radar, and read a book or write letters. Or whatever. I would daydream a lot. I must have downed five or six hundred enemy aircraft while on that CAP. If nothing else, I was well rehearsed. Standard procedure dictated that we go to a tanker at least once during a CAP period. Usually one at a time. The tanker was normally a marine KC-130, but occasionally we drew an air force KC-135.

Some probe and drogue pilots have a real fear of the KC-135. An air force tanker, it normally is configured for air force–style "boom" refueling but can be configured for probe and drogue refueling. This makeshift arrangement has been called a whole lot worse things than inadequate. A hose trails out from the boom for nine feet. Nine feet only. It does not extend nor retract but is simply static, with a basket attached to the end. At the basket attach point is a very heavy steel turnbuckle. If things go a bit awry, and they can, the turnbuckle can slam into the canopy or windscreen like a sledgehammer, shattering it and leaving the pilot exposed. I saw this happen to an F-4 Phantom at twenty-three thousand feet. The aircrew was not happy. Generally, however, things go smoothly. It's just that the potential for damage, and the reputation the evolution has earned, can scare pilots. There was a senior officer in the MAG who, if he found out the tanker on station was a KC-135, would bingo back to base with some imagined malfunction or another, rather than take fuel. He was a goof with second-rate nerves.

So the CAP was notoriously monotonous. Most of us never had so much as a radar contact on anything, other than an occasional helicopter flying well inside of Kuwait. But once in a while there was some excitement. Gary "Lurch" Thomas (he was kind of tall) was on CAP one day when a flight of Mirage F-1s flew south toward our northern limit, then reset back north about fifteen miles out. This happened one or two other times out of the thousands of hours we spent on station.

Every once in a while the Iranians would get into the act and decide to tickle the system. We would get vectors to intercept, but without fail they would always turn back well prior to coming within visual range. They really didn't have the jets or expertise to risk tangling with us.

Our rules of engagement for an unknown aircraft approaching the CAP were a mixture of necromancy, intuition, and guidelines put out by higher commands. Our group commander, Colonel "Fokker" Reitsch, did us a great service and boiled the rules of engagement down to a very simple formula: If we felt threatened, we were cleared to engage. He may have been making a very big mistake, but he did us a credit and trusted our common sense. And we had no problems.

Fokker was a great American success story. Born in Germany, his father had been killed in the tumult and confusion that was post World War II Europe. After much hardship and heartache, his mother was able to bring the family to the United States when Manfred was a teenager. He joined the Marine Corps and served as an aviator during Vietnam, where he flew the F-4 Phantom, and while there he accumulated a record number of combat sorties, jumping on every mission he could get.

As our group commander he hadn't changed, which may have been his only true shortcoming. It appeared that he liked to fly more than he liked being a group commander. He probably flew close to twice as much as the average pilot, which infuriated a lot of folks, as it took valuable flying time and experience from his younger officers. But no one could ever accuse him of not leading from the front, or not knowing what sorts of challenges his aviators faced.

He still spoke with a very noticeable German accent and would lean on his esses a bit. When he spoke to us he was very straightforward and to the point in his delivery: "Alright girlssss, thiss iss the way it'ss going to be." We used to love to mimic him. When he wanted to make a special point, he used to send handwritten, or drawn, memos to the individual squadrons. They were very short and to the point, leaving no doubt as to the message. We called them Fokker-Grams.

One Fokker-Gram left a particularly lasting impression. And the assurance that Fokker was, as surely as we were, a hunter. We were all warriors. There had been some dispute about how we should orient the axis of our CAP and where we ought to anchor it. We had several choices. A Fokker-Gram issued forth. Simple and handwritten, he could have composed it in the rest room if he had been able to find a toilet to sit on. It showed a map of the area, and two CAP positions. One was fairly well removed from the threat. The other was bumped up about as close to Kuwait as we could legally get, and pointed right at Baghdad. Next to the removed CAP he had penciled a note that "this CAP will not get MIGs." Next to the other he had written "this CAP will get MIGs." There was no doubt as to which CAP we would use.

The squadrons were rotated such that about every third week was free of CAP duties and time could be devoted strictly to training. We were given quite a bit of latitude, and our training was fairly varied. In an area south of us in Saudi Arabia we used to meet with RAF Air Defense Variant Tornadoes and engage in mock combats. Same thing with French Mirage 2000s and F-1s based out of the UAE. These fights against the Mirage F-1s were particularly valuable as this type was one of the principal aircraft in Iraq's inventory. It turned out to be a pig relative to our jets.

We particularly enjoyed our training missions with the RAF Air Defense Variant of the Tornado. They were very capable adversaries at BVR, spoke the same language (more or less), and were a blast to debrief with (beer, which they had plenty of, is an unequaled lubricant for moving a debrief right along). Air-to-air skills deteriorate quickly and are the most difficult to learn and grasp with any permanence at all. A four-versus-many BVR engagement is very challenging. Let's listen in:

Dash 1: "Swede 11, contact fifteen west bull's-eye, eighteen thousand, hot! Commit, Commit!" (Swede 11, the lead aircraft, has radar contact on an aircraft, or group of aircraft, fifteen miles west of a defined point, heading toward the Hornets. He has directed the Hornets to attack.)

Dash 3: "Swede 13, clean low." (Swede 13, who is clearing the lower altitudes with his radar, has no radar contacts.)

Dash 2: "Swede 12, contact, second group, five north bull's-eye, twenty-five thousand, hot." (Swede 12 has discovered a second aircraft, or group of aircraft.)

Dash 1: "Swede 11. Swede 13, target northern group." (Lead acknowledges Swede 12's call, then directs Swede 13 and his wingman to target a particular group of aircraft.)

Dash 4: "Swede 14, sorted left." (Dash 4 has a radar lock on his assigned target.)

Dash 2: "Swede 12, sorted right."

Dash 1: "Swede 11, Fox-1." (Lead has fired a simulated AIM-7 Sparrow.)

Dash 2: "Swede 12 . . . Fox-1."

Dash 4: "Swede 14, Fox-1."

Dash 3: "Swede 13 . . . clean." (Dash 3 has no radar contact, and so nothing to shoot his missiles at.)

Dash 2: "Swede 12 . . . shot's trashed . . . tally two, eleven o'clock low, six miles." (Swede 12's missile is unable to make an intercept and has been lost. He sees two targets six miles away, below him and a little to the left of the nose of his aircraft.)

Dash 1: "I'm tally your call, I've got the high guy." (Swede 11 sees the previously called targets and is going to attack the higher one.)

Dash 4: "Kill tornado, heading 145, fifteen thousand feet. . . . Train, come hard right, bandit three o'clock, level!" (Swede 14 on the common frequency has timed out his simulated missile and made a kill call. At the same time he sees an untargeted Tornado to the right and co-altitude with his leader, and directs him to turn into the threat. Note that the radio calls are becoming less structured and more frantic.)

Dash 3: "Swede 13, still clean, spiked nose." (Dash 3 still has no radar contacts and now has indications from his radar warning gear that he is being targeted.)

All aircraft: "Bandit's switched Kato. . . . Swede 11's extending . . . shit . . . OK, stay with him, I'll have a shot in ten seconds. . . . Guinness watch that guy below your nose. . . . Kill, Tornado, left-hand turn at ten thousand. . . . Who's that popping flares? . . . Kill, Hornet, left-hand turn at twelve thousand, popping flares. . . ."

And so it went. This was, and is, very typical of an engagement that starts at range and finishes in a dogfight. At the beginning the flow is very structured, and straightforward. The pilots are calm. As the intercept develops and both sides begin maneuvering, shooting, and reacting, things become more fluid (confused) and situational aware- ness begins to break down. Correspondingly, the pilots get more excited and frustrated as they work to keep pace with developments.

Finally, in the visual arena, things take on the appearance of a free-for-all as the fight turns into a giant "furball." Aircraft twist, pirouette, and arc about each other as pilots struggle for shots while working to make sure that neither they nor their wingmen get bagged.

Remember that at the same time the pilot is working his radar, employing his weapons, and exercising sound tactics, he is also flying his jet, watching his radar warning gear, and on and on. It takes a long time and a lot of Uncle Sam's (your) money to learn to do this well, and a lot of practice to keep the edge hard. Additionally, a good deal of time is spent in the squadron in lectures, tactics discussions, and book study.

It's not easy. A lot of guys never catch on.

We also were able to do some limited air-to-ground training on ranges in Saudi Arabia. One of our most valuable tools were what we called mirror strikes. After we had been in a theater only a short time, targets had been identified for us to strike in the event of hostilities. When all the planning had been completed for a specific target, we would validate our work by flying a mirror image of the mission in friendly airspace to the south. We did this using all the specific players, right down to the individual pilots if possible. This was quite useful in identifying potential problem areas, ranging from taxi and takeoff plans to fuel computations, aerial refueling evolutions, and target attack formations. Many times we would have these strikes attacked by fighters from the air force, or the French or RAF. Sometimes a combination of all of them.

Also conducted at this time were a number of combined forces exercises, which involved most of the coalition forces, including all of our own units. One particularly impressive show was named Imminent Thunder (or, bastardized by the troops, as all exercise names are: Imminent Blunder). This one was big enough that it received serious consideration by the Iraqis as a cover for the actual attack. At our level there were still a lot of kinks, particularly with command and control nets, so it was probably just as well that we didn't kick it off just then.

September and October were probably our worst months in terms of morale. We were bored and homesick. Things weren't encouraging on the diplomatic front. It wasn't clear whether the UN was committed to decisive action sometime in the reasonable future or if it was going to be satisfied by the status quo. There were rumors that we would be rotated back home in six months, and counterrumors that we were here for "the duration." Our absolute greatest fear was that after spending six or seven months in theater, we would get sent home and that someone else would get to do the fighting soon after.

The length of time wasn't what bothered us. Normally, deploying marine aviation units spend six months overseas or on an aircraft carrier, then twelve months in the States before leaving again. While in the States they deploy for two or three weeks at a time at regular intervals. So, unlike our air force brethren, we were used to long family separations. Navy pilots (poor souls) are away from home even more than us. The biggest bitch we had was the uncertainty of it.

I was unhappy and badly missed my family. I was also a bit resentful. Here I was, a grown man. Intelligent, educated, and trained. And I was stuck in a shit hole with nine other guys, being told at every turn what I could and couldn't do (many times by boobs and goofs). At times I envied friends who had left the service and were well on their way to successful, high-paying careers in the airline industry. They weren't bending over a hole in the floor to take a shit. It was one big pity party. And I, along with my squadron mates, still had it better than just about anyone else in theater.

A humorous incident during this period served to lift the spirits of the younger pilots, and to confirm our belief that the abilities, flying and otherwise, of some of the upper echelon officers were suspect. Taxiing about the flight line was still a bit dicey. The line was still very crowded, and some of the required turns were a bit tight. If you weren't careful you could get yourself into trouble. Well, we received a memo from the top admonishing us to be careful, and scolding us because we were taxiing too fast around the line. The first one who fucked it away and hurt a jet was going to hang.

Soon after, the general speared his Sidewinder-armed wingtip right through a guard shack adjacent to the line and dragged the

Typical flight line prior to the start of the war. Notice all the jets have air-to-air weapons for combat air patrol missions. *(Photo by Michael Garrison)*

whole structure down. Naturally, someone caught hell for setting the guard shack "much too close" to the line. We wanted to paint a miniature shack on the jet and credit the general with a confirmed kill, but that idea got squashed. So we satisfied ourselves by joking about our new "secret weapon," successfully tested by the general. The wood-seeking Sidewinder.

As we moved toward the end of the year, and hopefully a showdown with Iraq, conditions began to improve. The troops' GP tents had been moved onto concrete pads and erected over wooden frames with plywood sides. This got them out of the dirt and provided more protection from the blowing sand, which was a constant annoyance. They also were rigged for electricity and lighting. The operations area, where most of the pilots hung out, had been moved from the Bahraini buildings into mobile office units had been lent to us by the air force. Finally, they kicked us out (it's hateful to be a poor cousin), and we ended up in a compound of improved GP tents like the troops had.

Ancillary activities around the base improved as well. A chapel was erected, along with a weight-lifting tent. As mentioned earlier, a huge field mess was built, which improved the dining situation tremendously for the troops. MREs (meals ready to eat), our compact field rations, were rarely seen anymore. Occasionally, liberty was arranged for the troops and they were bussed into town, or to a recreation compound administered by one of the big oil companies.

One day the officers were invited to use the recreational facilities at a yacht club in Manama. We enjoyed the pool and took advantage of the tennis courts, sauna, and other features. Also popular was a restaurant located on the premises. We all ate big meals there, enjoying the change of fare. At the end of the day a group of us climbed into a car for the trip back to base. Ten minutes into the ride one of our pilots screamed for the car to stop. Mother nature was telling him that he needed to make a stop. And he had thirty seconds to find a place. Before the car had even come to a halt, he leapt out, ran twenty yards out into the sand and panicked when he couldn't find any cover. Unable to contain himself any longer, he gave up, dropped his trousers and exploded into the desert dusk. The rest of us burst out laughing, and "Moto" (Master of the Obvious: as sharp as he was, he sometimes suffered comical lapses of dull wittedness) Venden pulled the car around and highlighted our suffering comrade with the headlights. He was the victim of a common ailment we called Bahraini Revenge.

The fun lasted for about another thirty seconds. Then one of the other guys got a startled expression on his face. An instant later he was scrambling out of the car to join his stricken buddy. A third followed a moment later. Watching our pals crouched pitifully in the glare of the headlights, Moto and I were fairly certain that this was probably not the picture that the folks back home brought to mind when they thought of their valiant Flying Leathernecks.

Taking pity on them, we walked over a few minutes later and tossed them a big book of crossword puzzles. More for hygiene than entertainment. A book of puzzles was never more gratefully received.

The majority of our medical care was provided by our navy flight surgeon, Lieutenant Commander K. D. "Fingers" Klions. A slender guy with eight-inch fingers, he had a much appreciated commonsense attitude when it came to administering health care and medication. His responsibilities included everything from routine sick call to emergency response for more serious injuries. Additionally, he was responsible for the routine medical and administrative care of our unit's personnel, with particular attention to the health of the aircrew.

One of the medical problems that dogged the pilots in particular was getting enough sleep. A pilot might end up flying two three-hour missions in one night, one in the afternoon the next day, then be free for a couple of days. Rarely was there a good, solid routine for any length of time. For a lot of us, it was difficult to get enough rest.

If the pilot was willing, so was Doc. He tried a couple of different medications. One of these was a drug that later gained some notoriety back in the States for some alleged side affects. It worked fine for some and not so well for others. Our executive officer, Major David "Dip" Goold, swore off of it when he awoke shaking from a nightmare. He had dreamed that he was French-kissing his grandmother.

Another one of Doc's duties was giving us shots. Immunizations. His popularity would drop a notch or two when he broke out the needles. A month or two before the war, the Powers That Be decided that we needed to be immunized against anthrax. Iraq allegedly had the capability to expose us to this deadly bug. So like sheep (pun intended), we were lined up a couple of different weeks to receive our anthrax series. It was a painful ordeal as immunizations go. The initial injection was not too bad, but about two minutes later, your arm would burn like hell for another five minutes or so. Then it left a lump that lasted up to a month in some cases. To his credit though, Fingers saved us from a series of gammaglobulin injections intended to safeguard us against hepatitis.

For entertainment back at the base we watched a lot of video tapes. One of the most important people on base, tasked with the most thankless job, was the lieutenant (or as it turned out, string of lieutenants) who was responsible for selecting the feature tape for the evening. A goat, or a hero, depending on his selection, this poor guy survived at the leisure of a very fickle crowd.

A series that was popular back in the States and made its way to us was the PBS production on the Civil War. This was a very sobering piece of work that held our attention for hours. And it made us think. Those soldiers suffered a *real* war.

Chapter Ten
Approaching the Deadline

Thanksgiving came, and President Bush had turkey dinner with our troops in Saudi Arabia. As corny as it seems, we liked it that he came out and ate with "us." His men.

We liked George Bush. He was a naval aviator just like us. He knew what it was like to be away from home. He had flown in a great and just war and lost friends in combat while surviving deadly encounters of his own. At the time, the vast majority of us had never even been shot at. The president did it all before he was twenty-one years old.

Then Christmas came. Again, the attention and support from home was overwhelming to the point of embarrassment. More banners and decorations than we could ever hope to hang. Much of it went unopened. There were so many "care packages" that we were literally running out of room. I'm certain the infantry in the field were forced to dump most of them.

I'm not sure why America took such gracious care of us. Maybe it was a guilt trip over Vietnam. I think that the boys in Vietnam received a lot of heartfelt attention, but the negative things are what left the lasting impressions. Perhaps it was that we had a clear mission, against an obviously evil and ugly enemy. Whatever, we were grateful for the support and concern.

On the topic of evil, and ugly, and Christmas: evil and ugly was our mood toward Saddam on the day of Good Will toward Men. He was home; we weren't. Our holiday was not spent with our family and loved ones, and it really and truly was the fault of that one ugly and evil man. He was a point on which to focus our anger.

The USO came! That really means Bob Hope came. It was just like TV. In fact it was TV. A crew came to tape the show for a feature back home. It featured Bob Hope, Marie Osmond, Ann Jillian, the Pointer Sisters, Johnny Bench, and others. Because it was being taped, every time there was a gaffe, they would stop and redo the gag, skit, or whatever. It was fascinating to see Bob Hope lose his patience (at this point in his career he certainly rated that privilege) with a member of the cast or crew. He would snap at him or her, demanding a retake. What a great guy. We really enjoyed him.

Once again, we were more fortunate than our counterparts in Saudi Arabia. Because of Islamic sensitivities, only the male performers were allowed inside the kingdom. We, however, enjoyed the ladies very much. Marie Osmond was particularly endearing (I hated the show she did with her brother a hundred years ago), as was Brooke Shields, who toured through a few days later.

By now the air force had pretty much segregated themselves from the unclean, the "dark side of the force" (the marines). It had erected and moved its jets into an impressive set of aircraft shelters at one end of the airfield. In addition to its maintenance effort, the bulk of its operations and planning had moved there as well. Air force troops also had their own living compound (with air-conditioned tents!) and very nice ancillary facilities. Again, the general policy was NO MARINES ALLOWED!

I'm not sure why, but the Marine Corps has always played poor country cousin to the air force. No matter whether stateside or deployed, the air force has always had better facilities and newer and better equipment, and has treated its people better in terms of per diem (additional money for lodging, dining, and associated expenses while traveling) and other quality of life comforts. It would condemn a lot of the facilities we live in and work out of. This has been, is, and will be, the source of a lot of professional envy, at least on the aviation side of the Corps (traitors that we are). Even now, at this writing, in Aviano, Italy, as part of the NATO (North Atlantic Treaty Organization) forces enforcing the no-fly zone over Bosnia, air force personnel are drawing per diem and living in hotels. Marines performing the same mission are living in tents and getting their pay cut. The Marine Corps has always paid lip service to the slogan "We take care of our own." Well, we don't starve to death, but we could sure learn a thing or two from the air force. Like how to lobby for money.

Perhaps I'm being too flippant. Marines do take care of each other. We never leave anyone on the battlefield. Dead or alive. And I'm not saying that lightly. But in terms of the mundane, everyday stuff, the phrase "we take care of our own" is often a hollow boast. On a recent deployment our marines were working out of canvas tents in Thailand in one-hundred-degree heat and torrential downpours. Servicemen from a sister service were working out of air-conditioned portable units, billeted in hotels, and collecting per diem. I wouldn't have dared looked at our marines and told them "we take care of our own" with a straight face.

Much of the problem, I am sure, lies in the fact that the Marine Corps is committed to doing a wide variety of tasks with a budget that has never kept pace. The air force is primarily in the flying business. But the Marine Corps also flies. In fact, before the breakup of the Soviet Union, the air arm of the Marine Corps ranked in the top ten military air arms in the world in terms of size. But the Marine Corps also has artillery. And tanks. And amphibious assault vehicles, infantry, mortars, Hawk missile batteries, and assault vehicle battalions.

VMFA-451 F/A-18A over Manama International Airport, Bahrain, during Desert Shield. *(Photo by Michael Garrison)*

The air force doesn't. If it did, though, it would probably fund those additional tasks adequately.

In the end it doesn't matter. The enemy doesn't much care if the bombs falling on his head come from a pilot who's living in a five-star hotel or one who's living in a tent. America has gotten a lot of bang for the Marine Corps buck. Off of my soap box. The army established itself on the base as well, bringing its Patriot missile system, which, later, it would find an opportunity or two to test.

The Marine Corps had Hawk anti-aircraft missile systems on the island which were tested during this time. Right into the air. Oops! Evidently, at a missile battery set up between the base and Manama, something went awry during a test and a missile was launched. Fortunately, the crew acted quickly and was able to command the errant rocket to self-destruct.

Also during this time, we were given Escape and Evasion briefs. If, unhappily, we were unlucky (or unskillful) enough to be brought down, we had some idea of what to do and expect. It wasn't too

VMFA-451 flight line at Shaikh Isa as seen through heads up display of another squadron aircraft during Desert Shield. Aircraft during this period were typically armed with air-to-air weaponry for combat air patrol missions. Note the false canopy, designed to confuse the enemy in air-to-air engagements, painted on the nose-gear door. *(Photo by author)*

encouraging. The terrain we could expect to fly over was dry, hot, and unforgiving, brimming with snakes, spiders, and biting bugs. The people we could expect to encounter would be indifferent at best, downright mean at worst—which was what we were told to expect.

The equipment we carried was a mixture of what we normally had and some theater-specific stuff. We had in our survival vest, and flight gear, a number of signal and smoke flares, a signal mirror, high-intensity light beacon, survival radio, nine-millimeter pistol, some water, and a shroud knife. With a larger vest, individuals could opt to carry more, but it became cumbersome. Inside the seat pan, which would accompany the pilot upon ejection, was a radio beacon, more water, a space blanket, a first-aid kit, and other items.

One of the theater-specific items was a large chart intended for use in navigating to "safe areas." It had many other collateral uses conveniently delineated on the chart itself. These included use as a blanket, a catchment for drinking water, a floatation device (?), a bag, a splint for a broken wrist, and (I'm not kidding) a plug for a sucking chest wound! I wish I had a million of these and some late-night TV commercial time.

Another, perhaps more useful, item was the "blood chit." On this piece of very durable material an American flag was prominently printed. Below it, in five languages (Turkish, Farsi, English, Arabic, and Kurdish), there was a message and a promise to reward whoever presented a numbered corner of the chit (or the aircrew) as proof that he had aided an American flyer. Unlike the chart, the blood chit didn't say whether it would satisfactorily plug a sucking chest wound.

Representatives from the air force MH-53 helicopter units who would do the actual rescue work came to brief us. These folks and their equipment were impressive. Much of the briefing was classified, but we were comforted somewhat by the material they were putting out. One interesting point was made: There would be no repeats of the rescues from the Vietnam War, where all stops were pulled. There, all-out efforts were made without much regard to the cost in lives or machinery, just to rescue a single pilot. Neither the people nor the equipment could be afforded now.

What if we were captured? What were we to expect? No one really knew. Perhaps torture, starvation, rape, or even death. Perhaps not. The intelligence people knew what the Iraqis had done to Iranians, Kurds, and others, but they weren't sure how they would treat Westerners.

The media (press and TV) were allowed to visit with us more often. We weren't allowed to discuss in detail what we were doing, where we were doing it, and who we were doing it with, but to be honest, reporters didn't seem particularly interested. Nor did they stay very long. Maybe they weren't allowed to.

One day after tangling with some Mirages, a woman from *Newsday* asked me what I thought of the quality of the French pilots. I said that they seemed okay, but I didn't think they were as good as us. She looked at me like I was the world's biggest boor and walked off. Well, they weren't as good. But later we all were cautioned against denigrating the capabilities of our coalition allies. Good manners, I guess.

We devoured newspapers and magazines, though they were usually at least a couple of weeks old by the time they reached us. *Newsweek* and *Time* didn't score many points with our crowd. Too much of a liberal bent. You could almost see their staffs sniffling, and second-guessing the military, and the president. *U.S. News and World Report* seemed much more responsible and objective. The *Stars and Stripes,* the *Wall Street Journal,* and *USA Today* were popular newspapers.

It was during this time that an incident occurred that, for all the world, sounds like it was made up in a high school locker room. I never met the individuals involved, but the Doc insisted the story was true.

One morning a young navy corpsman went to his flight surgeon. He was complaining of headaches, and soreness and bleeding in his nether regions. The Doc examined him and asked him how long he had been a practicing homosexual. The poor kid may as well have been run over by a train. The surgeon insisted that his pain and bleeding were quite obviously caused by tears in the anal tissue from homosexual sex. The young corpsman called the Doc everything but a man and denied it all. The Doc brought in a colleague who confirmed the diagnoses.

A counseling session was called. The corpsman's denials were so heated that the flight surgeons began to have their doubts. After a few days and a little investigative work, a culprit was found.

That culprit was wearing a U.S. Navy uniform. In fact, the culprit was the corpsman's roommate. He had been getting up in the middle of the night and putting the poor kid under with some purloined ether (remember the headaches), then having anal sex with his unconscious bunkie. When the victim found out, he was so angry and violent that he had to be held in the brig until the offending homosexual was removed from the base. This will forever be remembered among us as the "Ether Bunny Inthident."

Just before Christmas, and through the New Year's holiday, our numbers were augmented. We were joined by the two other F/A-18 squadrons out of Hawaii; VMFAs 212 and 232. Also arriving was a Hornet squadron of a different flavor. VMFA(AW)-121 out of El Toro, California, was the Marine Corps's newest Hornet squadron, having just finished standing up only the previous year. It was unique in that it was the very first two-seat squadron, and as such would serve a valuable and distinct role in the next few months. Our heavy attack capability was beefed up even further when VMA-533 arrived with their A-6Es.

The Marine Corps now had over half of their entire F/A-18 fleet on the base at Shaikh Isa. Seven squadrons. And two out of three A-6 units. In anticipation of their arrival, the marines constructed an entirely new ramp out of expeditionary aluminum matting, designed for just this sort of contingency. Made out of lightweight, reinforced aluminum planks, the matting went together very simply. So simply in fact, that they even let me put a couple of pieces together.

The base now housed over two hundred jets. The air force had brought in additional F-4Gs, as well as a contingent of RF-4Cs for photo reconnaissance. We were loaded for bear. Not the Russian kind though.

The Soviets were scaring us. They weren't threatening us. Not militarily anyway. But as the UN-mandated deadline for the withdrawal of Iraqi forces from Kuwait approached, the Soviets were scrambling for prestige by trying to negotiate an honorable way for Saddam to save face and leave. We were petrified by the idea that they might succeed. We were sure that this would not solve the real problem, and would virtually ensure a large U.S. commitment to the area for the long term.

In our own minds we were more than ready to strike. Importantly, Hussein had by now released all the Western hostages, and removed a troubling obstacle (why he did that has always perplexed me). We had a tremendous number of troops, equipment, and supplies in theater. Most of the forces had had more than adequate time to train and prepare. The weather was relatively cool. Most of all, we were eager to engage, and smash the enemy. And go home.

We hoped the Soviet diplomacy would fail.

Chapter Eleven

Red Ropes

nd fail diplomacy did. Fortunately, the Iraqis exhibited no interest whatsoever in withdrawing from Kuwait, and final preparations were made for the initial strikes in the campaign to liberate that country. I was all for surprising Saddam by starting the war a day or two before the deadline. But the president didn't ask me.

Our aircrew made last minute changes to strike plans. The troops readied the jets, ensuring not only that the airframes were in good shape but also that the avionics suites (radars, weapons computers, radar warning gear, navigation systems, etc.) were perfectly tweaked. It was no good having a strong jet if the weapons system was incapable of putting bombs on target.

The plans for the initial phase of the war called for us to switch from air-to-air tasks, such as we were fulfilling on the CAP, to primarily an air-to-ground role, where we would perform deep air-support missions. Our targets would include power plants, oil refineries, airfields, and transportation links. No baby milk factories.

A day or two before the war, Lieutenant Colonel Dudley brought the squadron together and gave a sort of pep talk. This is what we had trained for. This was the entire reason we existed. This is literally what we had been getting paid for throughout the whole of our careers. He knew we were ready. Was proud of us and confident that we would perform commendably. Later, in another meeting with the pilots, he repeated the same thing. Additionally, he recalled his feelings serving in the Vietnam War. He told us we should be frightened. If we weren't, there was something wrong with us.

I'm sure that all of us were touched by a bit of nerves, and that it was a healthy, normal, reaction. All of us had trained for this for years. We had imagined what, and how, we would perform, and were a little frightened that maybe we would fail. For the most part, however, we felt confident and ready, more than a match for anything the Iraqis had to offer.

Most of us were not eager to kill. To destroy, yes. But as far as killing the individual, or the masses of individuals, was concerned, we were not bloodthirsty. But we knew we would kill—without hesitation. "I'll kill that smelly son of a bitch before he even has a chance to think about killing me." It was the nature of the beast.

Did we actually *want* to go to war? Yes, I think. Though we risked being killed, and would almost certainly kill, we knew we were right. Rarely has the justification for war been so cut-and-dried. For some of us there was also an egocentric reason for wanting to fight: no one wants to practice for the Big Game all of his or her life and never get to play it. Selfish, and childish, and just plain wrong. But very real.

On 16 January 1991 (the day *before* the war in our time zone), we were told to be ready to take fully loaded and armed jets airborne to launch a feint attack, in which we would turn back just prior to reaching the border. I'm not sure who that was supposed to fool. Later in the day, that nonsense was dropped, and we were told to get some sleep and prepare for the real strikes. Perhaps real heroes could

During the war, an ordnance tech prepositions ordnance for the next launch.
(Photo by Michael Garrison)

have wandered back to the rack and dozed off for a couple of hours just before starting a war. We couldn't.

There was an atmosphere of busy excitement on the base. We *were* ready, and well trained, and capable. Bombs were being loaded. For the ordnance crew, it was exactly the same, except different. The actual loading of the bombs was no different from what they had done many, many times before in practice. But this was the first time, for the vast majority of them, that they were loading bombs intended to destroy and kill. For the rest of the troops the feeling was much the same, if maybe a little less intense. The very jet they were fueling, or servicing, would be in combat tonight. Would be killing. Would be shot at. Might not return.

Though everyone knew the war would begin that night, it was not openly talked about. Everyone walked about as if they had a special secret, exchanging knowing glances with everyone else. Though we had expected commercial phone lines to go down, they didn't. No other really obvious signs of an impending action were evident either. It made sense from a security standpoint. Anything unusual may have tipped off someone who was watching.

The strike I was in was not going out in the first wave. For the first wave, I ended up drawing duty. I was going to be the first combat operations duty officer the Warlords had had since World War II. In peacetime, serving as the operations duty officer (ODO) is a crummy deal each company grade officer (lieutenants and captains) stands two or three times a week. It involves sitting at a desk in the ready room, tracking the flight schedule, watching the weather, answering the phone, and making coffee. In rare instances when an aircraft experiences mechanical or other problems, the ODO lends assistance over the radio by referencing an aircraft operating manual or coordinating with other agencies. Normally, though, it's a good time to do a crossword puzzle.

Tonight it would be different. There would be an edge. I didn't know if among the buddies I watched leaving the tent that night there might be some who would not return. My fervent hope was that every jet that went out would be safely on deck when I turned the duty over to my relief.

Sometime after midnight, in the early morning of 17 January, our crews walked to their jets. They would be part of the first wave of attacks to strike Iraq. Leading our squadron was Scotty, on his first combat mission in nearly twenty years. Their target was an air base in Iraq. The operations clerks and I watched the jets take off from outside our tent. Afterburner plumes are impressive at night. A light bluish violet, the glare blots out the aircraft so that all you can really see is a twin plume of exotic flame, racing through the dark. Tonight was extra special. I said a silent prayer.

After the launch there wasn't much to do. There wasn't anyone to drink coffee with, I didn't feel like doing a crossword puzzle, and our one field phone wasn't ringing off the hook. I didn't even have a radio. Somehow, surprisingly, five months wasn't enough time for the Marine Corps to track down a base radio. The clerks sat around and tapped on a game on the computer, and I just sat.

Our attention was captured a while later by the wail of a siren. Classic World War II, straight from the movies, just like *Twelve O'Clock High*. Scud alert. The first of three that night, and countless more later on. The clerks and I looked at each other. Big eyes. Procedure called for us to don chemical-warfare suits and gas masks. I didn't want to put that shit on.

We had been issued NBC (nuclear, biological, chemical) gear earlier on. A major part of that equipment was the suit. It consisted of a pair of trousers and a coat, both made of a charcoal-impregnated material. They were issued in sealed bags, and once they were taken out of their bags, were effective for only a couple of weeks. Worn with the suit were a pair of rubber overboots and thick rubber gloves. The gas mask completed the ensemble. Worn together, the various pieces created a terribly cumbersome, hot, and uncomfortable suit. It was almost impossible to do delicate work in it because of the bulkiness, and any strenuous work, particularly in the desert heat, would quickly cause the wearer to overheat. After being soaked in sweat, the charcoal material would leach out all over the skin causing a sweaty, black, mess. Just getting in and out of the thing was a struggle. It was not popular.

After a moment, deciding to set the example, I told the clerks to get their NBC gear on, and pulled out a set for myself that was lying underneath a bench. The thing had been there for weeks. It was impractical to drag the gear around with us wherever we went, so most of us just left our own sets underneath our beds. This set was there for whoever was around when the need arose. I wasn't convinced that the need had arisen, but after struggling with it, with some help from the clerks, I managed to get it on. I even had the trousers on my legs and the coat on my torso. Finally, after we had finished dressing each other, we donned our gas masks and stumbled out of the tent.

But we really didn't have anywhere to go. Once again, five months hadn't been enough time for us. We hadn't done much at all toward the construction of bomb shelters. Really, we'd done nothing. Our eyes adjusting to the dark, we clomped over to a couple of mounds of dirt and sat down between them.

Even then we knew that the Scud was a piece of junk. Notoriously inaccurate, I knew that for a Scud to even hit the base, much less a specific point on it, would involve more luck than anything else. The clerks and I sat around and looked at each other and tried to talk and make jokes through the gas masks. Finally, weighing the odds (risky for me, considering my track record in Vegas), I gave an unofficial "all clear" and we tromped back to our tent and got out of our gear. The siren sounded many more times that night. It was a case of crying wolf. And just too hard. I never so much as even put a gas mask on for the rest of the war.

As it turned out, we heard that Saddam had winged a few rockets our way. One had been engaged and downed by a Patriot battery in Saudi Arabia. The others, two I believe, were correctly judged to be no threat and left to fall harmlessly into the sea. He had tried, but hadn't succeeded, in bringing the war to us.

After about two hours the boys came back. Every single one of them. They were excited. I was excited. We were all excited. The strike had gone well. The skipper's inertial navigation system had gone a bit goofy, and he'd had to pass the lead to Z-Man. Z-Man, surprised, and youngster that he was, handled it very well and finished leading the package to the target without missing a step. Though there had been some weather in the area, it wasn't enough to preclude them from using their FLIR (forward looking infrared) pods to acquire and hit the targets.

Lurch Thomas brought back some tremendous video showing his bombs hitting a hangar which had been suspected of sheltering Scuds. Watching the tape was exciting. Our first taste of the "real" thing. On it you could hear Lurch call out "Good hits!" as his bombs impacted. He was obviously, and justifiably, excited. The tape was shown several times on television back in the States.

The enemy reaction had been fairly heavy. Lots of AAA (anti-aircraft artillery) and SAMs (surface-to-air missiles). No one had been hit, however, and the jets had come back in good mechanical shape as well. There hadn't been even the slightest hint of an attempt by enemy aircraft to counter the strike.

By now our crews for the second strike were briefing. It was almost morning, and as my strike was not scheduled until that evening, I went back to the barracks for some rack time. On the way to my bed, I stopped in the common room and watched some TV. It was amazing. Vietnam was the war that was brought into America's living rooms. This was the war that America watched in real time. The local Bahraini channel had given over its air time almost exclusively to CNN. So this morning, and through the rest of the war, we could fly a strike, debrief, and come back and watch it on TV. Talk about instant gratification for the Now Generation.

I managed to fall asleep for a few hours before I got up for lunch. On the way I stopped to watch some more TV and see who was winning the war. We were. It was as lopsided as any conflict in modern history. Losses were very light, and it appeared that we were going to be able to range over enemy territory at will.

At lunch I sat with Major Gil "Sluggo" Butler. Sluggo was our aircraft maintenance officer, and as such was responsible for ensuring our jets were maintained in tip-top shape. He also flew the jet smarter and smoother than anyone I have ever met. In one-on-one aerial combat against Sluggo, if you survived without getting shot, you were doing some tremendous work. Rarely did anyone best him. He was from northern Alabama and possessed uncommon common sense, dispensing it with the least amount of words required. When pressed about the best way to fight an F-16, his stock answer was, "Jus' get behind it and shewt it." Now, at lunch, on the first day of the war, Sluggo and I were sharing a common concern. We were worried. The war was going too well. Neither one of us had flown yet and we were terrified that Iraq would cave in and agree to terms before we had a chance to fly in combat. Our hope that Saddam would hold on until at least the next day was mutual.

The rest of that afternoon I spent hanging around the Operations tent, and the TV. Our successes mounted, though reports of some losses were now starting to come in. An F-4G Wild Weasel from our base had been misdirected in bad weather and had run out of gas before it could find a place to land. Both of the crew members ejected and were successfully recovered in friendly territory. An F/A-18 had been lost. Navy. I knew that one would drive my folks nuts until I called them. Official word was that it had been downed by a SAM, but now, unofficially, most feel it was bagged by a missile from an Iraqi MIG-25 that had been targeted by a number of different allied jets. But in the confusion, no one could get clearance to fire.

Additionally, we heard that a navy A-6E and one or more ground-attack Tornadoes had been shot down. The marines would lose an OV-10 (a two-seat, two-engined, propeller-driven observation aircraft) over Kuwait.

Significantly that day, the F/A-18 strike-fighter concept was validated in combat. Navy Lieutenant Commander Mark Fox and Lieutenant Nick Mongillo, flying from the USS *Saratoga,* each downed a MIG-21 en route to their target. After scoring their kills, they continued with their mission, dropping their bombs on an airfield in Iraq. The Hornet and its crews had succeeded in carrying out the mission the aircraft had been designed for.

As the day wore on, it appeared that Saddam was going to be able to hang on long enough for me to get my shot at him. I collected Kato, who was going to be my wingman on this mission, and we discussed a few items before we went off to evening chow. Finally, brief time arrived. My two-ship section was to be attached to a four-ship division from VMFA-314 led by Major Bob "Boomer" Knutzen. (In the navy and Marine Corps, a section is always two aircraft, a division, four. The air force calls a two-ship an "element.") We were all part of a larger strike package of about fifty aircraft that would all launch, and aerial refuel together, then press on to attack different targets in the same vicinity. Our six aircraft were assigned to attack a power plant in Iraq (Az Zubayr South), about ten miles south of Basra. The strike package would be composed of F/A-18s, A-6Es, and EA-6Bs, supported by KC-130s.

Kato and I would be carrying a loadout that would evolve as pretty much the optimum for the rest of the war. Our jets were loaded with two external wing tanks (which gave us a total of about fifteen thousand pounds of gas at engine start), five MK 83 one-thousand-pound bombs (two on each wing and one on the centerline station), one FLIR targeting pod, one AIM-7M Sparrow, two AIM-9M Sidewinders, and a fully loaded gun. For both of us, this would be the first time we would drop any kind of ordnance using the FLIR pod.

When the brief was over, Scotty met Kato and me and gave us a little pep talk. We were fine. The mission was a complex one. First of all, the entire evolution, from start-up to shutdown, was to be

"Hot" refueling operation at Shaikh Isa. After a sortie the aircraft would typically taxi into the "pits," where, engines still running, they were refueled. The jets could then launch again or park for the next sortie. This type of refueling reduced the time required to get aircraft ready for a follow-on sortie. *(Photo by author)*

conducted at night with no radio communication, with everything tied to a timeline. Just successfully taxiing that many jets around at night without talking, and getting them airborne in the right order, would be no small feat. I would be leading the last section of Hornets to take-off. After takeoff, I was to rendezvous with the tankers at the refueling track, find the right one, flex to another if need be, then get our aircraft refueled. From there we would proceed to a marshall stack (a gathering or "push-off" point), where the rest of the strike package would be waiting, and where I would attach myself to Boomer's four-ship. After getting joined, hopefully in time, we would push on the timeline to the target. Hell, everyone's biggest fear was just getting to this point without screwing up. The Fear of Embarrassment is a strong motivator for a fighter pilot, stronger than any other. For most of us, it would be our biggest and most complex evolution ever. And at night. On top of all that was added the pressure of first combat.

We had briefed about three hours prior to our takeoff time. This was about one to one and a half hours earlier than normal, in part due to the complexity of the plan, and also to allow time to overcome any glitches encountered prior to takeoff. As it turned out, we still had about a nervous hour or so to kill prior to our "walk" time. Finally, Kato and I put our flight gear on, checked the aircraft discrepancy books, signed them, and walked out to our aircraft. There we were met by our plane captains, who helped us with our preflight inspections. By flashlight, we checked the exterior of our aircraft for any discrepancies which might prevent us from safely completing the mission. At the same time we looked over the bombs and other loaded ordnance, ensuring to the best of our ability that they were safely and correctly hung.

The bombs had been decorated somewhere, or everywhere, along their trip from the ammo dump to the flight line. The graffiti ranged from the blunt "Fuck you Saddam" to the slightly more clever "Roses are red, violets are blue, U.S. Marines are here to kill you." Quite a few of the bombs dropped were more personalized. A typical message was: "To: Saddam, From: Aunt Louise, St. Louis MO." It seemed that everyone back home wanted to send a bomb with their name on it. Normally, white spray paint or chalk was used.

Preflight checks completed, we climbed into our cockpits and strapped in, again with the help of our enlisted plane captains. Upon starting the jet, my hands went about the cockpit fairly automatically. This is where training took over, and often made the difference between a successful mission or failure because of a missed switch or improperly programmed system.

After start, I checked to make sure the engines were operating normally, adjusted my digital display indicators (DDIs) and heads up display (HUD), set up the fuel transfer panel, adjusted the lighting (interior and exterior), turned on my radios, radar, and inertial navigation system (INS), and completed a number of smaller tasks. Then, most important, I entered the coordinates for the navigational points and the target into my INS. Last, I input all the data for the weapons I was carrying, including the type of delivery I wanted to make and how I wanted the bombs to come off and fuse.

For this mission, against the portion of the power plant I was targeting, I had set my bombs to come off one at a time, so that they would impact in a string with an interval of seventy-five feet between each bomb. With five bombs, this would give me a string three hundred feet long. The size of a football field. This would be one of the few times I would be targeting an area target rather than a smaller point target. The fusing was set so that the bombs would explode upon contact, rather than delaying an instant or two to allow for penetration into the target.

At the same time I was busy inside the cockpit, I was working with my plane captain outside the jet as he checked the aircraft over one last time. Also, I was keeping an eye outside on the flight line, checking off other aircraft in the strike as they taxied against the timeline fastened to my kneeboard.

Finally, with all my checks complete and a signal from Kato that he was ready, we taxied on time. Just prior to taking the runway we stopped while the ordnance men finished arming our weapons. That complete, we took the runway and rolled on time, with a ten-second interval between our jets. Because of the load, the jets were heavier than any we'd flown up to that point, and so the longer than normal takeoff roll was an eye opener.

I was nervous, and getting more so. My mouth tasted bad and it was dry. My stomach, widely hailed by family and friends as indestructible, was behaving like a sissy. I felt like I had swallowed a bottle of hot sauce. And I was a bit gassy.

Kato joined up and I set course for the tanker track. At takeoff we had seventy-one minutes to fly 140 nautical miles to the tanker track, refuel, join with the rest of our flight, make our way 160 nautical miles to the target, and drop our bombs. What we saw as we approached the aerial refueling track was intimidating. A galaxy of twinkling lights. At that time there were four tankers and at least twenty receiving aircraft, all loosely joined and engaged in one phase or another of refueling. Effecting a join-up at night into the middle of an evolution like this can be frustrating at best, fatal at worst. The potential for a midair collision was unnerving.

However, as luck would have it, the gaggle's direction of travel and our direction of approach allowed for a fairly expeditious rendezvous, and we were able to slip into position behind our assigned tanker with no problem. Once stabilized behind the tanker's left hose, I added a little power, made contact with the basket, and began receiving fuel. I looked over at Kato. He took a stab and missed. And another. Missed again. And again. Shit. The air was kind of rough and the hoses were waving erratically. I began to get concerned that Kato might not get in and that I'd have to leave him behind. I looked over again. Damn, in my concern for Kato, I'd fallen out of the basket before I'd taken a full load of fuel. Christ, it was rough. The tanker crew must have been letting the loadmaster do the flying. I looked over at Kato again. He was in. After a couple more stabs, and a lot more frustration, I finally got back in and finished taking fuel.

Finally, tanking complete, I eased the section out of the tanker formation and we headed for the marshall and push point. Approaching the strike package at the marshall point, I began to sort through the formations on my radar, and as we closed to visual range tried to correlate what was on my scope with what I was seeing, until I found Boomer's four-ship. Right where he was supposed to be, over our point, but two thousand feet low. Dammit. What was he doing down there? He was going to run into someone if he didn't get where he belonged. I'd pulled alongside the four-ship and was looking down at them from the assigned altitude.

I looked up in front of me and did a double take. There, at my altitude, heading the same direction, was another flight of four. Boomer. The jets below us were from another point and had wandered over to where our flight was supposed to rendezvous. I added a little power, and within a minute or so we were joined as a flight of six.

We orbited at the push point until time to go. As the time neared, we made final preparations for the run to the target. We spread out into three two-plane sections with four miles separating sections. Our anticollision lights were off, and the rest of our external lights were dimmed. Wingmen were stepped back thirty to forty-five degrees with about five hundred to a thousand feet of separation. This enabled them to keep track of their lead yet still run their weapons systems with little fear of running into him. FLIRs were checked, as were expendables, radar warning gear, jammers, and cameras.

Push time came, and we pushed. At twenty-nine thousand feet and .9 Mach we streaked over the water toward the target. About forty miles out as we approached the coast near Bubiyan Island, the airspace in front of us was filled with an incredible barrage of SAMs and AAA. It was much more intense than anything I thought the Iraqis could manage. I wondered what we were going to do, since we obviously weren't going to fly into that mess.

But we did. At any one time there were three or four SAMs in the air. They came continuously. Below us, and only reaching up to about half our altitude, were curtains of red and orange AAA fire. Adding to the terror of the whole show were our own high-speed anti-radiation missiles (HARMs) fired from F/A-18s tasked to suppress enemy radar-guided air defenses. These missiles were coming from behind and above us, and were just as frightening as the enemy rockets, though they posed no real threat.

I was scared shitless. I now wished that Saddam *had* surrendered earlier in the day. We'd been trained and drilled to defend against enemy SAMs by offsetting them to one side, and watching them, while putting out bundles of chaff to confuse the guiding radar. At the last instant, as the missile closed to intercept, we were supposed to barrel roll around it, causing it to overshoot and pass harmlessly by.

But it was dark. SAMs are typically powered by one- or two-stage rocket engines. The engine is designed to launch the missile and impart enough energy to enable it to intercept the target even after the fuel has been exhausted. In daytime a missile launch is generally easy to pick up visually, as there is a great flash of flame, smoke, and dust. After launch, the missile normally leaves a very noticeable smoke trail as long as the motor is still burning. After burnout, though, the missile can be very difficult to see, as it may still be miles away and, depending on the type, may be less than twenty feet long. Yet, still traveling at three times the speed of sound, or more, it has more than enough energy to intercept.

At night, after burnout, it wasn't difficult to watch the SAMs, it was impossible. What we saw was a brilliant flash at launch, and then a brilliant bluish white or yellow streak as the missile climbed toward us. The most terrifying moments followed rocket motor burnout when, unsure of whether I was being tracked or not, I scrunched down in the cockpit and waited for the SAM to hit. Or miss. Some of the missiles would self-detonate after a certain period. The explosions looked just like giant, cheap, molten bursts from a roman candle.

Actually, we weren't helpless. Far from it. Our mission included EA-6Bs, which were conducting standoff jamming to interfere with enemy acquisition and guidance radars. We were carrying our own jammers inside the aircraft, which were effective against certain types of radars. Also, bundles of chaff. These were innumerable metallic fibers discharged from the jet, which clouded enemy radars and presented false targets. Targeting the enemy radar sites were HARMs, which could be quite deadly and made for edgy missile crews. These were launched from specially dedicated Hornets within our strike package.

The radar warning devices we carried could give us some indication that we might be targeted, though in practice they were often overwhelmed, giving a constant indication that we were targeted. Annoying at best.

The most effective countermeasure was to maneuver the aircraft. This in conjunction with everything else would make us difficult to hit. We were limited, though, in the maneuvering we could do. First, we were heavy, loaded with bombs and full of gas, and the aircraft wasn't too nimble. Another factor was the timing into and over the target, along with disorientation and the attendant problems when trying to bring weapons systems to bear on the target. Probably most important, in the dark if we maneuvered at all, we would lose sight of each other, raising the potential for a midair. In the event, we maneuvered and lost sight.

Back to the mission. Crossing the coast, I spotted a SAM climbing toward us that didn't seem to be falling back or arcing off. It was coming my way. Next, its motor burned out and it disappeared. I started weaving like hell, pumped out chaff, and ducked low in my cockpit. (I don't know why guys try and hide in the cockpit when they feel threatened. It's akin to closing your eyes when hiding from someone. Doesn't do any good other than to make you feel better. But we all do it.)

Kato later told me: "All of a sudden I saw your jet going crazy and wondered what the fuck you were doing. Then I saw that SAM, heard my warning gear, and thought, *oooh, fuck!*" Kato started yanking his jet around, and that was the last we saw of each other until we were headed home over the gulf.

Neither one of us got hit. As I pressed in, I continued to react against those SAMs I considered a threat while trying to tend to the business of finding and bombing the target. First I punched up the target on the INS, then slaved my radar, in an air-to-ground mode, to the target coordinates. Just fuzz on my screen at first. Then the waterway adjacent to the power plant started to break out clearly. I switched to an expanded mode and the power plant started to become defined. First a bit blurry, then a clearly defined perimeter, with structures and grids inside. Perfect. Then I switched to the FLIR. Not perfect. A cloud layer obscured the target and would make it impossible to use the more accurate FLIR to bomb. Not a big factor. The radar was accurate enough for such a large objective. I was bound to hit something important.

Approaching the roll-in point for my dive delivery, I had no idea where Kato, or anyone else in my flight, was. We were all counting on the "Big sky, little airplane" maxim to keep us from running in to each other. The scene around me was terrifying. I could see the flash of bombs from under the clouds below, as jets from other flights hit their targets. There were a number of SAMs airborne, and the curtain of AAA fire below me was everywhere.

Reaching the roll-in point, I rolled over, pulled the nose of my jet down, and started toward the target. Temporarily disoriented, I took an instant to figure out which way was up, followed the steering on my HUD, and waited. There were no SAM threats, but the AAA was getting a lot closer. Suddenly bombs exploded under my aimpoint as Boomer's bombs, and those of his wingmen, impacted. If nothing else I was assured that I had designated the proper target. I heard one of his wingmen call out a SAM threat though I couldn't see it.

The AAA got even bigger as I started to descend into its effective envelope. I could actually see the tracers pulling lead on me as I dropped. Everyone comes back with the same description. It looks like the tracers are being sprayed out of a big garden hose.

For just an instant, I felt indignant. These guys were shooting at *me*. Not an airfield. Not a city. Or even a gaggle of airplanes. Me. Then I honestly had my feelings hurt. I was really a pretty nice guy, not the sort of person you'd want to kill.

All of that lasted for less than a second. I went back to being scared and mad. Approaching my release point, I mashed down on the red bomb pickle button and steered through my release cue. I felt the aircraft jump as the bombs tumbled off, then selected full afterburner and started climbing as fast as the jet would go. Looking back I got some satisfaction in seeing the flash from my bombs as they exploded below the thin layer of clouds.

Headed back toward the gulf I noticed that my jet seemed a little right-wing heavy. Looking out, I could make out the vague outline of a bomb still attached to my right wing. I thought for a second, shrugged, switched from air-to-air, back to air-to-ground, and dropped the bomb. After all, I was still over enemy territory. I watched it explode below me. I didn't, and still don't, have a clue as to what that bomb hit. (Later, as there was a shortage, we were told to bring our bombs back rather than dump them. Also, there was concern about hitting nonmilitary targets.)

Though the AAA still seemed heavy, the SAM activity had lessened. Looking at my radar, I picked out some of the closer targets, trying to figure out where Kato was. I could hear others talking on the radio trying to find each other. Minimum communication on the radio ceased to be such an important factor, now that the strike was complete. I locked one of the closer targets (this could be unnerving as it set off warning gear) and told Kato to light his burners. The target I had locked wasn't him, but I picked him up visually off to one side when his afterburners lit. I called his attention my way, stroked my burners for him, then had him join. All of this lighting up the night sky would have been dangerous had there been an airborne threat. But there wasn't. Besides, I hadn't even thought of it.

Joined, we climbed up above forty thousand feet and made our way home. As we neared Bahrain and checked through our reporting points, everyone turned up their external lighting, and the sky suddenly became full of aircraft. The airfield itself was well lit and would have been an easy target had Iraqi aircraft been able to mount a strike. Surprisingly, the recovery back to the single runway at Bahrain went smoothly despite all the returning traffic.

After landing, we taxied clear of the runway, dearmed (pinned and made safe the guns and missiles), and waited to hot refuel our jets. Adjacent to the taxiway, near the end of the runway, were enormous rubberized bladders of fuel. These things held thousands and thousands of gallons of gas and would have made one of the juiciest targets of the war. They were manned by marines and airmen, who worked proudly next to a sign which proclaimed, A.M./P.M., YOU KILL 'EM, WE FILL 'EM! During this period we were able to relax, reorganize our cockpits, and jot down some notes for debriefing with Intelligence.

Finished, we taxied back to our line and shut down. Before we could even be helped down from the cockpit, ground crew were scrambling to get the jets prepared and loaded for the next sorties. Making our way to the maintenance spaces, Kato and I were welcomed and congratulated by our squadronmates. We were almost giddy, excited that we had struck our target and survived such a barrage of enemy fire.

Kato was later interviewed for an article that appeared in the navy's *All Hands* magazine, which described how "during the first waves of attacks, the skies over Iraq were filled with intense barrages of anti-aircraft artillery (AAA) and missiles." The magazine went on: "'I had three or four SAMs fired on me the first night,' said Capt. John F. Marion, an F/A-18 pilot with VMFA-451. 'It was a busy time. Intense, very intense.' Marion described the incoming SAMs and AAA as 'red ropes' and a 'wall of white and orange lights.'"

Naturally, for sounding like such a hero, he caught a tremendous amount of verbal flak from all of us in the squadron. Even a year later we occasionally got his dander up by mumbling "red ropes" or "intense, very intense" whenever he was in the room. Those who have been in a squadron know that there is very little slack when it comes to teasing.

He was right, though. It had been very intense. And "red ropes" probably was a bit more succinct than "like a garden hose shooting out glowing red BBs that followed you wherever you turned." For all the intensity and effort, however, we never were rewarded with what we considered almost a right: a poststrike damage assessment report, if one was ever done, never made it down to us. For all we had gone through, we never found out how successful our portion of the strike had been. I still have no idea if the power plant was brought down by our bombs.

Nevertheless, the overall leader of the strike, Major "Rooster" Schmidle of VMFA-333, was awarded one of the very few Distinguished Flying Crosses allotted by the Marine Corps for action in the Gulf War. The citation made mention of the intensity of enemy defenses and effectiveness of the strike.

That we had no dedicated aircraft to conduct photoreconnaissance, or make poststrike recce runs, was a problem that would bedevil the Marine Corps for the rest of the conflict. Today it is still a problem. In the year prior to the war the Marine Corps had decommissioned its only photo reconnaissance squadron, VMFP-3. The Rhinos (who are famous for their role in the Tailhook scandal) flew RF-4Bs, a very fast but older aircraft that was relatively difficult and expensive to maintain. The Corps had no way of knowing that the conflict with Iraq was coming, and betting that the reconnaissance version of the Hornet was just over the horizon (it still was not operational in 1996), they dropped the RF-4B squadron as a cost-cutting measure. As luck would have it, it was a bad bet.

All through the war we would have poor, or no, photo intelligence of our targets. Often, when we were tasked to strike an enemy emplacement dug into the desert, we would get a black-and-white

photo of the area that had been taken before the war. Since the
enemy had not been there at the time the photo had been taken, the
picture would look just like a snapshot of a gray piece of construction
paper. Absolutely worthless. The air force had brought an RF-4C unit
with them. However, they were kept more than plenty employed by
the air force's requirements, and we received little support from
them. Even satellite imagery was rarely used, as it was often of poor
quality or outdated.

There was quite a bit of discussion among us as to why all the
SAMs the Iraqis had fired had been so ineffective. We had quite a bit
in the way of countermeasures, but my feeling is that the Iraqi SAM
crews weren't exactly major league caliber. All the countermeasures
we employed, poor or no communications with their command and
control centers, and the terror of being under fire probably degraded
their already questionable competency even further. There were
probably a lot of SAMs fired out of desperation without being targeted against anything.

I had to do one more thing before I could call it a day. The phone
lines had never gone out of service, as we had thought they might
for security reasons, and I was able to place a call home to Monica.
It was classic. Everything I wanted to say and tell her either came
out sounding not quite right or I forgot it. But she was in no doubt
that I loved her and the girls, and that I was alright. My parents had
both called her already, concerned about the F/A-18 (navy) that had
been downed early on. I asked her to call and reassure them. After
fumbling around on the phone a while, we said our I love you's, then
good-bye.

The first day finished, and having flown in and survived my first
combat, I went back to my rack for a good, hard sleep.

Chapter Twelve
Frustration and Satisfaction

When you think of the climate of Kuwait and Iraq, you probably conjure up a blistering sun set in a merciless, cloudless sky, radiating intense and inescapable heat over forbidding desert sands. So did I. But the biggest enemy to our air campaign had become bad weather.

The week after the initial day or two of the war was characterized by miserable weather for bombing. The F/A-18 can bomb in, or through, clouds with reasonable accuracy, but it is at its best when bombing visually, or with the FLIR pod. We were not inclined to accept "reasonable" accuracy because of a shortage of bombs in theater, and the uncertainty of when our ammo stocks would be replenished.

Another problem with flying in the weather involves defensive considerations. It is much easier to defend against a SAM when you're able to pick it up visually. When flying in the clouds, the

SAM's radar can easily track an aircraft, but the pilot of that aircraft is unable to see the missile being launched, or guided. A distinct drawback. And not a healthy one.

In the first week or so, weather figured prominently in our business. My second mission, on the third day of the war, was not, however, affected by the weather. I was leading a four-aircraft high value unit (HVU) CAP for four EA-6Bs that were part of a strike into southern Iraq. Our mission was to stay with and protect the Prowlers from any air-to-air threat while they were on an orbit off the coast of Bubiyan Island.

My wingman was Kato again. Flying in the other section were "Gramps" Peterson and Wolfy. Even this early in the war it was obvious that the Iraqi air force was not going to make a serious effort to challenge the overwhelming might of the coalition air forces. We had received no reliable reports of enemy fighter activity over Kuwait or southern Iraq, and so expected no opposition from enemy air on this mission. We weren't wrong. We were a bit jealous when we saw the other Hornets blasting off, laden with bombs to go do "man things" while we were going to drive around in circles shitting money out our ass ends (burning expensive jet fuel) while we baby-sat EA-6Bs (though they were well worth baby-sitting).

After leaving the tankers, we ended up separating into two CAPs while the mission went feet dry (over land) and the Prowlers did their "geek stuff." We monitored an air force AWACS (airborne warning and control systems) frequency for any data on enemy fighters. There was none. Just as briefed, we stayed with the Prowlers until the strike group went feet wet, then separated for a poststrike sweep to "delouse," or make sure the strike group wasn't being tailed by enemy fighters.

One problem we encountered on this mission, which would dog nearly everyone throughout the war, made itself apparent to us: discrimination of airborne targets. The scope of the coalition air campaign was so extensive that the sky over enemy territory was constantly filled with friendly aircraft. It was not unusual to be presented with a radar picture that displayed twenty targets. We were not equipped to easily discriminate between the targets, and even had we been, it would have been time consuming. Essentially, without information from other sources, we were committed to visually identifying every target we intercepted before we could fire. At any rate, on this, as with every other marine air-to-air mission I know of, the point was moot, as there were no enemy aircraft within range.

There was another reason to sweep behind our strike group, other than to clear it of any enemy air threat. An egocentric reason. Air Medal points. To be awarded a Strike/Flight Air Medal, you had to accumulate a certain number of points. The formula for awarding of points was some enigmatic mumbo-jumbo that few professed to be familiar with, and even fewer were truly familiar with. I know that if you got airborne and crossed into enemy territory, you received some sort of numerical credit. If you got airborne and were shot at, you got more credit. If you got airborne, were shot at, and dropped your bombs on target, you received even more. If you got airborne, were shot at, dropped your bombs on target, and did the hokey-pokey, you became eligible for a grand prize drawing of some sort. It could get goofy. We were awarded points each time we crossed the border on missions that called for us to fly into enemy territory, leave to aerial refuel, then reenter. I wouldn't be surprised to learn that sunspot activity somehow played a role in the way Air Medal points were awarded.

Anyway, Kato and I zipped inland toward Basra for ten or fifteen miles, spotted some AAA, decided we got shot at, and left. Instant credit. Again, no enemy aircraft. Hereafter, whenever we were assigned to a HVU CAP, we would try to wrangle some other role, as the CAP inevitably turned out to be a boring waste of time.

Marine aircraft never, throughout the entire conflict, had an opportunity to engage enemy aircraft. The predominant reason was that it was not the role of marine jets to achieve theater air superiority. That was the air force's reason for being. The sole purpose of marine aviation is to support that nineteen-year-old lance corporal hucking a rifle around. Whatever we could do to help him reach his objective is what we would be tasked to do. If that involved bombing petroleum-refining facilities to deny the enemy fuel for his convoys, then so be it. The troops on the ground might need an enemy-held bridge taken out. Or a closer threat might be artillery batteries, tanks, armored vehicles, or troops in the open. The overriding consideration in our mission assignments was the marine infantryman.

But very rarely would the marines on the ground need us to mount a fighter sweep to destroy enemy aircraft. If, during the course of another mission, we were presented the opportunity to engage, or if we were attacked, then we were to down as many of the enemy as we could. Much as Lieutenant Commander Fox and Lieutenant Mongillo of the navy did.

The air force, on the other hand, has entire units whose mission revolves about downing enemy aircraft. Flying mainly the F-15, these units are neither equipped nor trained for ground attack. As the air force ran the air campaign (makes sense), I am sure they assigned sectors of responsibility where the heaviest enemy air activity was expected to their own F-15 units. The F-15s were designed for air superiority, the crews were trained exclusively to it, and they were best equipped for it. To do otherwise would have been foolish.

As well as politically stupid. Imagine the embarrassment had the navy or marines downed more Iraqi jets than the air force. "What do we need the air force for?" I am not saying, though, that naval aviation had near enough assets in theater to fulfill their ground-attack requirements and still provide the same air superiority cover that the air force did. It didn't. But I am sure that if the air force had any inkling that there was, or was going to be, enemy aircraft airborne, they sent their own fighters first if they had a choice. Even if marine or navy fighters were handy. I would have too.

There may be some perception that, because it downed the majority of Iraqi fighters, the F-15 is overwhelmingly superior to the Hornet in the air-to-air arena. That this is definitely not the case was discussed earlier. The F-15 is simply the aircraft the air force owns for its air superiority mission. Had the air force for some reason been equipped with F/A-18s, I am sure that their score would have been very nearly the same. They'd do a great job regardless of the jet they used.

The large package strikes against the enemy continued. On the evening of the third day of the war, a large strike out of Shaikh Isa was mounted against the Iraqi airfield at Shaybah, as well as nearby rail facilities which supported a refinery. The strike included twenty Hornets and two EA-6Bs. Taking part in this strike was Major Jay "IV" (pronounced eye-vee) Bergstrom. Identified during Desert Shield as a replacement pilot in the event that aircraft and aircrew losses became significant, he had recently arrived from VMFAT-101 (the Hornet training squadron), in California, where he had served as an instructor. He fit in well, even though he was from Texas. Everybody knew and liked IV. So much so that VMFA-232 had hired him on. Not easy for a latecomer when there were so many other late arrivals scrambling for a squadron to call home.

This evening IV was flying as Dash 2 (the number two man or aircraft in a formation) to Keith "Champ" Champion. Champ was leading a four-ship of aircraft from VMFA-232. Their role was to cut a rail intersection connecting the airfield with the refinery and the city of Basra. IV tells his story:

The mission called for us to premission tank. It was a nightmare just finding the tankers and getting our gas. The weather was dogshit. I was more frightened of the embarrassment of having to abort because I couldn't get aboard the tanker than I was of getting shot down.

Finally, we got our gas and pushed toward the target. Approaching the IP [initial point], we started to draw fire from what seemed like hundreds of AAA sites. The border between Iraq, Iran, and Kuwait seemed to be outlined with anti-aircraft artillery. SAMs were everywhere too. For some idiotic reason we were using an SA-2 site as our IP for the run to the target. Kind of like stepping over the watch dog on the way to rob a house.

The weather got worse as we neared the target. The clouds made our FLIRs useless. Although we had technically reached our mission abort criteria due to weather, we figured that we had gotten this far without dying and we weren't going to drag the bombs all the way back just because we couldn't use the FLIRs, or see to dodge SAMs. Instead, we designated the target with our radars. The radar is good for attacking large targets, but isn't the preferred targeting device for cutting a railroad that's no more than three or four feet wide, from three or four miles up. Approaching the roll-in point, I was unable to find the targeted intersection and slewed my radar over to the rail yard inside the refinery.

Our attack profile called for us to release our bombs at fifteen thousand feet. Well, we went into the clouds at twenty thousand. It's not a comfortable feeling diving into the weather with a bunch of other bomb-laden jets. You can't see each other, the SAMs, or the target. In a perfect world you hope to miss the first two and hit the latter. All we had to rely on was cuing from our systems to put our bombs on target, and God, to keep us from running into each other.

I finally released my bombs and started back up. At least I was pretty sure it was up. I had vertigo real bad. As I started my climb I saw a bright flash in the clouds off to one side. It turned out that there was a big explosion underneath Champ's jet. It was either a SAM or one of his bombs had detonated prematurely. Anyway, I finally popped back out of the weather about forty-five degrees nose high. I looked over and saw Champ come screaming out, afterburners lit, headed nearly straight up. He looked for all the world like he wasn't even going to think about leveling off until he reached Jupiter.

A bit shaken, but still in one piece, and more importantly, mission complete, the flight rejoined and made an uneventful recovery.

Along with the weather, there was another factor that was frustrating some of us in the pilots' ranks. Because of a number of considerations, the equity of mission distribution among flyers was not what we would have liked. In general, the scheduling of missions happened something like this: The MAG would receive tasking for a given number of missions. Normally, once a day, the squadrons would send an Operations representative to a meeting where the MAG would divvy up the assignments. I am sure that an attempt was made to do so with an eye toward everyone getting their fair share of good stuff and dogs. Depending on the personalities at the meetings, however, sometimes there were differing interpretations of "fair." A squadron that sent only a junior captain to the meeting, who had to deal with majors and lieutenant colonels, would sometimes end up with a mission tasking that wasn't what they would have liked.

Popular missions were (as a *fighter* pilot, I hate to say this) bombing missions. Missions where we could directly hit the enemy. Had there been a lot of enemy action in the air, bombing would have placed a very distant second. But there wasn't. I am certain there are a lot of F-15 pilots who spent a lot of time on CAP and never had an opportunity to shoot who would have loved to have had the option to do a bit of bombing.

Unpopular taskings were the HVU CAP and HARM CAP. On the HARM CAP we would usually roam around with a couple of anti-radiation missiles, with the intent of taking down enemy radars as the opportunity presented itself. After the first couple of days, as the Iraqi gear was destroyed or the operators grew cagey, this was very infrequently, and so we spent a lot of time drilling holes in the air. There were periods of time when even the F-4G Wild Weasels were bored and looking to get into the bomb-dropping business.

Down at the squadron level, the job of writing the schedule fell mostly to everyone's favorite (or unfavorite, depending on how their own logbook looked), Hatch Borneman. This poor guy couldn't win. There is no way a schedule writer can please everyone (except himself and the skipper). Hatch was doing his best, but with weather aborts, pop-up missions, crew rest, and a myriad of other factors, there was no way to achieve absolute equity. By the third day I had flown two missions, while a couple folks had as many as four and some had only one. There were a lot of bruised egos, as no one knew how long the conflict would last and everyone wanted their fair share.

Aside from the actual mechanics of plugging pilots, jets, times, ordnance, targets, and other pertinent data into the schedule, writing it was something of an art. One pilot might bitch that he'd only gotten two missions, whereas the guy next to him had four. The guy next to him might point out that all of his missions had been crummy HVU CAPs, while the other pilot's missions had all been bombing strikes, which were much more desirable. So, try as he might, the poor schedule writer would never make everyone happy.

Looking back, it was all kind of petty, and maybe a little childish. We hadn't taken any losses. Had we been seeing ourselves being shot from the sky, and empty bunks at the end of the day, our attitudes would have been different. This wasn't World War II. It was more like a bunch of cowboys jostling in line for their chance to ride the mechanical bull.

My next mission was to be a strike against the Republican Guards in southern Iraq. Lurch Thomas was leading us. Lurch, the world's nicest guy, was from Texas. Very well mannered, he stuck out in a fighter squadron, where a classy guy was someone who didn't piss in the shower. Intelligent and well spoken, he was our pilot training officer and did what he could to educate our group of apes. He is exactly the sort that every mother wants their daughter to marry.

It was a morning strike. Once positioned on the runway, I could see a very thick layer of fog start to envelope the runway from the north. I impatiently wished the aircraft in front of us airborne, before we got stuck in the quickly approaching fog. Finally, as my turn to roll came, I released brakes, selected full afterburner, and blasted right into the fog. Damned if I was going to get left behind. It was thick. Though I managed to get safely airborne, with the visibility at zero, it was too late for the rest of the strike and they aborted.

As it turned out, my impatience was for naught. We hit the border at an altitude of close to forty thousand feet. The weather extended from the ground almost all the way up to us. There really was no way to accurately bomb troops and equipment through it. And certainly no way to visually pick up SAM launches. We aborted the mission.

On the return trip, we found that the visibility at Shaikh Isa was still nil and decided to divert into the airfield at Dharhan in Saudi Arabia. The air force had a strong presence there, and it was only about thirty miles from our base in Bahrain. We would be able to quickly hop home once the weather cleared. We got into the field without much problem and soon were parked neatly together by the air force. As soon as we climbed out of our jets, Colonel McBroom, commander of the First Tactical Air Wing, came out by himself to meet us. We didn't really have any idea who he was, other than some air force colonel (to us marines it seems like they're a dime a dozen in the air force) who came out to see how we were doing. He turned out to be a very personable guy, and we had a good time jawing with him while we waited for the weather to clear and got some fuel squirted into our jets.

Moto Venden let it slip out that he was a Texas A&M Aggie, and the colonel spat a big wad of tobacco juice on his boots. Perfectly accidentally on purpose. We got a big kick out of that. Moto took a lot of crap for letting a Zoomie spit all over him. Still does. Didn't matter that he was a wing commander.

The colonel told us about his wing's kill on the first night. A young captain named Tate had bagged a Mirage F-1. But lately it was the F-15 pilots in western Saudi Arabia who were getting all the action. Right place, right time sort of deal. Oh well, he still had more kills than we did. We soon got word that the weather at our own base had cleared, and we parted company with the colonel. The short hop home took less than ten minutes.

About this time during the conflict, our group came under siege from a different direction. Every marine aviator in theater (and some from outside theater) was making his way to Shaikh Isa, all after the same thing. The same thing we who were already there were fighting over: combat missions.

This was a very touchy issue. Every combat aviator wants to test his mettle in the Real McCoy. And we were the only game in town. There were those of us, though, who didn't like it one bit. We had been there since August, put up with all the crap, suffered the family separation, and suddenly here comes a bunch of sons of bitches who had only been in the area since after the holidays trying to steal our sorties. We were hot (and selfish), but admittedly, and to the last man, had the roles been reversed, we would have tried the same thing.

Marine Corps aviation is a small community. Loyalties stretch a long way and take a lot of twists, for many different reasons. Like just about any organization, there is a good old boys' network (this isn't always bad), and we try to take care of each other. So many of the PHDs (post holiday deployers) were authorized to fly missions. I am certain there has been a similar story in every service, in every war.

Professionally, it probably wasn't a bad idea to spread the wealth around a little. Everybody who was able got a little taste, and it helped soothe some egos. Tactically, it probably wasn't the greatest idea in the world. Some of the latecomers weren't very current in the jet, and certainly weren't familiar with flying around the area. As it turned out, the threat wasn't as deadly as it could have been, and we didn't lose any people or equipment because of it.

One particular group that comes to mind whenever this is discussed is a handful of pilots from Marine Aviation Weapons and Tactics Squadron One. These are the aviation tactics gurus of the Marine Corps who, among other things, help develop and standardize tactics, train aircrew, and evaluate equipment. A few of them had deployed with us initially when we had first come out. When it was obvious that things weren't going to get hot for a while, they went back home. After all, they still had work to do in the States. Rationally, it makes sense. But a lot of people weren't feeling real rational when the tactics folks rolled back into town just before the war. Earlier they had "abandoned" us. We had had to squat to shit while they had been home with Mom, the kids, and MTV. And now the varsity was back in town to save the day. Lots of bitterness.

Some of the "higher ups" were also getting into the act when perhaps they shouldn't have. Our guard-shack smashing general decided to fly a strike mission with VMFA-451 one day. As he rolled in to bomb the target, all the HUD symbology slewed over to one side, because of crosswind effects at altitude. This is exactly what is supposed to happen, though it can be a little disorienting the first time or two. Well, the general wasn't familiar, and he aborted his run without dropping his bombs on the target. Enemy soldiers lived, and/or equipment wasn't destroyed, because he was in over his head. He brought the jet back and griped it as "down," blaming what he had encountered on a mechanical problem. The general may have done some good work at the elephant staffing level, but he wasn't impressing too many people with his Hornet prowess.

The weather continued to hamper us. Moto and I were scheduled as a night HVU CAP to cover a strike going into Iraq. We took off into what was turning out to be a mess. Because we weren't carrying heavy ordnance, Moto and I weren't scheduled to hit the tanker. Thankfully, because the weather was atrocious. Embedded thunderstorms, lots of cloud layers, and poor visibility, even outside the clouds.

Listening to the communications, we could tell things were falling behind the timeline. We could hear Lurch and Z-Man talking as they and the rest of their package played a cat and mouse game with the tankers, trying to rendezvous in a patch of clear weather. Finally, after too many unsuccessful attempts, a close call or two, and doubtful weather over the target, they aborted the mission. Everyone made an uneventful return to base.

We were frustrated. Me probably as much or more so than anyone. It had been a week since the start of the war. So far I had flown on one strike, two missions which were scrubbed for weather, and one HVU CAP. We knew this was going to be a short campaign and wanted to do as much damage as quickly as possible. It was infuriating to be stymied by bad weather in the desert of the Middle East. It just wasn't supposed to happen that way.

Finally, on 24 January, we got a break. I was scheduled as the second section leader of a four-plane division being led by our executive officer (XO), Major David "Dip" Goold. We in turn, were part of a much larger strike, hitting targets in the Kuwait City area.

Dip had joined the squadron only a month or so before we had deployed. From Wyoming (which he still wrongly insists is God's country), he had a "regular guy" mentality and a good reputation as a pilot and officer. He fit right in. As the XO, his role as second-in-command was to be the skipper's counselor, alter ego, and enforcer, all rolled into one. Dip had the unusual knack of being able to fulfill all these roles yet still maintain an easy relationship with the rest of the squadron.

We were directed to destroy a building located in a former Kuwaiti army complex in Kuwait City. The building housed the Iraqi army's III Corps Forward Headquarters element. Staffed with top brass, its destruction was certain to have a demoralizing effect, as well as a very real effect, in a tactical sense, on the command and control of III Corps. It was, in a way, an assassination mission.

VMFA-451 executive officer Major David "Dip" Goold at
Shaikh Isa, February 1991. *(Photo by author)*

For this effort, our S-2, or Intelligence section, was uncharacter-
istically able to produce some photographic intelligence. We were all
given photos of the target area, which we pored over for some time,
until we were certain we would be able to find the target. When
studying routes, charts, and photos for a target attack, you generally work from large to small. For instance, on this mission, we
started out with a map of Kuwait. From there we focused on Kuwait
City. From that point we narrowed the scope down to that portion of
the city which held our target, and all the readily identifiable features that we could use to define it from the air. From there, we
relied on the supplied photographs to pick out the specific building,
and even portions of the building, we were to strike.

For wingmen, I had Kato, and Dip had Bill "GQ" Buckey. GQ fit his
call sign to perfection. Regardless of where he was, or what he had
been doing, he looked like he had just stepped out of a men's magazine. And he could do a tremendous East Coast, Old Money, Yacht
Club, spoiled-brat imitation. Complete with stuffy accent. He had a
good deal of experience in both the Phantom and the Hornet, and so
was quite knowledgeable.

Dip split targeting assignments within the division. He and I would hit the headquarters building, while GQ and Kato would bomb adjacent structures. This would keep us out of each other's way, while ensuring that enough bombs would impact the target to ensure its destruction. We would be carrying five one-thousand-pound bombs, two external wing tanks, one or two AIM-7s, and two AIM-9s each. The length of the mission would not require us to aerial refuel.

Acquisition and bombing of the target would be demanding. It was located in a fairly congested portion of the city, so just locating the specific complex was going to be difficult. From the air, it's very easy to make yourself believe that what you're looking at is what you're looking for. It was bounded on the side that we would be attacking by a major street, across from which was located a heavily built up area of apartments. We were specifically directed to avoid damaging these structures. Because of the expected heavy anti-aircraft fire and SAM activity, we would be dropping from an altitude of around fifteen thousand feet, which meant that, due to the effects of wind, we would not be as accurate as we could be at a lower altitude. The longer a bomb has to fall, the more time it will be exposed to the wind, and the farther off target it will be. Additionally, from a higher altitude (greater distance), the pilot is less able to "fine tune" his aiming point, because he is able to see less detail.

The F/A-18 is a very accurate bomber. I've seen guys go out to the practice range and hit twelve out of twelve bull's-eyes, or "shacks" (as in "the bomb went right into his little grass shack"). I've also seen guys go out and get an average seventy-five-foot miss distance. There are a lot of variables. Ability and experience are big players. The condition, or "fine tuning," of the components on the jet are also crucial to success. An aircraft that consistently delivers good hits is said to have a "tight" weapons system. The type of delivery, that is, a high release versus a low release, also has an impact on accuracy. A pilot who releases his bombs from a lower altitude is able to see the target better. There also is less time for the wind to affect his bomb after it's been released.

Steeper dives also tend to be more accurate in the Hornet. The aircraft uses its radar for ranging information and gets a better, more accurate return from the ground in a steep dive, as opposed to a shallow one. Imagine pointing a flashlight at the ground right at your feet (steep dive). The spot is fairly bright, crisp, and clear. Now point it at an angle at a spot about ten feet away (shallow dive). The spot is more vague in shape, clarity, and brightness. It works the same way with the radar.

Visual deliveries in the daytime are the most accurate. The pilot is able to see the target directly rather than through another sensor such as the FLIR or the radar. Generally all squadron pilots will have a circular error of probability (CEP) of less than fifty feet when bombing visually. For example, if a pilot has a CEP of thirty-seven feet, that means that half of his bombs will hit inside a circle with a radius of thirty-seven feet and half will hit outside. This is a quantum leap in accuracy over what was generally seen in World War II, and even in Vietnam.

A bombing derby held by MAG-31 in Beaufort illustrates this point. Teams of two aircraft each are required to fly a tactical low-level navigation route over two hundred miles long, then strike a target at a given time. The winning teams usually score two bull's-eyes and hit the target on the exact second. The top five teams are generally on target with timing errors of less than ten seconds. The traveling trophy moves quite a bit between F/A-18 and F-16 units. (The F-16 is as accurate as the Hornet; however, with the money, maintenance manpower, and time they have, I believe the air force "tweaks" their jets a little more finely than we are able to do—hats off!)

FLIR bombing is the next most accurate. With a tight system it is not unusual to get a few bull's-eyes. Certainly CEPs of under one hundred feet are the norm. Sometimes much better. But FLIR bombing is much more demanding of the pilot in terms of workload. It's disorienting as well. More on that later.

Radar bombing is not nearly so accurate. I wouldn't want to try bombing something smaller than a football field with the radar. And then, I'd want to drop a stick of five bombs with one-hundred-foot spacing between each bomb. Several missions were sent up to Basra to bomb bridges through the overcast. Radar bombing was the only option. There was a miserable lack of success. The cloud cover forced very high drops at altitude where the winds were high. That combined with the inaccuracy inherent in radar bombing was the major contributing factor to the ineffectiveness of these strikes. Recently I was told that a software glitch was uncovered and fixed, which greatly enhanced the accuracy of radar bombing. I personally haven't tried it yet.

With global positioning satellite (GPS) equipment, which is only just now being put into new jets, blind bombing off nothing more than navigational coordinates promises CEPs of under fifty feet. This system uses triangulation (i.e., ranging and bearing information from three or more satellites) from a system of navigational satellites that provide extremely accurate positional data.

Anyway, back to the mission. The takeoff and flight up to the push point and into Kuwait went without incident. Our route took us generally from Bahrain, up through Saudi Arabia, to western Kuwait, then east to Kuwait City. Pushing across the border, the communications jamming became annoying. This was one of the few sorties I flew in which it was evident that we were being subjected to deliberate comm jamming. It really was not that debilitating, as we were so thoroughly briefed that we could have flown the mission with no radios, but it was irritating. Just like listening to a mother-in-law.

Approaching Kuwait City, I had radar warning indications that I had been locked onto by an enemy SA-2 missile guidance radar, but I did not detect a SAM launch. I believe they were truly petrified of our HARMs and didn't want to risk taking a shot, or holding a lock for very long, because of the HARM threat. The HARM is blind unless the targeted system is up and operating, hopefully emitting energy from its missile guidance radar. At any rate, I don't believe I was fired at.

The AAA was light to moderate on the way in, and didn't seem to be directed at anything in particular. It was almost as if they knew that there were aircraft in the area, but not exactly where, and just decided to send up barrage fire, hoping to get a lucky hit. Most of it was the smaller fifty-seven- and thirty-seven-millimeter stuff and was detonating below us.

By now we were working to pick the target up visually. Recalling what I had committed to memory, I picked up what I believed was the target area. Nearing the complex, I was able to pick out the specific building we were to destroy. My guess was confirmed when I saw Dip and GQ start their roll in on the same target. They were in fairly close formation a couple of hundred feet apart. Kato and I were in the same type of formation, spread about a half mile out at their three o'clock position. I put out chaff as I began my own dive. For the entire run, I had my FLIR on, with my camera on and recording. During my dive, I rechecked it. On and working. Scotty had earlier made a bombing run on an ammo dump near Kuwait International, where the strike had caused the Explosion of the Century. We'll never know what that looks like because he forgot to turn his tape on. We all had, or would, at one time or another.

The run looked good. I can remember looking out at Dip and GQ as the bombs separated from their jets. There goes Dip's bombs . . . there goes GQ's bombs . . . and there go my bombs! We all pulled off hard, safely away from the AAA, and watched. The bombs hit and there was a tremendous flash. Then an enormous cloud of black smoke, dirt, and lighter smoke from secondary explosions, and burning debris. That entire side of the complex seemed to disappear beneath it all. We were ecstatic. To top it off, we hadn't slung anything into the apartment complex.

Turning east, out over the water, we raced like hell, dumping chaff all along our route. There was more sporadic AAA. Like the last strike I had been on, I could see smoke, and explosions, as the other flights hit their targets. Behind us, and not far from our own scene of destruction, I could see a single SA-2 screaming skyward, seemingly in pursuit of nothing.

Safely back home, and on deck, we exchanged excited high fives as we greeted and congratulated each other. We almost knocked each other over as we rushed over to debriefing to take a look at our FLIR video. What we saw was disconcerting. We hadn't directly hit the building we had targeted. Because of the high winds aloft (over one hundred knots), our jets had miscomputed the correction factor. We had hit a couple of adjacent structures, as well as the parade deck (at least we stopped them from practicing their marching). There was murmuring about mounting another strike. Soaring spirits suddenly sagged (nice alliteration, huh?).

Luck was with us, though. The structures we had hit were actually the ones that contained the staff. Radio traffic had been intercepted that said a general and several other ranking staff, along with a number of garrison troops, had been killed. The survivors of the headquarters element asked for and received permission to leave. They feared another strike. Also, they were fearful of time-delayed bombs, which they said had been dropped during the strike (a couple of our bombs had dudded).

Later we learned that a remotely piloted vehicle (RPV), launched to collect data for a battle damage assessment (BDA), recorded video that showed the place was in a shambles. Another strike was definitely not required.

A week or so later we received a treat related to this strike. While watching the news, a CNN segment came on which was showcasing the precision of allied air strikes and their ability to limit collateral damage to civilian areas relative to earlier wars. Sure enough, much to our excitement, among the featured tapes was the FLIR video from our jets during this strike.

There was some consideration later to awarding the flight a Distinguished Flying Cross. But in reality, the mission really had not demanded any special skills or courage. The bombing run had been fairly straightforward, and though we had accomplished our mission of destroying the command element, we actually had missed the targeted building. Additionally, enemy resistance wasn't such that the mission could really have been called heroic. But the mission had been a success, and finally, I felt like I was actually contributing something to the effort.

Chapter Thirteen
Prepping the Battlefield

he sole reason for marine aviation's existence is to support
infantry on the battlefield. Although we were smaller players,
as part of a huge campaign we were obligated to provide a certain number of sorties to bolster the larger, overall effort. The
first week had been characterized by these sorts of missions. Particularly the more strategic ones, directed against power plants, airfields, and so on. As the campaign progressed, more and more of the
marine effort would be directed toward the actual battlefield our
troops would be fighting on. Specifically, Kuwait and southern Iraq.

The day after the strike against the III Corps Forward Headquarters found me on Z-Man's wing as a HARM shooter, in support of a
large Hornet strike against Republican Guard units in southern Iraq.
Wingman assignments were a "luck of the draw" sort of thing; we
didn't have assigned wingmen. Though we flew more often with

some than others, it was more chance than anything else. Among the captains, unless an individual wasn't qualified as a flight lead (junior guys like Kato, Wolfy, and Fattie), we all led or were wingman, pretty much at random, depending on how it showed up on the schedule. If it was a section and there was a major or higher in the flight, then the ranking pilot would usually lead. Though many of the larger strikes were led by captains.

And this was not at all unusual. Captains, or their equivalent rank, form the backbone of the pilot ranks in the marines, air force, and navy. First, there are more of them than any other rank. Second, they have been around long enough (five to ten or twelve years) that they generally have good, current experience and training. It is mostly captains who are sent to their respective service's "high-zoot" tactics and weapons schools. This enables them to return to serve as instructors within their own units. Probably most important, captains are not generally bothered with the type of non-flying-related distractions and demands placed on higher ranking officers. This allows them to devote that much more time to learning to fly their aircraft, and tactics. Few would argue that a solid high-time captain is more suited to lead a complex strike than a lieutenant colonel from some staff who has been dogged by and tasked with solving all manner of administrative problems.

Z-Man and I, after getting airborne, proceeded to the tanker rendezvous point in Saudi Arabia. This at times was the hardest portion of the flight. The sky was literally full of aircraft. Many times you could look in all directions and see aircraft, all from different flights, coming, going, joining, splitting up, and so on. Beside the obvious danger of a midair collision (we didn't have the equivalent of U.S. air traffic control), with so many aircraft about, it was often difficult to find and join on the right tankers. It was quite common for a lot of gas and time to be wasted by chasing down the wrong aircraft. Generally, there was a prebriefed refueling track, but often aircraft would stray a bit, or there would be different sets of tankers at the same track, deconflicted (separated) by altitude. Additionally, some types of aircraft looked a lot like others. An A-10 (an ungainly looking but very effective air force attack aircraft) at six miles looks very much like a KC-130 at fifteen miles. There isn't much difference between navy, marine, and air force KC-130s, either, except that in general the marine KC-130 is the only one that gives fuel. That can make a big difference.

Anyway, after sorting through the throngs, Z-Man and I found our tankers. We were the first ones there, and as we took fuel, we listened to the "big picture" as the air force AWACS aircraft controlled various parts of that day's air war. At the same time we kept a lookout for the rest of the strike group. We finished at about the time they showed up and pulled to the side to wait for them to take their fuel.

Watching something as seemingly mundane as a strike package refueling was, if not awesome, certainly interesting. It was a choreographed production in its own right. The tankers took their cues from the air tasking order (ATO) passed down from the wing, with little or no exchange with the strike leader. Sometimes up to six tankers. The fighters as well, knowing that the tankers would be at a given point, at a certain time, at a particular altitude, with the right amount of gas, had little or no need to coordinate with the big aircraft. The fighters, seemingly out of nowhere, laden with their tools of destruction, would arrive. On cue the tankers would stream their hoses, the fighters would nuzzle up, and "gas would be passed." Never did I hear of a mission that was botched or scrubbed because one side or the other was unable to meet its commitments. And all of this was done without any communication over the radio.

With the strike group finishing their refueling, Z-Man and I pushed on to sweep ahead of the strikers to the target. Our mission was a sort of SEAD (suppression of enemy air defenses) sweep. We were to push ahead of the package with our HARMs, looking for indications of enemy radar-guided SAM activity. If any activity was detected, and we could target it with our HARM, we were to destroy it. Sort of a Wild Weasel mission, Hornet style. Additionally, as we were the first ones over the border, we would be the first to encounter and destroy any enemy aircraft.

VMFA-451 F/A-18As refuel from a KC-135 on day one of Desert Storm. The bombload of two two-thousand-pound bombs was atypical; the normal load was five one-thousand-pound bombs. *(Photo by Tom Clark)*

We were able to pick up a good deal of activity on our sensors as we approached the border. None of it was particularly threatening, and some of it was ambiguous, that is, unidentifiable as either friend or foe. The Iraqi SAM crews had pretty much gone to ground by this time. Every strike package up to this point had taken with it some sort of HARM protection, as well as jamming from airborne systems. On top of that, the SAM sites themselves were often targeted, instead of the targets they were supposed to protect. By this stage of the game, they weren't using their radars for long enough periods of time to guide a missile to intercept an aircraft. By doing so, they were ensuring that they weren't emitting energy long enough for a HARM to guide to them. In effect, just the threat of the HARMs was keeping the Iraqi SAMs from being effective. If we could do it without shooting anything, that was fine with us.

For once the weather was beautiful. I could see fifty miles in any direction. Z-Man led us deeper into Iraq toward the Republican Guards. What surprised me was how much stuff there was to be bombed. En route, we flew right over several concentrations of men and equipment that were at least as lucrative as the target we were going to hit. There was stuff everywhere. I took notes as to location, size, and types of formations we overflew. I even took pictures with my own camera, which I had brought on board.

I was dying to shoot something with those damned missiles. Kind of like a kid with a big firecracker. Itching to blow something up. But the Iraqis weren't playing. And the HARMs were (are) very expensive. Earlier, we had been shooting them preemptively during a strike to ensure that the SAM sites would be targeted if they attempted to engage us. Now with the threat largely beaten down, we were launching them only against an emitting threat. It was hard to justify sending such an expensive piece of weaponry downrange against a questionable target—though a few guys did.

A frustrating aspect of this weapon was that it was typically employed from fairly long ranges. Usually the pilot never saw the impact because of the distances involved. As a result, we rarely had any firsthand evidence that the missiles were actually striking their targets. And, as with BDA, we rarely if ever received any intelligence information as to the effectiveness of the missiles. One hardly refutable piece of evidence, however, was the obvious reluctance of the enemy missile crews (those that were still operational) to engage us. The relatively small number of our aircraft brought down by radar-guided SAMs (no marine aircraft) was a testimony to the effectiveness of the HARM that we would have to be satisfied with.

Approaching the Republican Guard positions, Z-Man and I swept off to the side and watched the strike group roll in and drop their bombs. There was quite a bit of AAA fire. There were also quite a few man-portable, infrared-seeking SAMs fired. These were relatively small missiles that could be carried and launched by a single individual. They carried a comparatively small warhead and had limited range and speed, but their relatively low cost enabled them to be deployed in large numbers. The sheer numbers of these missiles fired, in combination with AAA, was the most effective anti-air system the Iraqis employed.

Leaving the target area, I could see secondary explosions and fires, which indicated the effectiveness of our attack. Never did a fighter pilot wish so fervently for a planeload of bombs.

After we got back I gave the data on the enemy emplacements and equipment we had seen, as well as the roll of film, to our intelligence personnel. Perhaps it was useful and was put to some good. Maybe it was information they already had and was considered redundant. I never heard. But I'll bet money that our Intelligence shop was so overwhelmed with day-to-day activity, and so inexperienced, that the information was never forwarded up the chain of command. I want my roll of film back.

The air campaign had a full head of steam going by now. Through our careers, we marine officers had been told that once we went to war, our staff noncommissioned officers (SNCOs) would step up and fill most of our ground job obligations. Amazingly, it worked. My gunnery sergeant and two corporals were handling all of the logistics matters very well. I rarely had to get involved, and instead was able to direct all my attention to planning or flying missions. And resting in between. Or more likely scrapping with other pilots to get more missions.

Talking with my mother one day on the phone (a luxury marine fighters on Guadalcanal surely never enjoyed), she told me that she had seen my airplane on a news clip. We didn't really have personal airplanes. Generally, a squadron will paint the pilot's names on the sides of the aircraft just below the canopy. This is more of a perk, or an incentive to boost morale, than an actual assignment. Everyone flies everyone else's jet, and aircraft assignments on the daily flight schedule are made fairly indiscriminately. This is far more practical, as a pilot whose jet is waiting two weeks for a part before it can fly would be missing out on a lot of flying. Also, a pilot whose jet really needed maintenance would be reluctant to "gripe" it for the needed maintenance if he felt it was going to keep him from flying for any length of time. Most important, our squadrons have twelve jets assigned and usually eighteen or more pilots. The more junior pilots have to share airplanes. That is, one pilot's name on one side of the jet and another pilot's name on the other side.

During this time our squadron was part of a mission striking targets in and around Kuwait City. Sluggo and GQ were part of this mission as strikers. In the target area they encountered the heaviest enemy response they were to encounter during the war. The AAA and radar-guided SAMs were very thick and unusually well directed.

At the same time they were running their mission, they were surprised at seeing a strike group composed of F-16s hitting targets in the same area. Sluggo described watching and listening to a stricken F-16 pilot calmly make his way out over the water so he could eject. Sluggo was impressed with the coolness of the pilot. He sounded just as if he were in a landing pattern on a Monday afternoon somewhere in the States. While this was going on, he was urging GQ, who was leading their section, to roll in so that they could drop their bombs and "get the hell out of there." Sluggo joked that it was about then that he "saw Jesus come up on my DDI telling me to 'run like hell, Gil!'" (Thereafter, this mission was always referred to among us as the "Jesus mission.")

This was one of the few missions in which some pilots had actually emergency-jettisoned their wing tanks and other loads so that they could get to speed and escape faster. I remember getting excited when, on my way to chow, I passed by these same aircraft (which had just returned and were refueling) and noticed they didn't have any AIM-7 missiles. I thought that perhaps they had gotten engaged with enemy aircraft. But instead, in their excitement to get out of the target area, they had jettisoned everything, including the missiles.

On the night of 26 January, I had Moto on my wing. We were a roving HARM CAP stationed off the coast of Kuwait. The idea was that we would patrol off of the coast and target any enemy radars that might start emitting or targeting our strikes as they made their runs. Kind of like a cop on the beat. Also on patrol, performing its own jamming mission, was an EA-6B CAP. Prior to the mission, I had coordinated with our ordnance officer, Chief Warrant Officer Bob Conquest, to load us each with a one-thousand-pound bomb, in addition to our scheduled load of HARMs. Those who had flown these missions earlier hadn't had too much excitement because of the inactivity of enemy SAMs. I wanted to ensure that we didn't just end up boring holes in the sky.

Before we briefed the flight, Moto and I went down to the group S-2 (Intelligence) shop and went over their target list. This list was a group of targets we were authorized to hit as alternate targets, if for some reason our primary couldn't be struck. With the help of the Intel folks we settled on an enemy-occupied army barracks within a couple miles of the southern coast. Once we had been relieved on our HARM CAP we would make a bombing run on this barracks.

The HARM portion of the flight went about as expected. Neither Moto nor I could find anything we could justify loosing a missile at. At the end of the CAP period we were relieved as expected and went about on our own to set up for our ministrike. It was dark, and neither one of us had a FLIR pod. This meant we would have to drop our bombs using a radar delivery. While not as accurate as a visual or FLIR delivery, it was adequate enough for a barracks complex. As we were not pressed for time or fuel, and there was little AAA activity, we both made a practice run to ensure the best targeting and delivery possible. I can remember talking to myself, taunting "Abdul" in a bad Bill Murray accent (the movie *Caddyshack* is something of a cult favorite among us), while I sweetened my radar designation. Finally, with everything perfectly set up, I made my run with Moto about a minute behind me. The radar presentation couldn't have been nicer, and the actual drop went perfectly. I pulled up out of the dive and waited for the flash of the bomb explosion. As it was night and we weren't being particularly targeted by AAA, we were dropping from a lower altitude, and so the explosion came sooner than normal. Moto called out when the bomb went off and already had his own on the way to the same point.

Like most of our missions, particularly the ones at night, where we couldn't see firsthand, we never learned anything about the damage we inflicted. This was the only mission that I had a pang of conscience about. I hadn't been directed or ordered to hit this target. In fact, I wasn't even supposed to have the ordnance to do so. I had purposely gone out of my way to scam a couple of bombs to kill somebody. Almost like premeditated murder. But this clandestine sidetracking of bombs for personal strikes wasn't that unusual, and was something that I and others would do many times in the future. In fact, I gave it another shot a couple of hours later. No luck this time. The ordnance folks weren't able to waylay any bombs for our own personal effort. This wasn't too unusual, as they were pressed for time loading bombs for legitimate missions and there was somewhat of a shortage of ordnance.

I had Dave "Bull" Durham on my wing for this mission, which was a copycat of the first. Bull was our safety officer, a billet that at first glance seems a bit out of place in the middle of a war. But it had its place: we weren't going to be doing much damage to the enemy if we were breaking our necks or crashing our jets doing the mundane stuff.

Little SAM activity made for a fairly uneventful night. Uneventful didn't always mean uninteresting, though. With our radios we could follow other missions as they made their strikes. We were also able to watch the flash of their bombs and see an occasional SAM being fired in the distance, as well as the trails of AAA tracers and small-arms fire. Rockeye cluster munitions also made a unique sparkling pattern as they blanketed their targets. But still, without employing a weapon, we felt more like spectators than participants.

On 27 January the weather was back in town. I flew as part of a strike which Scotty was leading against an SA-3 (a Russian-built surface-to-air missile) site in Kuwait. The cloud layers reached all the way to thirty thousand feet. Though some of us had pretty decent radar designations, Scotty elected to save the bombs for a sure thing and we aborted. The weather would continue to be a factor, off and on, throughout the entire war.

The next day I flew the first of several missions I would fly in company with the two-seat F/A-18D. The "Ds" were envisioned as a quasi-replacement for the A-6 as the older bomber was phased out of service. This would be the first and only war in which the two types would fight in the same conflict wearing the marine mantle.

As an attack platform, each type has advantages and disadvantages. The A-6 is much older and more difficult to maintain. The F/A-18D is newer and designed with maintainability in mind. The A-6 is slower, but it also has a longer range and greater bombload. The F/A-18D has newer avionics but does not have all-weather attack capability. Most important, the Hornet is a very formidable air-to-air weapons system. The A-6 isn't much more than an air-to-air target. The Marine Corps looked at all the tradeoffs, including the commonalty with its single-seat Hornets, and decided to replace the A-6 with the F/A-18D. Since the war, the A-6 has been retired from both navy and Marine Corps service.

The Marine Corps has the two-seat Hornet filling a number of missions. The Marine Corps views the second crew member as enabling the aircraft to perform the night low-altitude mission. The pilot can concentrate on flying, while the backseater, or WSO (weapons system operator), can work on targeting. But in real life the crews are not always perfectly honed. The same pilot and WSO do not always fly together, and less than optimum crew coordination sometimes results in miscues. Unfortunately, one plus one can sometimes equal a big fat zero. The other role that has been assigned to the two-seat aircraft is that of the airborne forward air controller, or FAC(A). In this role the two-seat aircraft finds and marks targets, then controls bomb-laden aircraft as they fly in to destroy them.

To be honest, though, the very existence of the F/A-18D confuses many people. The two-seat F/A-18D is an outstanding jet because it's an F/A-18. Some argue it is inferior to the single-seat jet because the extra crew member takes up space that would otherwise be occupied by about one hundred gallons of fuel. The two-seater also performs no mission that the single-seat aircraft cannot do. In fact, because of crew coordination problems dividing tasks that can be handled by the pilot alone, the two-seaters at times do not perform as well as the single-seat aircraft. And finally, young two-seat pilots do not develop or mature as quickly as their single-seat counterparts because they don't carry the entire workload on every flight.

The role to which they are better suited than the single-seaters is that of the FAC(A). Two people can truly handle this task better than one. They did this superbly during the Gulf War. But realistically, the single-seater can do the job. Air force OA-10s do it. And forward air control does not make up the bulk of the F/A-18D's mission, so it's doubtful that the Marine Corps has procured six squadron's worth because they are marginally better airborne FAC aircraft.

Well, why have them? Some suspect a dark and selfish motive. The F/A-18D was supposed to be a replacement for the A-6. But it does not have all-weather attack capability as the A-6 did. Indeed, it is absolutely no more capable than the single-seat Hornet. Some suspect that the F/A-18D was an idea fostered and furthered by senior nonpilot bombardier navigators (BNs) of the A-6 community and radar intercept officers (RIOs) from the F-4. Sort of a vehicle with which they could ensure the survival of their own kind (in the back seat of a Hornet).

A telling comment on the entire issue is that the navy has no interest in the F/A-18D and feels that the marines' two-seaters are too short on fuel to deploy aboard aircraft carriers.

The FAC(A) mission is how the Marine Corps decided to use the F/A-18D in the Gulf War. And it was a good decision. The Ds would primarily prowl around Kuwait, looking for targets in designated areas. On finding the targets, they would call for bomb-carrying aircraft, usually F/A-18s or AV-8Bs, which would be orbiting on station nearby, to come destroy them. As the bombers came within visual range, the two-seater would roll in and mark the target, usually with a 5-inch or 2.75-inch white phosphorous rocket. With the marking round in sight, it was usually an easy matter for the bombers to adjust their aimpoints and destroy the enemy.

During the daylight hours, Ds would usually have a single-seat F/A-18 assigned as an escort. The idea was that the single-seat Hornet would carry a HARM or two for self-contained suppression of enemy SAMs, and a bomb or two for added effect on target. Most important, though, the escort was to provide high cover and give warnings of enemy hand-held SAMs and AAA. Two was also better than one in the very unlikely event that the pair was engaged by enemy aircraft. In addition, the escort could help out with the communications and perform other wingman-type duties.

If you could get some decent ordnance loaded on your jet, these were a pretty decent mission. You got to see a lot, drop some bombs, and usually go to the tanker a couple of times, so that the flight time often approached four hours. It was an escort mission that I was flying this time.

The pilot of the two-seater I was escorting was one of my former students from my days as an instructor in Beeville, Texas. George Zamka was a great guy. Funny, and he knew his stuff. This was early on in the D escort business, and though I honestly don't remember much about this mission, I do remember that we mostly just stooged around looking for targets. I know that we flew around the very southern border area of Saudi Arabia and Kuwait and that it was pretty much devoid of everything. Finally, we found a lone artillery emplacement, and I dumped three bombs into the thing. Lots of smoke, sand, and dust, but no fire. It was kind of hard to tell what kind of damage we did. We were still dropping from up high, with horrendous crosswinds, which didn't do our accuracy much good. We were still releasing our bombs at around fifteen thousand feet. At this altitude there were sometimes winds of up to one hundred knots. When we designated our targets, the aircraft computers would figure in a one-hundred-knot correction. The problem was that the crosswind was not at one hundred knots all the way down to the ground. This would throw our accuracy all out of whack.

After releasing my bombs, I decided to give the gun a go. I hadn't used it yet in the war. Most people hadn't. We were staying too high, and at altitude it wasn't really that effective. Anyway, I selected and armed the gun, rolled in, and squeezed the trigger. *Pop!* The gun fired one round and jammed. It was that kind of day. A relaxed, sunny afternoon, "lookin' around" kind of day. I don't know that I could have hurt somebody if I had crashed on top of them.

Late in January, the marine aircraft group in Shaikh Isa launched a strike to Baghdad. The target was a solid rocket fuel facility in the southwestern part of the city. Already hit by the air force, the plant was a huge and difficult target, and still needed more attention. Twenty Hornets made up the strike group. Four were tasked as air superiority MIG sweepers, twelve were bombers, and four were HARM shooters.

Fokker was in the four-ship of MIG sweepers. He was excited. The strike was going right into the heart of Iraq, a tremendous opportunity to bag an enemy jet. And he wanted one. Badly. Him, and every other fighter pilot in the world. Responsibility for the successful completion of the mission was squarely set on the shoulders of "Baja" Oltorik of VMFA-235. Leading the gaggle airborne before first light, he proceeded straight northwest out of Bahrain toward the tri-border area, where Kuwait, Saudi Arabia, and Iraq meet.

The border area, because of all the tanker traffic, entry and exit points, and control points, was typically jammed with aircraft. After an aborted run on the wrong set of tankers, the flight (with the help of a FLIR ID) finally rendezvoused with their dedicated refuelers. Well, clashed might be a better description of the encounter. They were supposed to meet up with a mixed bag of KC-130s and KC-135s. Evidently somebody zigged when they should have zagged, and the timing and join-up got all fouled up. Aircraft were everywhere as tankers were chased down, joined, and plugged. To make matters worse, the tankers didn't have enough fuel to meet the mission requirements. Two aircraft were mission-aborted for fuel.

Finally, after considerable delay, the package was refueled, reconstituted, and accelerated toward Baghdad. Major Bob "Boomer" Knutzen, the operations officer of VMFA-314, was leading the four-ship from his squadron behind Baja. He carries the story from here:

Because of the mess on the tankers, we had three thousand pounds less fuel than what was required for the mission. I wasn't going to turn back. We had orders to destroy the target. I figured that by taking a more direct route home, and with the help of tail winds, we could still make it back to Bahrain. If not, we still had the option of landing short somewhere in Saudi Arabia.

The run in was actually pretty quiet. No enemy air activity at all. I'm sure that Fokker was disappointed. Ironically, we used the same IP that the Israelis had used in the early '80s when they had bombed and destroyed Iraq's new nuclear plant. I guess a good idea is a good idea, regardless of who thinks it up.

A little ways out from the target, the HARM shooters offset and deployed in a wall. A moment later, I looked behind me and almost had a heart attack. What I had thought for an instant were SAMs were actually seven beautiful smoke trails from the HARM shots. Right on time, they would target and take down any SAM emitters that might try to guide missiles into us.

As we approached the fuel plant I was able to get a nice radar designation, which I handed off to the FLIR. The picture was beautiful. A huge industrial plant. It consisted of enormous blocks in rows that all together looked like an inverted egg carton. The bomb delivery would be difficult. Too shallow an angle would cause the bombs to impact the sides, doing little damage to the actual target at the bottom of the sloped blocks.

As we got closer to the target, the whole area above the plant erupted at about fifteen thousand feet into one solid, gray-white, sparkling cloud. Thirty-seven-millimeter AAA. It was obvious that they were tracking us by radar, as there was no way they could have seen us at our altitude of thirty thousand feet. After rolling in, I concentrated on making sure my dive angle was right. It was obvious that I was going to fly through the barrage of AAA, and I scrunched down in my seat as I passed through. We were carrying two MK 84, two-thousand-pound bombs each. I pickled these at twelve thousand, started my pull back up through the flak, and kept one eye on the FLIR.

I could see the two bombs hit simultaneously. The first one impacted the side of one of the blocks without much effect, but the second one hit right in the middle, creating a violent, brilliant, cylinder of light blasting out both sides as the rocket fuel exploded. One of my wingmen, "Rock" Collins, hit a pipeline that ran around the complex, and this also erupted into a giant sheet of flame.

After climbing up through the flak, my division was able to join up again so that we could look each other over. Everyone was okay, though one of my boys had somehow inadvertently pickled one of his wing tanks. We were feeling pretty good about ourselves. This had been briefed as a pretty tough mission. The AAA had truly been wicked. Before the flight we had joked that they should have scheduled all single guys for this one. Anyway, we blew off the preplanned egress route and put home on the nose for fuel considerations. As it turned out we made it back with enough gas to get safe on deck.

The mission was a success. Though there hadn't been nearly enough aircraft on the strike to destroy the entire plant, the facility had been very badly damaged. The explosions from the detonated rocket fuel showed up clearly on satellite imagery. In fact, Baja was awarded one of the very few Distinguished Flying Crosses given out by the Marine Corps for his role as the flight lead on this mission.

Chapter Fourteen

Khafji

Don't let the word "Khafji" fool you. Our unit never bombed into, or even very near, Khafji, but we flew some missions directly related to the action there, and some that perhaps influenced it.

Early on 30 January the duty clerk came into our rooms and woke us up. It was a travesty that more than five months after we had been in theater, the only way we had of communicating from the operational side of the base to where we were quartered was by sending someone in a vehicle three miles with a message. Iraqi troops had penetrated into Saudi Arabia. It didn't sound like a major effort to penetrate into the country and drive the coalition out, but nonetheless they had attacked and were there. We were to get aircraft airborne armed for CAS (close air support), and get on station close to Khafji as soon as we could. Four pilots were sent early. Lurch, me, and our wingmen would finish sleeping, then brief and take off at first light.

That is what happened. We got airborne with a ridiculously small load of three Rockeye CBUs (cluster bomb units) each. When it worked, the Rockeye was a neat weapon. Designed to be dropped from relatively low altitude, after release the bomb unit would separate in half and release hundreds of smaller bomblets. These bomblets would then disperse as they fell to earth, covering an area about the size of a football field. The bomblets were particularly effective against "light-skinned" targets such as trucks and APCs (armored personnel carriers).

At that time, because testing had never been completed, we were unable to load two Rockeyes per bomb rack. Though we had room for five in our normal configuration, we only carried three. Later in the war we either got clearance to carry five, or we just ignored the directive, because we launched with five.

Once airborne we headed north and checked in with the marine Tactical Air Control Center (TACC). This was an air-to-ground problem within the marines' area of responsibility, and so we were handling the command and control of all the air-to-ground sorties. It was a fiasco.

Marines are supposed to be the masters of CAS. It is one of our primary reasons for being. There is an elaborate command and control structure which is supposed to work like clockwork, as it smoothly controls the flow of sorties into, and out of, the battlefield. The problem is that it rarely ever works. It's not practiced enough, people are not well trained, and the equipment, particularly radios, stinks. On nearly all the exercises I had participated in throughout my career, including ones during Desert Shield, the command and control had been botched. And as we were expecting, it was messed up now.

For one thing, there were far more aircraft airborne and ready to play than the system was able to handle. There were several different types, and lots of them, from the marines, navy, and air force. When we checked in with the DASC (Direct Air Support Center) after being handed off from the TAOC (Tactical Air Operations Center), we were sent to a point to hold until we could be used. While holding, we could hear other flights checking in and also being sent to hold. As time went on, flights were sent to the tanker

VMFA-451 Logistics Department (S-4). *Left to right:* Captain liams, Corporal Cunningham, Corporal Davis, Gunnery Sergeant Rosenberg, Captain Stout. Note the purple heart ribbon painted on A/C nose above Captain liams. This was the same A/C liams was flying when he was struck by an enemy missile. *(Photo by U.S. Marine Corps)*

for refueling, in order to give them enough time on station. Occasionally aircraft would get lucky and get a mission assignment.

We were holding over a point just south of the border. Looking down, we could see various vehicles and ground units. Our preflight Intel briefing had given us very little information. We had no way of knowing whether the units below us were friend or foe. We didn't know if the enemy had penetrated on a broad or narrow front. When queried as to the identity of the units below us, the DASC told us in no uncertain terms not to drop on anything, or anyone, until directed. That was only common sense, and we wouldn't have anyway. It was obvious, though, that the DASC was uncomfortable and unfamiliar with what was going on below us.

The radio communication was extremely frustrating. Pilots were constantly stepping on each other as they tried to pass or receive information. There were so many aircraft that the DASC was getting confused. Some flights were able to communicate in an encrypted mode, while others weren't, further jamming the radios. People were missing radio calls, which had to be repeated. Others were constantly pushing DASC, trying to bully it into giving them a mission. Aircraft were running short on fuel, and pilots were whining. It was a Command and Control Carnival. That Lurch, our unflappable flight lead, was able to maintain his composure was inspiring.

We were sent to the tanker. Then back to holding. And more holding. Listening to the mess on the radios was infuriating. We were low on gas again. Back to the tanker. Back to holding. Finally we were assigned a mission. We were sent to join up with an F/A-18D working the coastal road across the border in Kuwait. The pilot had used up all his marking rounds and was verbally trying to talk our eyes onto a target alongside the highway. The backseater very professionally described it as "stuff underneath some camouflage netting." That was good enough for us. You can't run a war without good stuff, and we were just the group of guys to deny the enemy his stuff.

Particularly if we had been carrying the right weapon. But we weren't. At that point in the war we were still supposed to be bombing from relatively high altitude to stay away from enemy AAA. But Rockeye was designed for low-altitude delivery. The weapons system was unable to give accurate bombing solutions from high altitude. Additionally, the dispersion pattern for the bomblets was ineffective at altitude. But we were game. In we rolled. And dropped. The Rockeye went everywhere. We didn't see any effect on target and went home. The enemy's stuff was safe for now. Over four hours of flight time for virtually nothing.

Later, many of us from all different units would get together to try to solve the high-altitude Rockeye delivery problem. We never came up with a satisfactory solution. But soon enough we abandoned our high-altitude tactics and used the weapon down low, where it was intended to be employed. And we enjoyed a good deal more success.

Aircraft providing CAS attack enemy troops who are in close contact with our own. Because of the proximity of friendlies to the targets, this air support must be closely and expertly controlled, either by a marine on the ground (FAC), or by a FAC(A). The whole chain of command, communication, and control of CAS aircraft is beyond the scope of this book, but at end game is very simply boiled down. A FAC establishes radio contact with nearby aircraft armed and ready to provide close air support. He briefs them on the type of target, its location, the location of friendlies, and so on, as well as the exact time to drop bombs on the target. The target is then marked, usually with a white phosphorous mortar round, but occasionally by tank or artillery rounds, or lasers. Or if the FAC is airborne, by a white phosphorous rocket. When the attacking pilot visually acquires the "mark," the FAC adjusts his aimpoint from there. Usually bombs are on target within ten seconds of the assigned time. This is what was supposed to happen during the mission I had just flown with Lurch.

The marines are the avowed masters of this trade. Just read any newspaper or magazine article on the subject. True, we in good measure pioneered the tactic before, during, and after World War II. And we have continuously touted our prowess to help justify our reason for being. But the marines weren't and aren't the only experts. The Brits did plenty of it in World War II. The U.S. Army Air Force too. USAF in Vietnam. Gobs of it. But it's considered unglamorous work and the air force didn't need it as a primary mission to flesh out its budget.

Things have changed. Forces are being cut back and every service is scrambling for every mission, and every budget dollar, it can get. The air force pays a lot more attention to CAS now. The navy too. Who would have dreamed of F-14s lugging bombs in support of embattled Leathernecks when the movie *Top Gun* came out? Well, it's a reality now. The Marine Corps's response has been to beat its chest and scream louder than ever that its pilots are the very best at providing CAS.

Well, probably. But not by much. You see, it's just not that hard. With a two-week CAS "summer camp," air force pilots could be our equals at CAS, if they're not already. With global positioning satellite navigation systems, they're probably better equipped. At this writing, of the approximately one hundred sorties I have flown in the last six months, less than five have been CAS. Though to be honest, the Harriers and two-seat Hornets fly more CAS than us single-seat folks.

At the time of this writing, F-16s patrolling over Bosnia are equipped with Martin Lockheed's Sure Strike system. This system allows a FAC on the ground to get laser ranging and GPS positioning to a target, and link that information up to the F-16. The pilot then designates and steers a course to the target for a weapons delivery that is accurate inside of tens of feet. Indeed, he could make the delivery in clouds or at night with the same accuracy without ever seeing the target. It is a quantum improvement in terms of capability.

The true yet intangible value in marines providing CAS for marines is just that. That marine pilot is hell-bent on aiding that company commander on the ground. The Marine Corps isn't that big. They may well be friends. And being ground trained as well, he knows exactly what his "Band of Brothers" is going through. He's worked with them before and he's not going to let them down.

Back to the war. After all the practice and our supposed mastery of the art, classic fixed-wing CAS was used very little in the conflict. The reasons were many. Before the ground war, positions were fixed and there was little ground contact with the enemy. A significant portion of the CAS during Khafji was provided by air force A-10s. Once the ground war started, our troops encountered little resistance that they couldn't handle on their own. Also, the weather was so atrocious that target acquisition would have been very difficult. Additionally, the troops' line of advance was so quick, and frenzied, that it was difficult to keep track of who was where. The potential for "friendly fire" casualties was high. But mostly, the need for a lot of CAS simply did not exist.

To be fair, during the time of Khafji, there was some good CAS done. The poor guys in the DASC were trying their hearts out—and with some success. Probably none of them, though, had ever worked a problem as large and difficult as this one. It should be remembered, however, that we had some failures at Khafji. Men were killed by friendly CAS. They were a significant percentage of the total casualties from the war.

Later on we heard that one of our F/A-18D buddies had played an important part in stopping the initial push into Khafji. Bob "Tanks" Turner, one of my pals from Officers Candidate School over ten years earlier, and his WSO, were on a mission when the Iraqis pushed across the border toward the town. With his night vision goggles he was able make out the enemy formations as they rumbled on. Firing white phosphorous air-to-ground rockets designed to mark targets, he was able to cause enough confusion to singlehandedly stop the advance for some time. This, and the information he and his backseater were able to provide, were invaluable.

On the night of 31 January, Dip and I went on a mission into southern Kuwait that proved to be one of our more effective sorties during the war. We were scheduled for an armed reconnaissance mission, with Dip as the lead.

The preflight briefing, start, taxi, and takeoff went fairly uneventfully. By now everyone was into a pretty good routine and we had stopped scheduling ourselves for extraordinarily long briefs with details planned to the tiniest degree. We had been doing it for about two weeks now, and knew what was important and what was not.

Upon arriving on station off the coast, just south of the border, we went through the drill of checking in with the command and control network, ending up on the Direct Air Support Center frequency. Things had not changed much. Confusion reigned supreme. We listened in frustration as other flights checked in and were assigned missions, sent to the tanker, or just told to hold.

This particular evening the navy fliers were the unrivaled "boobs of the airwaves." Their radio comm, procedures, and preparation were lacking to the point that it was impacting their ability to perform the mission. They were checking in with the wrong call signs, at the wrong points, at the wrong time. They didn't have the day's code words or numbers and were unable to switch to an encrypted mode of radio comm. At the same time, because the DASC was spending so much time trying to unscrew them, everything else was suffering.

It seemed to us who saw or heard them that the navy sometimes just didn't get "the word." The major portion of the aerial campaign was coordinated and directed by an air tasking order, which was published daily. All inclusive, this very thick document was the Bible from which all participants drew their missions, and all the pertinent data needed to complete them. This data included items such as target types and locations, radio frequencies, IFF (identification, friend or foe) codes, code words and numbers, special instructions, and on and on. Evidently sometimes the navy didn't receive the document, or was off on its own program. That was what seemed to be happening this particular evening.

After wasting half an hour, we were sent to the tanker. Upon our return the situation hadn't changed. I was going nuts inside my jet, and I knew that Dip was doing the same. Finally he couldn't stand it anymore and raised Blacklist (DASC) on the radio: "OK guys listen to me. *I* know who *I* am. I know *where* I'm supposed to be. I know *what* I'm supposed to *do*. Now *give me a mission or I'm on my way home!*"

I cheered. We had been holding for so long that if we didn't get a mission soon, we would have had to return to base so that our jets could be readied for the next scheduled mission. It seemed like we had been forgotten. We probably were. There was a pause from the DASC. After a moment, almost apologetically, they gave us our mission particulars and we were on our way, glad to leave the confusion behind.

We had been given coordinates for a group of enemy vehicles in southern Kuwait. The Iraqis had not been completely routed from Khafji yet, and it was possible that they might try moving troops and equipment down from occupied Kuwait. We were excited about being turned loose to find and destroy the enemy. As it was night, and we were without night vision goggles, the only effective way for us to locate and destroy the enemy was with the FLIR pod. For bombing at night, this is the neatest gadget going. With its camera it senses infrared, or thermal energy, and transmits a continuous picture, similar to a black-and-white TV image, to the pilot. It is cleverly integrated with the rest of the aircraft's weapons delivery systems, and enables the pilot to find, designate, and attack a target.

Being dependent only on thermal energy, as opposed to the night vision goggles, which require small amounts of ambient light, the FLIR pod is effective on even the blackest of nights.

But tonight we had a problem. When the Hornet was purchased, the navy and Marine Corps only bought about one FLIR pod for every three aircraft. Dip's aircraft had a FLIR pod mounted, mine didn't. But we had worked out a plan. Our idea was that Dip would locate the target with his FLIR and bomb it. When his bombs exploded, I would note where his bombs hit, roll in, and drop my load. In practice, this plan really does not give the wingman much of a probability of success. It's difficult to visually fix a spot on the ground at night and keep it fixed. Much less maneuver an aircraft, at night, under "G" and effectively bomb it. This night, though, luck was with me.

It was the clearest night we had seen since we had been in the Middle East. From fifteen thousand feet I could look down through the dark and make out the darker ribbons of roads against the lighter background of the sand. There was enough ambient light to see significant detail on the ground. With the FLIR pod integrated so well with the rest of the jet, Dip was able to simply plug the target coordinates into the inertial navigation system and slave the FLIR pod to look directly at that spot on the ground. Nothing. The coordinates had either been inaccurate or the vehicles had moved on. Dip widened his search and I clung close, careful not to lose my lead. A few miles away from the original coordinates we hit pay dirt.

Hallelujah! Dip was really excited. He carefully related to me in detail what he had found, trying to help me build a picture in my mind's eye. Just off of a road running roughly east to west, there was a large horseshoe-shaped group of about sixty vehicles parked in bunches of five to six vehicles each. The vehicles appeared to be light armored fighting transports, or tanks, of some sort. Dip briefed me very carefully on just how he was going to attack the group, from what direction and altitude, and how I should adjust my bombing run after his.

Feeling exactly the same sort of excitement I felt when hunting, and that a covey rise was imminent, I separated from my lead so he could attack the target. Watching the point on the ground where I judged the target to be, I also listened as Dip told me when he was beginning his dive and when he released his bombs.

His bombs exploded. He shouted that he had good hits and I should hit the same spot. The bombs had exploded a little bit off from where I had expected and I told him that I was going to readjust my run and come in from a different direction in about thirty seconds. I was able to see the road next to his hits, as well as a few pinpoints of fire from burning vehicles. Dropping a wing, I flew away from the point for a moment or two to give myself enough room to make the run. Then, very carefully turning in and lowering my nose so as not to lose the target, I started my dive. At the same time I reached up to the HUD and dimmed the brightness of the display so that the target would still be visible through it. I was able to make a good designation and delivery. The aircraft shuddered and leapt as it quickly dumped its load of five one-thousand-pound bombs. Pulling out of my dive, I watched my bombs explode and simultaneously heard Dip shouting, "Good Hits! Good Hits!"

We rejoined and made our way home, checking out with the command and control net on the way. Our recovery back at the lighted air base was uneventful. It surprised me a little bit that throughout the entire war the airfield was kept lit. It would have been no problem for an enemy aircraft to find it at night, in the very unlikely event that he would have been able to get through. We didn't, however, have a whole lot of other options. Landing at a darkened field would have been nightmarish, and very dangerous.

After parking our jets, stopping through the maintenance department, and shucking our flight gear, we went to Intelligence to debrief. We crossed our fingers as Dip rewound his video tape so that we could watch the hits. Occasionally we would goof up the switchology for the camera, or the camera simply wouldn't record, for a number of different reasons. A lot of super work went unrecorded for these reasons. Fortunately, everything had worked perfectly. The tape showed the large cluster of vehicles that Dip had described. Our hits were beautiful. In slow motion the bombs were visible, looking like fish in formation as they fell through the air and found their marks. When the bombs exploded amid the targeted vehicles, the tremendous heat from the explosion blanked out the video. We were more lucky than good with my bombs. Considering the extremely crude targeting method we had devised for my drop, the fact that my bombs hit right in the middle of another group of armor was probably due in part to pure luck.

The Intelligence marine who debriefed us was even more excited than we were. He rolled the tape over and over. When we left he credited the two of us with twenty of the sixty vehicles we had seen. He kept the tape to forward it up the chain of command. Unfortunately, Dip never got the tape back, but we were rewarded a week or so later when we saw the tape featured in a news segment.

It's always nice to see your work appreciated.

Chapter Fifteen

Killing Boxes

A round this time, though we still continued to fly some large strikes, the emphasis and tactics for prepping the battlefield evolved a bit. We began to exercise the concept we called the killing box. The killing box was an area defined by longitude and latitude. I don't remember the exact dimensions, but ten miles by twenty miles seems about right. Just big enough so that if you paid attention, you wouldn't accidentally fly out of your box into someone else's.

The idea behind the killing box was to assign it to a given number of aircraft for a certain amount of time. During that period, the aircraft were free to roam throughout the box without fear of conflict with other aircraft or of bumping into a strike group. Though targets within that area might be highlighted for the mission, generally the pilots were free to pick and choose among whatever they might find.

The emphasis was, as it had been for some time, on artillery, armor, or whatever could directly harm our troops when the time came to storm Kuwait. But if something else particularly juicy presented itself, it was open season.

That we were able to do this was due in part to two factors. First, the threat from radar-guided SAMs was practically nil because of all the damage inflicted earlier, as well as the HARM and EA-6B umbrella that existed over Kuwait. Second, the air-to-air threat from Iraq over Kuwait was nonexistent. While airborne, I never heard of any Iraqi aircraft within a hundred miles of Kuwait. Certainly, I don't believe that any allied aircraft were ever molested by Iraqi fighters while operating over Kuwait. That is not to say that the skies over Kuwait were completely safe. Already, several aircraft had been brought down over the country, and more would be. The threat from hand-held SAMs and AAA was very high.

There was an area along the coast south of Kuwait City that was defined by two pointed bulges which extended into the Persian Gulf. Their appearance caused them to be tagged "the Tits." Simple, crude, and very descriptive. What else could a fighter pilot have called it? The Pointy Peninsular Projections? This area was notorious for very heavy AAA.

Hand-held SAMs were everywhere. Anywhere there were troops, it seemed they were armed with these relatively cheap and simply employed weapons. Pilots were coming back and reporting up to ten launches against a single aircraft. They would continue to plague allied aircraft until war's end.

My next couple of missions were killing box sorties. I believe they were officially called "armed reconnaissance." On the evening of 1 February, Vector and I were paired with Major Mike "Walt" Garrison and Fattie for a night mission into Kuwait. Walt, also known as the "Man Mountain" because of his tremendous size, was our assistant operations officer. With a wealth of Hornet experience, plus the Weapons and Tactics Instructor and Top Gun schools under his belt, he was a long-ball hitter for the squadron. On top of all that, he was a lot of fun, as well as protection, in the bar.

Mike Garrison, Bill Buckey, and Rick Hull return from the flight line at Shaikh
Isa, February 1991. *[Photo by author]*

The air tasking order called for four aircraft to cover an area for
half an hour. Because the area was a bit too small for four aircraft to
go milling around in the dark, looking for something to blow up, we
split the time in half. Walt and the Fatman would take the first fifteen
minutes, while Vector and I would follow and cover the second half.

In the brief, Vector and I worked out a plan similar to the one Dip
and I had used, and trailed Walt in getting airborne by about fifteen
minutes. After the usual command and control drill, we crossed the
border and contacted Walt. They weren't having any luck. No bad
guys anywhere. It seemed to them as if the Iraqis had simply packed
up and left the area. Anyway, they departed the box and took a cir-
cuitous route out, hoping to spot a lucrative target on the way.

Vector and I were a bit suspicious. How could there be nothing
worth hitting in an area that size? We established ourselves within
our assigned sector and started looking. The responsibility for finding a target belonged to me; Vector did not have a FLIR pod. I started
my search by first looking at some coordinates provided by Intel that

supposedly marked some artillery tubes. Nothing. We followed the main road, which ran along the coast. Nothing.

I was starting to get a bit concerned. Missions were hard enough to come by already, and I sure didn't want to lug five one-thousand-pound bombs all the way back to Bahrain. I didn't want to let Vector down, either. But I couldn't find a damn thing. My FLIR pod was a bit cranky as well. It wouldn't slew in direction very well and was difficult to fine tune. Still, I was covering a good chunk of countryside and not finding anything.

We flew down the coast for a way. Along parts of it, as we flew over, the ground would suddenly start sparkling and tracers would reach up toward us. We couldn't figure out what it was. Finally, we decided that perhaps another jet was violating our box and dropping cluster munitions. Later, I realized that we were flying over concentrations of troops, and that they were reacting to the sound of our jets by firing wildly into the air, hoping to get a lucky hit. We were only a few thousand feet up, and the sound was easily carrying down to the ground. Had I realized this at the time, or been able to find them on the FLIR, the enemy troops would have made a perfect target.

We were out of time. But we still had gas. So we just hung around for a couple of more minutes. And then a couple of more beyond that. We were yakking on our interflight frequency as I struggled to find a target.

"Vector, I can't find shit."

"OK, do you want to make another run down the coast?"

"Yeah, hey look at those explosions right below—"

I stopped before finishing my sentence. Directly below us a huge string of explosions was making its way across the desert. The number of explosions was indicative of a bombload far greater than any aircraft in the Marine Corps inventory could carry. As we were relatively low, we both instantly realized that if those explosions were occurring right below us, then the bombs must be coming from straight above us. To get from above, to right below, they had to be coming very close to us as they fell.

Captain John "Vector" Hartke, an air force exchange
officer with VMFA-451. It rained surprisingly often
during the winter of 1990–91. *(Photo by author)*

We had flown right under a B-52 mission. We had overstayed our
time in the box and now it had almost cost us. The chances of being
hit by a bomb were probably fairly small, but still big enough that
we had had the shit scared out of us. We made a hasty exit, still
loaded with bombs, and made an uneventful recovery. Upon arriving back at the squadron we found that Walt and Fattie had brought
their bombs back as well. No targets. At any rate the ordnance crews
got a break, in that they had four less jets they would have to reload.

The ammunition situation had gotten worse. Despite that evening's
dry spell, we were dropping bombs quicker than we could be resup-
plied. We were directed, in no uncertain terms, not to drop our
bombs unless good effect against an identifiable target was certain.

To have simply dumped them over enemy territory would have been unconscionable.

The use of B-52s on troops and equipment in the field was a little puzzling to us. We had seen long strings of craters criss-crossing the desert. I'm not sure how they actually designated and attacked the targets. Some of the strings of craters were near nothing at all, or came only close to something that might be considered a target. Or the string might cross a line of entrenched positions at an angle where only one or two bombs out of the entire load might have had an effect. I never saw an enemy position that appeared to be completely devastated by a B-52 attack.

Since then I have heard a plausible explanation for these seemingly errant strings of bombs. The U.S. military, and pretty much everybody else, uses many different sets of charts and maps. Unbelievably, some of these are based on data from surveys taken during the previous century. Variances from one set of charts and data to another can be close to a mile, more than enough to cause these miss distances. Whether this was the case or not, I don't know, but it is an interesting explanation.

So, on one hand it seemed to be an inefficient use of a very expensive strategic asset. On the other hand, there was no doubt that it had a tremendous psychological impact on the enemy. We heard stories from POWs captured during and after the war, about how the booming raids from the big bombers had a tremendously demoralizing effect on the troops in the field.

An hour or two after debriefing I was airborne again. This time Scotty, our squadron commander, was the flight lead with me on his wing. We were headed back to the same killing box, on the same type of mission. With the same results. I have no idea where the enemy had gone, if he had gone anywhere. Or why we were having such a hard time finding decent targets. But we were. It was extremely frustrating, racing back and forth over enemy territory with the tools and ability to hurt him, but unable to find him.

Finally, frustrated and tired, we headed back. During the flight my aircraft had been having bleed-air system problems. This system draws hot air from the engine and uses it to pressurize the cockpit and fuel systems, as well as provide air for the cockpit air conditioning. Evidently there was a leak, and extremely hot air was blasting somewhere it shouldn't. With warning lights starting to flash, and smoke in the cockpit, I secured the system as we made our way home.

Upon landing, an inspection revealed some badly burned ducting. The aircraft needed major repair, and in fact did not fly again for the rest of the war. It was used for the rest of the conflict as a parts bin. That is, it was cannibalized by our maintenance effort for parts to keep the rest of the jets in good working order.

The air force had done it again. They were too good to use a sawed-in-half fifty-gallon drum as a toilet. That just wouldn't do. That lifestyle was too pagan. Too marine. They had recently erected a modern, modular, environmentally controlled complex of rest room facilities. It was beautiful. We were nothing except jealous until a sign appeared one day at the entrance: NO MARINES!!! Well, when a marine sees a sign like that he gets kind of dyslexic. To him it says something like "Abuse the shit out of this since they won't let you use it." And we did. First, the plug on the holding tank was mysteriously pulled. Several times. That our own working spaces, downhill from their facility, were getting flooded didn't matter. Deep in our hearts we knew that our air force sisters were being denied the use of their shitter. The sign was torn down too. The air force responded. Barbed wire went up around it. And more barbed wire. We were reduced to throwing fluorescent sea-dye markers into the tank. They put a cover over it. A number of other different attacks of varying sorts were mounted. In the end we lost. We ended up having to guard their latrines with our own marines (latrine marines . . . sorry, I couldn't resist). By the time the cease-fire came about (the Shitter Wars cease-fire, not the one with Saddam), that place was more secure than our MAG Intelligence section. More useful too.

On 3 February I briefed and led a group of eight Hornets against an army installation northwest of Kuwait City. The target was described as a commando barracks. As the lead I made target assignments, briefed the flow across the target and the egress, and took care of the more mundane particulars. We were all much more experienced by now and the atmosphere was almost relaxed.

The bomb supply at this time had gotten to the point where we had virtually run out of the MK 83 one-thousand-pound bombs. They were being saved for those missions where they were an absolute requirement for destruction of a target. For this mission we were going to be loaded with five MK 82 five-hundred-pound bombs instead of the usual five MK 83s.

The smaller bombs, at half the size of what we were used to carrying, looked almost like toys suspended from our jets. They were used mostly by the Harrier units because the smaller weight and size was better suited to their capabilities. At the time there happened to be many more of the MK 82s than the larger MK 83s, though, and so that is what we were loaded with for awhile.

While preflighting the bombs we made a surprising discovery. They were old. Real old. The date of manufacture of the bombs loaded on my jet was 1957. Two years before I had been born. Those things were five years old when I was potty trained. When I was pitching in Little League baseball, they had been sitting around somewhere for fourteen years. They had escaped the Vietnam era without being used. They had survived thirty-four years of continuous military training. *My kids* had been potty trained for over five years before they were finally pulled from some bunker somewhere, shipped overseas, and loaded on my aircraft.

The routing for the strike did not require us to do any aerial refueling. I led my eight-ship airborne a little early and thus ended up dragging them along at a wallowingly slow airspeed through Saudi Arabia, so that our timing would not be off as we struck the barracks. Sorry guys.

The weather was back. Crossing the border and accelerating, it wasn't immediately evident whether we would have the weather to bomb visually. With my radar, I was able to get a good picture and designation on the target. My own personal target, and Wolfy's (my wingman), was a fuel depot just out the gate of the compound and down the road a bit. The radar picture was very clear, and I was easily able to pinpoint the exact location.

This was one of the sorties where Intelligence had been able to give us good photographic intelligence of our target. They had marked a number of points inside and around the compound, and because of it we were able to do some good targeting even with the radar. Approaching our roll-in point, we could see breaks in the clouds, in and around the compound. There was some electronic interference on the radios, but no AAA or SAMs yet. Considering the good radar pictures, the size of the target, and the considerable footprint our strings of bombs would cover, I made the decision to press the attack. Additionally, there was a good possibility that as we arrived overhead, there would be enough of a break in the cloud cover that we would be able to employ our weapons visually.

While I had my head buried in the cockpit, sweetening my radar designation, I ended up flying a bit close to the barracks, and so ended up in a very steep dive following my roll-in. With a dive angle approaching sixty degrees, my weapons release point came up very quickly and the airplane jumped as the five bombs were dropped. Pulling out of the abnormally steep dive, I could see through a hole in the clouds as my bombs exploded exactly where Intelligence had briefed the fuel depot location. Looking around, I could see other jets in various parts of their bombing dives, as well as bombs exploding in and around the compound.

Exiting the area, and rejoining over the gulf, we could see AAA just starting to come up to try to knock us down. It was obvious that none of it was radar assisted, as it was very inaccurate. It was likely they were only reacting to the explosions on the ground. Too little, too late, too stupid.

Back on the ground during debriefing, I learned that every one of Wolfy's bombs had dudded. This was a problem that had bothered us consistently in ones and twos since the beginning. We weren't sure if the problem was with bad fuses, improper loading procedures, employment, or a combination of things. But this was the first time we had experienced a whole bombload not exploding.

Also, I found that in flying too close to my target I had dragged a couple of guys along with me, and they hadn't been able to get to a steep enough dive angle to deliver their bombs. I felt a little bad about this, and I filed it away as a learning point for later. As with nearly every one of our missions, we were never able to get a battle damage assessment from our S-2 folks. I guess that if we had destroyed ten thousand Scud launchers, or dropped a bomb on Saddam, they would eventually have gotten around to letting us know.

I don't know how much effort was expended trying to collect post-strike data. Very little is how it seemed to us. In general, if we wanted to get information after a strike, we would have to hound the already overloaded S-2 folks until they were able to produce something, or until we, or they, just gave up. Mostly we just gave up. This was bad for morale. It didn't do much for us tactically, either. During and just after a strike, there was often so much smoke and dust that we were unsure of the effect of our weapons on the target, and whether the type of weapon and fusing we used was effective on that type of target. Fortunately our superiority in other areas was so overwhelming that we were able to operate and prevail with a less than adequate Intelligence capability.

It was not the fault of our enlisted marines. During peacetime in the squadron they generally don't have a trained Intelligence officer for guidance and supervision. Most of the time they spend moldering away in an office where their talents and skills aren't exercised. Little is demanded of them other than an occasional training lecture, which is rarely critiqued and usually amateurish at best. A good presentation is one which doesn't cause the pilots to squirm with embarrassment for the poor corporal and his stumbling delivery. Occasionally they do get tasked during an exercise, but this is usually so canned that the training value is questionable. The majority of their peacetime duties do very little to prepare them for what is needed during war.

Let me talk for a moment about our enlisted marines and a couple of the dramatic changes I have seen in just under fifteen years of service. One of the most obvious and positive improvements has been the almost virtual elimination of drugs from the Corps. In my first squadron, during the early to mid-1980s, it was not unusual for fifteen to twenty marines to "pop positive" for some sort of drug use during unannounced urinalysis sweeps. Now it's unusual to uncover a single incident in an entire year. I believe this is a product of the military's "zero tolerance" attitude, the better education of the young people recruited, and a better drug awareness in our culture. I think the near nonexistence of drugs in the Marine Corps has made a significant difference in our performance and capabilities.

The services recruiting arms have done a tremendous job drawing in talented, bright, young people. Well over ninety-five out of a hundred are high school graduates who are eager to work, learn, and lead. Had I been placed in this group at their age, I would have been a middle-of-the-pack performer. These sharp young people are probably the primary reason we have been able to pare numbers in the service and still fulfill our mission (though we're hitting bone now!).

I have had the pleasure to serve with them in literally every clime and type of place. Winter in Norway above the Arctic Circle, the jungle environment of the Philippines, and the stinging desert of Kuwait. They have never let me down. Though they do complain. We all do. It's human nature, and to a marine, it's an art. That they were the backbone of marine aviation's success in this war is a given. However, I'll never underestimate (overestimate?) the average marine's talent for getting into trouble. Give him time, half an excuse, a six-pack of beer, perhaps a paper clip and a wad of gum, and stand by. He'll get into situations that Stephen King, paired with Lucille Ball and a good dose of LSD, would be hard pressed to match. I love marines.

The next day, 4 February, I again had the opportunity to lead. This time it was a twenty-aircraft strike against some sort of Republican Guards regiment with an unpronounceable name. The targets were mostly artillery emplacements in south central Kuwait, near Ahmed Al Jaber Air Base. Because the AAA, and particularly the radar-guided SAM threat, had been so ineffective against us up to this point, I made the decision to break the strike up into divisions of four aircraft. These divisions had separate target assignments and times on target. There was enough time built in for each division to loiter over its target and drop its bombs in pairs or singly if desired. This would allow us to be more careful, and, we hoped, more effective, with our selection of targets.

Again, the brief and flight up were fairly standard and uneventful. We were getting to the point where we could have flown the route with our eyes closed. Approaching the enemy positions, we were met with some light and sporadic AAA and not much else. We broke up for individual attacks. The idea was that while one aircraft was in its dive delivery, the others would be watching him to warn of AAA, or more importantly, hand-held SAMs.

These SAMs would prove to be the biggest threat to the Hornet. Most of them could be easily decoyed with flares. Technically, the F/A-18 could carry up to sixty of these decoy flares. The SAMs were infrared, or heat seekers, and were designed to home on hot jet-engine exhaust. The flares put out a more intense source of heat and so were able to decoy most of the hand-held missiles.

One of the problems with the flares was that they were very visible to the naked eye. If the enemy on the ground didn't see you initially, he almost definitely would once you started popping out flares. The idea was that it wouldn't really matter since the flares would decoy any SAM the enemy put up. The problem with that was that the flares were absolutely worthless against AAA. If the AAA gunners could see you, they would shoot at you.

This didn't matter to a lot of pilots. They would rather put out flares from the time they started their dive until they had dropped their bombs and were safely at altitude, or out of the target area, and take their chances with the AAA. This used a lot of flares. Others, myself included, preferred not to highlight themselves with the flares. I would normally not employ my flares until I had already dropped my bombs, was down at low level, noisy and readily visible, and on my way up and out. Or not dispense any flares at all unless I had been shot at. Here, I was betting that I would be able to pick up the SAM visually at launch and get some flares out before it could guide to impact. Not always a safe bet, but it saved flares for subsequent runs.

Also, to increase our chances of survival, we arranged our attacks so that we would never come from the same direction two times in a row. This kept the enemy gunners guessing, as it is very difficult to visually detect a fighter coming in from higher than five or six thousand feet until it gets down to a lower altitude. And that lower altitude would often vary as well, depending on sun angle, haze, cloud background, and so on. Sometimes it's tough to see a jet at only a couple of thousand feet. In fact, looking down from high to low, it was sometimes difficult to keep our own wingmen in sight.

Sometimes adding to this difficulty of keeping sight was a problem unique to the Warlords of VMFA-451. Within the previous year our unit had painted false canopies on the bottom side of its jets. The idea was that outside of about half a mile, if one of our jets went belly up to an enemy aircraft, the enemy pilot wouldn't be able to tell whether he was looking at the top or the bottom of the jet and would become confused. Well, it worked. But it worked both ways. Sometimes it was hard as hell to tell what in the world your wingman was doing. This idea of false canopies has been attributed to the great aviation artist and historian Keith Ferris, and is still widely used by the Canadian air force.

On this mission we weren't receiving much attention. I rolled in to release a pair of five-hundred-pound bombs on a battery of artillery guns. The delivery was good, but as I pulled off target, I was disappointed to see both bombs dud as they impacted in the battery and kicked up a sad little cloud of dust. Duds again. Vector rolled in and dropped a pair of bombs with good effect, as did the rest of the division. Picking up a new target, I dropped down and released my remaining three bombs. Dust, dust, *ba-boom!* Two more duds and a good hit with secondary explosions. A couple of tubes in the battery were gone with some good secondary explosions, probably from ammunition stored with or near the guns.

Discriminating among good hits, poor hits, and secondary explosions amid the explosion from the bomb itself is not as easy as it might seem. It's almost an art form. Obviously, if the target is small and you see it explode from a direct bomb hit, you can assume it was destroyed. Particularly since there is normally nothing left after a direct hit. If a bomb hits the ground nearby with no incendiary effect, there will be the usual flash as it explodes, followed by black smoke and billowing dust. I had my own personal observations and criteria to help me decide whether something besides the ground was hit. The explosions were different. If something volatile such as fuel or ammunition, or a vehicle carrying one, the other, or both, was hit, the explosion often was asymmetrical with fuzzy extensions or arms of smoke extending from the center of the explosion. These "fuzzy arms," as I liked to call them, were chunks of burning material being "blown to kingdom come." The explosion generally would last a bit longer with a sustained fire after the initial blast. Secondary explosions were obvious, as fuel or ammo would cook off and burn long after the initial blast.

I don't think we ever satisfied ourselves with a good explanation as to why we were getting so many duds. Some folks thought it was the age of the bombs. Others thought that perhaps they were being loaded improperly, as most of the time it was just one airplane during a particular mission that would experience the majority of the duds. Bad lots of fuses were also suspect. Our ordnance personnel resorted to double-fuzing the bombs with both contact and electrical fuses. Earlier, we had been relying almost exclusively on the electrical fuse. Because the contact fuse was so reliable and exploded instantly upon impact, it pretty much defeated the purpose of the electrical fuse, which gave us the option of selecting delays after impact to detonation. Fortunately, against the types of targets we were striking this wasn't important. And our dud rate seemed to drop after we started using double fuses.

After we had finished working over the target, we checked out with the command and control net as we made our way back home. One of the reports the Tactical Air Control Center always wanted from us was our estimate of the BDA. We would always give our best guess, or if we had been working with a FAC(A), we would pass on the BDA he had given us for our bombs. Most of us took this very seriously and erred to the conservative side rather than trying to make ourselves look good by making bogus claims. It was very disheartening, then, when we listened to the news and heard reports of the higher ups in Riyadh and the Pentagon discounting pilot claims and counting only those kills which they could verify through hard film or video evidence. If they could get that kind of information after a strike, why couldn't they pass it to us? And why couldn't they get good photo Intel to us before a strike?

This was one of the reasons we preferred having jets loaded with a FLIR pod, even though it meant we had to carry one less Sparrow missile (there was virtually no air-to-air threat). The FLIR pod would automatically slave to a designated target and stay slaved as the bombs impacted. Pilots could bring this video back as irrefutable proof of their success. However, only a third of our jets were so equipped. A good deal of fine work went unacknowledged and unrecognized because no video was brought back. A picture carries more weight than a marine officer's word.

Chapter Sixteen
Night Intruders

Marine F/A-18s weren't the only jets doing good work out of Shaikh Isa Air Base. If ever a war was a perfect fit for a given airplane, it was the Gulf War for the A-6E Intruder. Designed and built with 1950s technology, the Intruder had proven itself long before in Vietnam, and more recently over Libya. It was intended to fill the night-attack, bad-weather role, but was effective day or night, bad weather or good. The marines had two squadrons at the base, VMA(AW)-533 and VMA(AW)-224 (VMA[AW] stands for Fixed-wing Marine Attack All Weather).

Now retired from navy and Marine Corps use, the A-6E had a two-man crew consisting of a pilot and a BN, or bombardier-navigator. As you might guess, the pilot flew the jet while the BN did the navigating and handled the bulk of the weapons systems. Because the aircraft was older, its systems were not quite as advanced as those of later aircraft, and so were more manpower intensive. Both crew members earned their pay.

"Ease of maintainability" was not a phrase which came to mind when the Intruder was mentioned. Again, the older design and the age of the airframes demanded a great deal of attention and work from the maintainers. The maintenance hours per flight hour were quite high relative to the newer jets.

Because the jet was slow and big relative to the Hornet, it was employed mostly at night. With the radar SAMs largely taken out of the picture, and the enemy virtually blind at night, the biggest threat to the A-6Es was a lucky hand-held SAM shot or AAA barrage. Or, more realistically, running into another aircraft in the crowded skies over Kuwait or Iraq.

But the Intruder could haul a load of bombs. And deliver them accurately. On some sorties, the Intruders were taking off with over twenty five-hundred-pound MK 82 bombs or a similar load of Rockeye CBUs. It also carried a great deal of fuel, which gave it tremendous range and loiter time. Whereas the Hornets would go on night sorties, the tremendous payload and fuel specs of the Intruder allowed it to go on night "adventure safaris." A typical mission would be a night armed-reconnaissance sortie into Kuwait or southern Iraq. Once established over enemy territory, the Intruders would fly about, "trolling" for lucrative targets. Because of their payload, they could afford to work a target over, finish with it, and go hunting for more. Fuel consumption was not nearly the concern that it was for the Hornet drivers.

Intruders also had a FLIR set. Called the TRAM (target recognition and attack multisensor), and permanently mounted underneath the chin, it was operated by the BN and equipped with a targeting laser. This enabled the A-6E crews to carry the hugely successful laser-guided, or "smart," bombs, which were the stars of so many of the "hit videos" featured during press debriefings of the air war. Typically they would carry one or two of the expensive bombs on each sortie and save them for the best targets.

Unfortunately, the video recording system they had on board was old and didn't deliver as clear a picture as the video systems on the newer aircraft. Nonetheless, they brought back some tremendous footage. One particularly impressive tape recorded an attack on an enemy barracks. There were troops scurrying everywhere, trying to escape the Intruder as it delivered a planeload of Rockeye cluster bombs. There was no doubt that they were the kings of nighttime attack over Kuwait.

But their missions weren't all night solo sorties. They played a big role in many of the large strikes, particularly early on in the conflict. More than one of their flyers was decorated for flight leadership while executing these large strikes. The Marine Corps should be very proud of the contributions that the aircrew and troops of these two units made as they helped close out the final chapters of the Intruder in Leatherneck service.

Chapter Seventeen
The Running Man Tapes

More and more, we tended away from the large strikes, concentrating more on battlefield preparation in Kuwait itself. Word was that the invasion was scheduled for 22 February, and so there was still a lot of work to do. This information was general knowledge and came right from the top. If we had ever been captured by the enemy and interrogated, we would have had to make stuff up to tell them. They would have known everything else. I'm not sure if the twenty-second was planned disinformation, lax security, or what. Perhaps it was felt that it really didn't make any difference whether Iraq knew or not.

The weather was back and kept me from flying any missions on 5 and 6 February. On the seventh I had Kato on my wing as part of a four-plane mission into east-central Kuwait. Z-Man was leading it with Vector on his wing. We had been briefed by Intelligence that there was an artillery position at a certain set of coordinates, and that we were to destroy it.

When we got there, we didn't find much. Z-Man and Vector separated a couple of miles to the north while Kato and I wandered south. We came upon a set of trenches dug into the desert shaped like giant Ws. We didn't know what they were. There were variations in their shapes. Some of them looked squashed, some stretched, and others had offshoots. Some of the offshoots led to other positions and others led nowhere. At the junctions, or points of the Ws, there were dug-out holes, which we guessed may have been command and control points for troops, supply points, or gun positions. Whatever they were, we knew that they were freshly dug, Iraqi, and fair game.

Kato and I set up an orbit around the positions and started our runs. We were still fairly close to Z-Man and Vector, who had found fresh game of their own, and so had to be careful not to run into their pattern. On this day we were carrying two MK 84 two-thousand-pound bombs each, one under each wing. This was a manly weapon. Though we were only carrying two, they were twice as big as the bombs we normally dropped, and they created a tremendous explosion. I had never dropped one before.

I picked my first target, and dropped a bomb. The airplane, instantly two thousand pounds lighter, almost leapt as the bomb fell away. The now unladen wing flipped up because of its lightness relative to the other. Looking over my shoulder, watching the trench, and putting out chaff and flares as I climbed toward safety, I was surprised at the size of the explosion. That was a *big* bomb! The trench disappeared in the blast.

An instant later I felt my aircraft shudder. Oh shit! In a panic I kept my jet turning toward the coast and looked it over. Now it seemed to be flying okay; the engines were operating fine. Kato hadn't seen anything hit me. I could find no damage to any part of the aircraft. It finally dawned on me that what I had felt was the shock wave from the bomb blast catching up to me and rattling the airframe as I climbed. I had never before dropped a bomb of that size and was unprepared for the jolt.

I regathered my wits and repositioned the seat cushion, which had gotten pinched halfway up my back end during my panic. That finished, I let Kato know I was okay and turned back toward the positions to drop my other big bomb. The second delivery went the same as the first, except that this time I was ready for the big thump from the bomb concussion as it caught up with my jet.

Debriefing with Intel upon our return, I wasn't surprised that they weren't able to tell me what the big trenches were. My guesses were as good as theirs. We subsequently encountered and attacked these types of positions many more times. To this day I have never received a satisfactory explanation as to what they were. I did bring back a tremendous sequence of FLIR video from my second bomb delivery, and was quite pleased when this one was later shown in a news segment.

We had mixed feelings about the two-thousand-pound bombs. The effect on target was outstanding. If the bomb was delivered with anything near normal accuracy it had a devastating effect on the target. However, because of the way our jets were configured, with one fuel tank hung under each wing, we could only carry two of them. If the delivery was goofed, then that left only one more bomb to finish the job. The same thing applied if one of the bombs dudded. If we were going to go out plinking tanks or artillery positions one bomb at a time, it really didn't matter if they were hit with a one-thousand- or two-thousand-pound bomb. The only difference was that the pieces flew further if they were hit with a two-thousand-pounder. It was to our advantage then if we carried five of the one-thousand-pound MK 83s. We could destroy more stuff. The two-thousand-pound MK 84s were better suited to bunker busting or sorties of that nature.

Since the war's beginning we had filled our time with a number of activities. If we weren't flying, we spent a good deal of time eating, sleeping, or writing letters. Hanging around the Operations tent was a great pastime. Here we could gossip with our buddies, review their missions and tapes with them, and find out the most recent goings-on over our operations area. Our ground duties also took some time, as did preparing for upcoming missions. Forays into town just about stopped. I think I made one trip into Manama during the war. We were just too busy, or tired, and there was some concern about the terrorist threat.

As the war continued, security on the base was stepped up but from our point of view was never much that would have deterred a resolute and trained foe. The terrorist threat to us as individuals affected each person in different ways. Most guys didn't really give it much thought. Though of course during the slow time, which was most of the time, there wasn't one of us who didn't imagine himself holding off a gang of terrorists with his trusty nine-millimeter pistol. But mostly we just didn't give it much thought.

Kato was an exception, however. He was constantly cleaning and fingering his weapon, as he was certain that heavily armed terrorists were going to ambush us at every turn. He also pulled his mattress off his bed, which was close to a window, and put it on the floor so as not to present an easy target. I can remember one day when a bunch of us were gathered together and Kato was cleaning his weapon for about the fourteenth time that day. Major Rick "Train" Hull set him up perfectly.

"Kato, do you know what you really ought to do with your pistol?" Train said.

"What's that, sir?"

"You ought to file the front blade off of the gunsight," Train answered.

Kato's interest was piqued. Maybe this was some sort of sharp-shooting technique. "Why's that, sir?"

"Well, that way it won't hurt nearly as much when the Iraqis jam it up your ass!"

The rest of us laughed so hard we couldn't breathe.

One of my favorite activities was cards. Specifically, euchre. Kind of a poor man's bridge, it's a favorite in the Midwest. Initially there weren't many folks in the squadron who knew how to play it. However, between myself, an Indiana boy (God's country, you know), and Chuck Seaver and Earl Bellon from Michigan, we made quite a few converts. Both of these guys were chief warrant officers. They made things happen while the rest of the officers were flying. "Pearly" Bellon ran the unit Administration Department, while "Chuck-San" was the assistant maintenance officer. Another regular was "Wild Bill" Hidle, our avionics guru. Pearly played cards by a system of maddening intuition and wild guesses. But he won more often than not. Chuck was good at cards because he was extremely smart. We would play for hours at a time. Some of my best memories from this period are of a bunch of us sitting around in various stages of dress (or undress), having a drink, and throwing cards around the table and at each other. Just like the movies.

The ninth of February was an exciting day for the squadron. Late in the morning Wolfy came back from a mission on which he had been hit. He had been part of a four-plane sortie on which they had been "circling the wagons," working over an Iraqi position. After a bomb release while he was climbing up to altitude he felt a thump and the aircraft yawed over to one side. Sluggo, who was part of the division, was above him looking down and asked, "Who's that on fire down there?"

At the same time Hatch started screaming at Wolfy, "Get out, get out, get out, . . . *over the water!*" He had a panicked note in his voice as he added the last part, realizing that Wolfy might have miscon-strued the meaning of his "get out" call and ejected right there over enemy territory. If Wolfy had gotten into more trouble and had actu-ally needed to eject, he would have been much safer, and would likely have ended up in friendly hands, if he ejected out over the coast.

No one saw what had hit him. It was likely a hand-held SAM. What-ever it was had detonated underneath his jet and had perforated the bottom of his fuselage, a fuel tank, and his flaps. The fire that Sluggo had seen was caused by the rocket motor from one of Wolfy's fuselage -mounted AIM-7 missiles. The motor had been hit by a hot piece of shrapnel and had cooked off while still attached to the jet. This sent a huge trail of flame aft as it burned. The heat from the burning motor had scorched the aft fuselage of the jet on that side and had badly burned the engine bay door.

Fortunately, though, the jet was still flyable. Wolfy made his way out over the gulf and was joined by his comrades. They looked him over carefully as he made his way back to base and gave him a report

Rick "Train" Hull over Manama, Bahrain, January 1991. *(Photo by author)*

on what they could see. He ended up jettisoning the burned-out AIM-7 prior to landing and made an otherwise uneventful recovery.

Wolfy was a bag full of mixed emotions (though until he emptied his trousers, he smelled more like a bag full of shit). First, I think he was happy to be alive, never mind happy that he had gotten the jet back safely. Second, he was worried, or concerned, that he had done something wrong. He spent quite a bit of time in front of the VTR machine reviewing his tape, checking for clues as to why he had been hit. But there wasn't much there. His airspeed and altitude certainly weren't any slower or lower than those of other pilots. We finally decided that it must have had something to do with the way he was holding his tongue.

The damage to the jet was not as extensive as it had first looked. The troops were able to patch the holes in the flaps and the fuselage. The burnt aft fuselage and engine bay door were quickly repaired as well. In fact the aircraft was flying the very next day. We never figured out exactly what had hit him. Some chunks of sheet-metal-type fragments were pulled from a few of the holes. These were about one inch by one inch in area and were burned and twisted. This sort of shrapnel seemed consistent with the material that would come from a hand-held SAM rather than an explosive AAA shell.

This incident marked the first time that a jet from the base had been hit by enemy fire. That we had gone so long without suffering any damage or casualties was a testament to a number of things. For one, it validated our tactics. We had tailored our flying and bomb deliveries to the threat. We had successfully inflicted heavy damage on the enemy while still giving ourselves some measure of protection. Another factor was our use of countermeasures, which took the form of expendables such as chaff and flares, as well as HARMs, onboard jamming equipment, and of course the EA-6Bs, which provided a protective ECM (electronic counter-measures) umbrella. The successful integration of all these factors, and more, was a validation of our training, and a justification of the vast sums of money spent on our equipment (though the sum spent on marine aviation was a lot less vast than the sums of some of the other services).

The same day Wolfy was hit, I flew an escort hop with an F/A-18D. We spent some time over central Kuwait working with some Harriers, marking and directing strikes on some revetted armor positions. The drill was fairly simple and typical for the entire conflict. As the Harriers got airborne and checked in with the command and control net, they would be directed to a control point. Once there, they would switch frequencies and contact the FAC(A), which was the two-seat Hornet. If the two-seater wasn't working a group of aircraft already, he would give them a set of coordinates to the target he was concentrating on. Or if he did have aircraft currently working the target, he might direct them to the area with instructions to hold overhead.

Once established in the target area, the F/A-18D would briefly describe the target he wanted hit, and how he wanted it done, along with a quick "heads-up" as to what the enemy response in the form of AAA or SAMs had been. Then, if he hadn't already expended them all, he would dive on the target and mark it with a white phosphorous rocket. For the Iraqis, this must have been "one of nature's most fearsome warning signs." Something akin to a rattlesnake's warning just before the strike. If he was out of rockets, the FAC(A) would simply do it the good, old-fashioned way and try and talk the bombers' eyes onto the target. In this case, the comm could get fairly colorful. Frustrating, as well:

FAC(A): "OK, see that road intersection next to the burning truck?"

Bomber: "Uh, no. . . . Oh yeah, I got it."

FAC(A): "OK, that's not it. Follow the eastbound road out of that inter-section for about half a mile until you get to a burned-out build-ing. Do you see that?"

Bomber: "Um, no . . . you mean by this antenna farm?"

FAC(A): "Aaah . . . No! That's west! Look *east,* about a half mile. See that burned-out building?"

Bomber: "Oh yeah. You want me to hit that?"

New bombers checking in: "Four Harriers at the control point, five minutes time on station before we need to push." (The Harriers were *always* low on fuel.)

FAC(A): "Standby! No, don't hit that building! Look north about two hundred yards. Christ, who was that who almost ran into me?!? Everybody stay at your assigned altitude! See those brownish bumps north of the building?"

New bombers: "Understand you want us to come in now? We're still at the control point."

FAC(A): "No! You wait! If you don't have the fuel, then go home!"

Original bombers: "Hey, I think I've got the target. . . . Looks like revetted vehicles?"

AWACS on-guard frequency: "Reef 41 turn north now. I say again. . . ."

FAC(A): "That's your target. Cleared hot!"

And on and on it would go. Obviously it was much to the FAC(A)'s advantage, and much easier for everyone else, if he had plenty of Willie Pete (slang for white phosphorous) marking rounds.

On this day I was fortunate enough to have a pair of MK 83s loaded. During lulls in the activity, the escorts would do some free-lance work of their own with the FAC(A), or use the bombs to sup-press AAA emplacements. I used mine to work over the same emplace-ments that everyone else had hit. Unfortunately, one of my bombs dudded, and so 50 percent of my entire load was useless.

As discussed earlier, dudded ordnance was not unusual. I have no doubt that a hundred years from now, they will still be finding tons of unexploded bombs, newly uncovered by shifting sands. One horrible effect of the effort to liberate Kuwait is that the country-side was, is, and will be for a long time littered with numberless pieces of unexploded devices. Kuwaiti families who used to journey into the surrounding desert for traditional nomadic holidays now travel instead to the explosive-free sands of Saudi Arabia. Rockeye bomblets have been particularly devastating. A significant number of U.S. casualties were caused by inadvertent contact with these deadly little bomblets.

The nature of the environment, with its moving sands, makes it particularly difficult to find, mark, and remove all of the errant ordnance. When I deployed to Kuwait more than three years after the war, they were still engaged in clearing operations on the air base we were flying out of. The method seemed crude, but evidently was effective. A long line of conscripts would move slowly across the desert with probes or sticks, gently probing the earth in front of them. They didn't experience any casualties while we were there, but we heard that it was not uncommon for someone to be hurt or killed while conducting these operations.

We had experienced other problems with the bombs as well. Or more correctly, the fuses. Electrical fuses can be set to detonate when they sense that the bomb is in close proximity to the target. This gives an effect which is devastating on certain targets. For example, a bomb which explodes ten feet above the battlefield has a more deadly effect on troops in the open than one which explodes as it hits and continues to bury itself in the earth. The problem occurs very, very infrequently when bombs are released in a cluster or at very close interval. The fuses sense the other nearby bombs as the target and prematurely detonate. This happened at least once in our squadron, and I understand that it happened elsewhere (including with the air force). Most of the time the bombs were well clear of the aircraft before the fuses fired. This didn't always happen in Vietnam, and aircraft and crews were lost. Fortunately, the Marine Corps didn't lose any jets in this manner. Indeed, as missions changed more toward surgical battlefield interdiction, and bombs were dropped in ones and twos, the problem went away.

At any rate, after I had dropped my bombs, I circled overhead to help direct traffic and watch for enemy fire. While stationed in my orbit, I made radar contact with a low, slow-flying target about thirty miles north. This was well clear of the area we were supposed to be working in. Hoping for a chance to bag an enemy helicopter, I called AWACS and queried them about my contact. They replied that they were getting intermittent "hits," or radar contacts, in that area, and that there were no known "friendlies" operating there.

My FAC(A) felt fairly comfortable as he had plenty of company, and he cleared me off to give chase. In an instant I was on my way. I was excited. Sometimes the radar would lock onto fast-moving trucks and give the same indications, but this lock was holding nicely and indicating a bit too fast for a truck. As I closed within ten miles of what I hoped would be my victim, the radar broke lock. Damn! If it was a helicopter it may have set down, making my radar worthless. Perhaps it had ECM gear on board, warning of my approach.

The area in which it had disappeared was obscured by a shelf of low-lying clouds. To get below them I would have to get down below a thousand feet. The thought of rooting around so low, highlighted against a cloud background, and within the lethal envelope of everything from AAA to water balloons, didn't much appeal to me. I wasn't even sure that I would be able to find what I was looking for. And if I got shot down, they'd kill me. Not the Iraqis, but my command element if I ever made it back. They wouldn't have thought much of my risk assessment skills. To lose a Hornet while looking around for a helicopter that maybe wasn't even there, and certainly wasn't menacing anyone, would have been foolhardy.

So I chickened out. On my way back, though, I spotted a couple of large, camouflaged transport trucks. I gave the FAC(A) a holler to let him know what I had found. No good. Too far north for the Harriers. They didn't have the gas and weren't allowed up so far north. My God, it was only up by the bay.

The trucks were rolling along. They were on what looked like a hardened dirt track. There were quite a few revetments and positions dug into the desert alongside the road. I didn't have any bombs left. But I still had my gun. And over five hundred rounds of twenty-millimeter cannon ammunition. That could certainly stop a truck. Later we found that it could stop a tank.

No one in our squadron had done any serious strafing yet. Though we were now dropping our bombs much lower than we had earlier, we weren't yet down to the altitudes where we needed to be to effectively use our guns. I was in a little bit of a dilemma. We hadn't been told we couldn't strafe. But we had been told that we had better not trash a jet because we were doing something stupid. And it wasn't exactly an Einstein-caliber idea to go blasting around down low in and among the enemy. Particularly without a wingman to keep an eye out for me.

Well . . . those *were* enemy trucks down there. If I didn't shoot them, then they were going to get away. And we were here to kill the enemy. And no one was shooting at me. Yet.

I swung around to dive on the trailing truck from behind. Other than my abortive "one-shot" attempt a week or so earlier, this would be only the second time I had ever fired the gun. This was not a factor, though. The systems on the Hornet made shooting the gun a "no brainer." All I had to do was to put the reflective gun reticle illuminated in my HUD over the intended target. As the jet came within range, automatic cuing would appear. All that I needed to do then was to pull the trigger. If the reticle was centered over the target, then the twenty-millimeter rounds would hit it. The gun was deadly, and accurate.

My plan was to dive steeper than normal to minimize my time at lower altitude. This steeper angle would also make the footprint of the impacting rounds on the ground more concentrated. Rolling in, I could literally feel the hair on the back of my head trying to stand up under the helmet. There were enemy positions everywhere, and they became clearer and more evident the lower I got. As I closed within range I squeezed off a short burst, started my pull-up, and began dumping chaff and flares like a madman. Climbing back up to altitude, I saw the smoke from my impacting rounds cover the truck and the surrounding dirt. The truck came quickly to a halt and I distinctly saw the driver jump out and run away.

Circling up above, I felt like a shark circling blooded prey. The other truck was gone. The one I had shot was smoking, askew in the road. We found that when strafed, even when solidly hit, most vehicles didn't explode in a violent burst of smoke and flame. Mostly, they just sat and smoldered and burned. Not like the movies.

Wanting to ensure that the truck was indeed finished off, I decided to attack from the opposite direction. Diving head-on at the vehicle, I gave it another burst and saw the front enveloped by the twenty-millimeter rounds. Pulling out and dumping expendables again, this time my attention was captured by twinkling AAA guns as well as larger AAA rounds exploding above and behind me. Their aim had been off, but this time they had been ready.

The truck was finished. I turned south, found my FAC(A) and non-chalantly worked my way back into the confusion. Like a naughty school boy who doesn't want to be caught. I had successfully destroyed the enemy, but wasn't sure whether I would be disciplined or not. (A week or so later we were all routinely racing around at a thousand feet, blasting away at whatever we could find. I believe we were the only service that went so low.) I simply debriefed Intelligence that I had destroyed a truck.

While reviewing my video tape after debriefing, I was in for quite a surprise. During my second strafing run, I had been locked onto by a missile guidance radar from a French-built Roland missile system. Though the aural warning tones and flashing indications on the HUD were very obvious, I had been oblivious to it all, perhaps distracted by the AAA. I don't know if this could be properly classified as the fog of war. More likely "the haze of stupidity." My case of nerves wasn't helped much when I learned that a Harrier had been bagged that day south of where we had been bombing.

I didn't say anything about this strafing evolution to anyone for days. Didn't want to get grounded. Showed my tape to only a couple of people. But soon, people senior to me were running across the same situations and making the same decision. The cannon was just too valuable and effective a weapon to not use. Soon it became common practice to drop our bombs, then drop down lower to employ the gun. I considered a one-second burst of the gun to be analogous to a super-accurate Rockeye bomb. Though a one-second burst was only about one hundred rounds, half that of the two hundred bomblets carried by the Rockeye, its greater accuracy more than made up for the smaller explosive mass. And it was much more reliable.

Around this time we coined the term "Running Man Tape." Major Rick "Train" Hull, our very inventive operations officer, had brought back some unusual FLIR video. He had made a Rockeye run on a truck surrounded by a number of troops. As his aircraft flew over the truck, the men took cover around and under it. Then one of the men got up and ran away from the truck. Changing his mind, he turned and raced back. Just as he reached the vehicle the bomblets from the Rockeye began to envelope it and the surrounding desert. The area was perfectly covered by the bomblet pattern. Almost as if by a quirk, an instant after the shower of bomblets ended, one last bomb landed right on top of the man who had been running earlier, and now was laying next to the truck. There was no doubt as to his fate.

It is perverse, and probably sick and cruel, but everyone wanted to come back with the same type of footage. From that point on, nearly everyone who was flying with a FLIR pod did their bombing with an eye toward bringing back a Running Man Tape. It was almost a sport. Many pilots were successful in their efforts. It wasn't as if we could actually seek out manned targets on the ground; that was still very difficult. But as the nature of the battlefield changed, we flew and bombed at lower and lower altitudes. From these lower altitudes we could more readily make out scurrying troops on our tapes. Their reactions differed widely. Some of the enemy ran like hell, while others would walk away seemingly unconcerned. Either they were unaware of the threat or they were putting their trust in Allah. Many of them died.

The next day was a doubleheader for me. I was fragged to fly with Scotty, "T. C." Clark, and Moto. Scotty would lead the division with me on his wing, while Moto flew as number four on T. C.'s wing. T. C. was one of our maintenance officers. Smart, and a veteran of the squadron's Mediterranean cruise, he was also quite the computer geek. He was constantly organizing and compiling our daily briefing items and other data on handy little computer-generated kneeboard cards. If it hadn't been for his work, the war probably would have lasted another week or two.

We were fragged to fly two missions that day. After the first, we were to quickly refuel, reload, and go on a second. The initial mission was against a suspected headquarters element located in a community south of Kuwait City. This particular settlement had a peculiar five-sided shape and so earned a very obvious nickname: the Pentagon. The area around here was noted for its AAA.

Though we did get a photo of the area we were to hit, we didn't get much else in the way of intelligence. A circle on the photo denoted the exact building we were to hit. Scotty briefed a couple of other targets in the complex, assigning Moto and me the headquarters building. For all the enemy reaction there was, we could have been on a training flight in our old desert stomping grounds near Yuma, Arizona. Crossing the border from west to east, I was able to get a very good radar depiction long before I could see the settlement. The radar reflectivity of the target was excellent. I was able to spend quite a bit of time refining my designation. Coming within visual range of the community, I was able to see the area where my target was located. My plan was to roll in, break my radar designation (which I didn't really need, and was less accurate than a visual designation), designate my target visually through the HUD, and make my attack.

That's exactly what happened. My HUD video showed a solid textbook designation and delivery. Pulling up from my dive, I saw the skipper's bombs explode and complimented him on his hits. By the time I had finished gabbing, my bombs were impacting exactly on target and he was commending me for mine. We were a very supportive, sensitive bunch that day. Ahead of our time. We probably would have even welcomed women into the fighter community during that brief instant. Maybe not. Moto and T. C. also had nice deliveries. We easily rejoined and made our way back with little reaction from the enemy.

As was so often the case, we never got any BDA. For all we knew, we had destroyed a geriatric ward, or the local tennis club.

After landing, we were quickly refueled and reloaded. We conducted a quick brief and were airborne again. This time we played with the FAC(A). The target was an area of artillery and armor emplacements in southern Kuwait. Once established in the target area, we dispersed into a circular bombing pattern, taking turns rolling in to drop singles or pairs of bombs. The idea was to come in from a different direction to confuse the enemy and remain unpredictable. This tactic was commonly called "circling the wagons."

The flak was unusually thick and accurate this time. At one time Scotty was encircled by what looked like a cloud of popcorn. T. C. and I spotted a truck going like hell, trying to clear the area. We raced each other to get to him first. It's not easy to bomb a speeding target. The first bomb stopped him and we could see the occupants get out and run, no doubt as fast as they could go. The second bomb sent the truck tumbling end over end out of the explosion, but it still never blew up Hollywood style.

We continued to work the emplacements with good success. The AAA continued to dog us. There were a lot of "Hey! Hey! Hey . . . watch out!" and other heart-in-the-throat calls, but luckily none of us were hit. It was hard to give a wingman any kind of useful calls to counter accurate AAA. It really didn't do a guy much good to shout a warning at him when rounds were exploding all around. He usually already knew. But SAMs were different. They took a little bit of time to get there, and a timely call from a wingman could get an endangered pilot turning in the right direction, and putting expendables out of his jet in a timely fashion.

One of the very real dangers was that of running into each other. With the four of us and the FAC(A) working over the same area, not always with everyone else in sight, the danger of a midair collision was very real. That no allied aircraft were lost over enemy territory due to a midair still amazes me.

Anyway, this mission worked out very well. It was very satisfying to leave an enemy position in smoke, fire, and ruins. After checking out with the TACC and passing our BDA (for whatever use they made of it), we made another uneventful recovery.

Author testing a field-expedient armrest (two AIM-9M Sidewinder air-to-air missiles). Typical air-to-air weapons load was three AIM-7 Sparrows, four AIM-9 Sidewinders, and five hundred rounds of twenty-millimeter cannon ammunition. *(Photo by author)*

We had our recoveries back to base down to a science. At start-up, before takeoff, we had about fifteen thousand pounds of fuel. This allowed us to fly the 250 miles to Kuwait at about thirty-five thousand feet, then descend and work a target at fairly high fuel consumption for about twenty minutes. We used a "bingo," or "time to go home," fuel figure of about fifty-five hundred pounds. With this fuel state we would climb to about forty thousand feet for our return trip. This enabled us to land with about two thousand pounds of fuel. Fifteen hundred pounds was considered an emergency fuel state.

Being at war wasn't all work and no play. A gathering of fighter pilots often differs little from a pack of adolescent boys. Especially when they have idle time on their hands. And between missions, there was indeed idle time. The boys from VMFA-212, the Lancers, built themselves a surefire guarantor of "madcap, zany, good, clean, fun." It was an All-American, college campus–proven instrument of power projection. A water balloon catapult! Capable of hurling a six-inch, fourteen-ounce, water-filled balloon up to one hundred yards with absolutely no accuracy whatever, this "weapon" was primarily directed against the Death Angels of VMFA-235. The Death Angels weren't targeted because of any slight committed against the Lancers. Their "crime" was that they were perfectly situated, slightly downhill, and about fifty yards from 212's tents. However, the boys from 235 weren't the only targets. To be honest, anyone within a hundred-yard arc was at risk. Particularly if they weren't being aimed at. The balloon catapult was only marginally more accurate than the Scud, but a lot more fun. In fact, the catapult had other Scudlike qualities. It was mobile and could be set up and taken down with ease, which frustrated all attempts at its destruction. And with the coming of the cease-fire, the water balloons, like the Scuds, never flew again.

The weather on 11 February was poor again. Vector and I were airborne on a night mission making our way north when we were called back. Evidently the weather over the entire theater was crummy and unworkable. It was hard to believe that in the entire area we couldn't have found somewhere to work. Unfortunately, the system was efficient enough to catch up with us and call us back.

Yes, the command and control system had made improvements. With missions coming up at a fairly regular though heavy pace, the TACC, TAOC, and DASC had worked out a lot of the bugs and gained a lot of experience. They were now usually able to handle us fairly expeditiously. If we were on an armed recce mission to work with a FAC(A) and the FAC(A) wasn't able to handle us, they would usually send us to a prebriefed target or a killing box. Much preferable to stacking up and waiting. This saved gas, eliminated confusion, kept pressure on the enemy as well as destroying him, and eased our scheduling problems. The improvement was marked.

Vector and I got a consolation prize and were sent up the next day to work with the FAC(A). Our jets were ready well prior to our scheduled takeoff, so we grabbed a couple of cans of spray paint and a camera and entertained ourselves a bit before the mission. We found that a few of the bombs hadn't been dedicated or decorated yet, and so fixed them up ourselves. I did a couple of bombs to Saddam from

Example of a dedicated bomb. *(Photo by Peter B. Mersky)*

"Big Al" (my Dad) and my hometown (Danville, Indiana). Vector did a couple from his relatives. We took a bunch of pictures posturing in front of our jets and bombs, and otherwise looking like a pair of goofs. Had to have "Hero" pictures for the folks back home.

After getting airborne and making our way up to the border, we made contact with our FAC(A). The two-seater had found a large enemy logistics point just north of an area we called "the Elbow." As we became more and more familiar with our operating area (mostly Kuwait and southern Iraq), we began to coin nicknames for each particular area. The Elbow was that portion of the western border of Kuwait which made a sharp left turn from north-south to east-west. "The Crotch" was that portion of the same border where it turned back north again at the junction of Kuwait, Saudi Arabia, the Neutral Area, and Iraq. "The Jacks" was an oil-producing area north of the Elbow that was demarcated on our maps by a set of symbols that looked exactly like children's toy jacks. "The Icetray" was a huge set of livestock pens north of Ahmed Al Jaber Air Base. "The City," "the Bay," and "the International Airport" were obvious. There were many more. In south-central Kuwait at Al Wafrah there was quite an extensive area of agricultural activity. As the only real green area in the entire country, it earned the appellation "Kuwaiti National Forest."

On this mission we were working north of the Elbow. The enemy logistics point consisted of a great many semitrailers, tents, and stock-piles of equipment arrayed in a huge square about one-half mile per side. The center of the square was bare desert, but the sides were composed of bermed soil, lined with the trailers, vehicles, tents, and equipment. The entirety of the equipment was covered with camouflaged netting so that the position looked like a huge square with fuzzy brown sides.

Upon our arrival the F/A-18D gave us a brief description, told us there were numerous hand-held SAM shots already observed, and cleared us in. Not quite grasping the Big Picture yet, I very cleverly dropped my first bomb smack dab in the middle of the square. Probably didn't do much except give them a good start toward a swimming pool. The D crew finally got it through my fat head that all the goodies were aligned along the sides of the square. With that revelation, Vector (who probably never was confused) and I went to work. Very methodically we made our runs, dropping a single bomb on each dive.

The depot was soon a smoking shambles. There was lots of smoke, fire, and dust. The damage was incredible. It was a textbook illustration of something. A failure of defense, a misestimate of the capability of our air power, or an overestimate of their ability to counter us. Whatever it was, it was gross. Two plain-vanilla jet fighters had arrived, and virtually unmolested, had destroyed millions of dollars (or dinars) worth of equipment and supplies. They quite literally had nowhere to hide, and very little ability to protect themselves.

Our very pleased FAC(A) gave us a 100/80 BDA. This meant that 100 percent of our bombs had hit the target and 80 percent of the target had been destroyed. Though I considered this to be a very successful and noteworthy mission, it didn't create much interest when we debriefed, and Vector and I were soon on our way back to the chow hall.

Around this time Colonel Reitsch, the MAG-11 commander, came out with one of his famous Fokker-Grams. Essentially it said that we were now going down as low as we needed to get the job done. No more wasting bombs. Hoo-ray. While we had been pretty effective in the past couple of weeks as we gradually lowered our bomb release altitudes, now we were cleared down as low as we felt was required. The ground invasion was approaching and we needed to ensure that every piece of armament we loaded was killing something. I didn't have to be a closet strafer any more.

How low did we go? Well, in peacetime we train to a three-thousand-foot strafe pattern. Starting a fifteen-degree dive at about one and a half to two miles from the target, we begin firing at about twelve hundred feet and start our pullout at seven hundred. Typically we bottom out at no lower than five hundred feet. This gave us adequate clearance from the ground as well as protecting us from most of the twenty-millimeter frags and ricochets.

Yeah, but what about during the war? We did the same thing. After the war we found that the other aircraft and services did not employ their twenty millimeter in classic strafe as we had. The F-16s generally weren't allowed nearly low enough to do it. Eagles and Tomcats didn't strafe. They navy wouldn't let their Hornets down there. Too dangerous. In the heart of about every weapons envelope the Iraqis had. In fact, just a simple, heated barrage of well-aimed dirty words at that altitude might have been deadly.

The A-10s were quite effective with their thirty-millimeter cannon. However, with this huge gun (a beautiful monster) they were able to adjust their dives so that they didn't have to root around nearly so low to be effective.

With our smaller gun we did, though. The dive angle we used allowed us to shoot through the tops of the more vulnerable rear ends of enemy tanks and armored vehicles and was suitable for everything else as well. To make ourselves less vulnerable we didn't jump right into an area that was already wickedly hot with AAA or hand-held SAMs unless friendly troops were in contact with the enemy. When we attacked we had at least one other aircraft stay high to call out threats. Generally we tried to attack from a different axis or direction each time to keep the enemy guessing. These tactics, combined with the intelligent use of chaff and flares, helped ensure that we never lost a single Hornet. We considered our very low altitude work with the twenty-millimeter cannon to be a testament to our courage and machismo (others would call it an indicator of our idiocy; I think the record speaks for itself).

Major Garrison flying north for a CAS mission. Due to a shortage of water, the jets were rarely washed. *(Photo by Major Garrison)*

There was, however, a fine line between what was considered tactically sound yet aggressive and what was considered brash and foolhardy. One of our department heads came back from a mission with some amazing video footage. After dropping his load of bombs, he descended to low altitude for strafe. Very low altitude. And he stayed down there. His video showed him setting a number of tanks on fire. But he had stayed down too low, and too long, for Scotty's liking. Our commanding officer thought that he had needlessly exposed himself and his jet to enemy fire, far longer than what was required by the mission. He grounded him for several days.

A commanding officer does not lightly ground one of his own department heads. The move by and large was not popular among the other pilots. The aggressive pilot was a leader; he was well liked, funny, and a super pilot. Our mission was to destroy the enemy and, by God, that's what he had been doing. Perhaps Scotty had expected a more conservative example to be set. I don't know. In his defense, he knew that the other man's life and his jet were more important than any number of enemy tanks. Perhaps there is, or was, more to the story that I'll never know. I do know that we all walked on eggshells for a while during and after that episode. It was confusing too. They were both great men and well respected. I think we younger pilots expected a different outcome from this clash, and were just a tiny bit demoralized to see one of our "heroes" sidelined so ignominiously.

On the same day that Vector and I had hit the supply depot, a 747 and a DC-9 had appeared on the tarmac at Kuwait International Airport. Evidently they had been pulled out of hangar spaces somewhere on the airfield. There was concern that the Iraqis might try to ferry them home, so it was decided to destroy them.

The 747 was bombed at altitude by an F/A-18 from one of the other squadrons. The weapon used was Rockeye. Rockeye is impossible to deliver with any accuracy from high altitude. As might be expected, the delivery was horrible. The 747 was hit by just one bomblet out of the entire load of two hundred. It didn't matter. The bomblet struck just forward of the horizontal stabilizer and started a small smoldering fire that eventually caught and spread, consuming the entire jet. Everything was reduced to ashes except the small tail section. Moto and Bull were directed to attack the DC-9. From very high altitude Moto dropped his stick of five MK 83s. They impacted next to the passenger aircraft, which was completely destroyed by the resultant fire. Easy as pie. When talking with some McDonnell Douglas personnel later on, their response to Moto's destruction of their fine product was unexpected: "Bomb some more, we can use the business!"

On 13 February, I took part in a strike against troop and armor positions north of the bay. This would turn out to be the last large strike mission I would fly during the war. With our attention almost wholly shifted to surgically removing the Iraqi army, tank by tank, and gun by gun, from the battlefield, the large strike had become almost a dinosaur over Kuwait. Too cumbersome.

In fact, this strike, which consisted of sixteen aircraft, had been allotted a time over target of thirty minutes and could have been broken down into smaller groups with five or ten minutes over target each. As it turned out, the strike leader opted not to. The plan was to run all sixteen aircraft over the enemy positions in five minutes. This in retrospect was probably not the most efficient use of our assets. Dropping a string of five bombs on dispersed positions was akin to what the B-52s were doing. They dropped a huge string of bombs and only took out one or two pieces of gear. It was much more efficient to make multiple runs against individual targets.

This was borne out during the strike. We all streaked across the enemy position and dropped our bombs in one run against the first target we picked up. This tactic didn't allow us to evaluate which targets were the most valuable, or to coordinate with other aircraft in the strike as to which targets to hit. There were some close calls as more than one aircraft rolled in on the same target and others, having aborted their runs, circled back to make another run.

The enemy reaction was heavy. There was a great deal of AAA and a good many hand-held SAM shots. Egressing toward the bay, I encountered for the first time the type of AAA that came close to approaching what the beleaguered bomber crews of World War II had called a "carpet of flak." Exploding in angry flashes of orange, leaving puffs of gray smoke, it was set to detonate at about fifteen thousand feet. Once we climbed through it, it posed no threat. They weren't adjusting any of the rounds to detonate above that.

Once at altitude flying south past the city, we saw a small naval vessel leaving the harbor. There was no way to tell if it was friendly or hostile, but odds were that unless our sailors were taking shore leave in Kuwait City, it was Iraqi. We didn't have any bombs left, and had no idea of who to ask, if we needed to ask at all, to attack it. I doubt that AWACS or the navy's Red Crown (the radio call sign given to whichever naval warship is providing airborne intercept control) would have had a clue. We still had our cannons, though we were running short on fuel. To attack it we would have had to drop down low, where we would have been well within lethal range of the heavily defended coast. A Harrier had already been bagged earlier in the same area. In the end we passed the ship's location to the TACC and continued home. I've often wondered since if we could have sunk that boat with twenty-millimeter cannon fire. And not gotten downed ourselves.

Getting shot down, though it wasn't something we talked about, or dwelled on a lot, was still a dark possibility that was always somewhere in our minds. We'd seen some of the POWs on TV, and while they appeared to be upright and generally all in one piece, they also appeared to be fairly well "used up." We argued about whether or not they were being tortured. They looked bruised and beat up, though that could have been caused by ejection seats. Most of us thought that they were being beaten. God knows the Iraqis aren't famous for their humane treatment of anything. Kind of the Klingons of the Middle East.

We argued about how they might be tortured as well. Simple beatings? Electric shock? We didn't know. The horror stories that had come out of Vietnam didn't do much to reassure us. And just as we had been nervous about how we would react when exposed to combat, we were just as nervous about how we might act in captivity. We were frightened of it.

Valentine's Day saw me as part of a four-plane, or division, mission against revetted artillery and armor in west-central Kuwait. An area we called the Jacks. Crossing the border into this area, we crossed over a line of oil trenches. These were trenches dug by the Iraqis that appeared to overlap each other. Each one seemed to be about a mile in length. The enemy had filled them with oil. They were an additional obstacle designed to delay our troops when they crossed the border to liberate Kuwait. These trenches, which would be ignited at the crucial point, along with the minefields and barbed wire, were part of an elaborate deathtrap. They were intended to entangle our men long enough so that the enemy artillery could zero in and butcher them while their advance was slowed.

Dip was leading this mission with Wolfy on his wing. Hatch was flying with me. It was another "circle the wagons" massacre. Dip and Wolfy had a moving truck cornered and blasted it to smithereens before working over a group of revetted tanks. They sounded like kids, whooping and shouting over the radio.

I also had cornered a truck that had made a run for it. My first bomb didn't do much more than scare the shit out of its occupants. They stopped the vehicle, got out, and ran like hell. A familiar pattern. Smart too. By now, Hatch, who hadn't spotted "my" truck yet, was trying to get me to talk his eyes on to it so that he could have a go. I started describing the area to him, got all jumbled up (those D guys had a tough job), then stopped. Why the hell should I tell him where "my" truck was? I rolled in on my own and finished it. From there I moved onto another position and shacked a tank and another semitrailer. The AAA was very light that day. Only a few sporadic puffs. We may as well have been bombing worn-out hulks on one of our desert targets in the States.

Nearly every strike mission I flew after this was as part of a two-plane flight. A section of aircraft was much less cumbersome than a larger flight, and more suited to the surgical destruction of battlefield weaponry. This was now where the primary emphasis of marine fixed-wing aviation was directed.

On 15 February I took the Fatman north of the Elbow on an armed recce mission. Again primary prey was revetted armor and artillery positions. The Iraqis had a curious habit of burying their tanks all the way up to the turrets. It made the tanks very difficult, if not impossible, to find from the air, but defeated the purpose of having the tank. Buried as they were, they were not very mobile and were little more than fixed-gun positions. These positions could be easily outmaneuvered, or bypassed. Sort of a poor man's Maginot line. And just as stupid.

A better idea they had was that of scooping out a short, wide trench and putting a sand-covered top over it. They were able to drive in and out of these, and it was impossible to tell from the air whether they were occupied. From the ground they would have been hard to spot as well. Additionally, they didn't lose much mobility by using these "drive-in garages." A less sophisticated practice was simply driving them into shallow revetments or trenches, which were easily spotted from the air.

Arriving over our targets, we took separation from each other to set up a wide circular pattern, and make it easier to select our prey as we wouldn't have to worry about running in to each other. There seemed to be more equipment and vehicles than ever. I'm not sure if they had moved more equipment in during the past few days or moved it out where it was more visible. Regardless, there was plenty of it.

Fattie and I had a bright idea for this sortie. We had the capability to set the Hornet up so that whenever we pressed the bomb release button, it would transmit a tone over whichever radio was selected. We figured that upon hearing this tone, we would know when the other pilot was about to drop his bombs, be closest to the ground, and be in the biggest danger. We would thus be easily cued as to when to keep an extra sharp watch on each other. Kind of a neat yuppie gadget.

Well, it was a bust. The tone was so damned loud that it drowned out any attempts to talk over it. We couldn't have warned each other if we had shouted. After that sortie, we never used this option again.

Our attacks went well. I found some light armored vehicles holed up with multiple rocket launchers. I was able to work these over pretty well, as I kept an eye on the Fatman and his attacks on some tanks. With a FLIR pod on board, I was able to record each one of my runs. I was dropping my bombs singly and having good luck as I moved from position to position.

With my bombs expended, I selected my gun and dropped low to strafe some artillery positions. I was careful to slave my FLIR pod to look straight ahead so that it could record the effects of the twenty-millimeter ammunition. The gun was quite effective. With it, I was able to set two separate positions ablaze. I was very pleased with myself.

Fattie now had quite a bit less gas than I had, so we called it quits and started home. He had dropped all his bombs, and I had too, as well as having shot about all of my gun ammo. He was lower on fuel because of our two conflicting philosophies. He, along with many other pilots, liked to engage his afterburner after each bombing run. This kept his speed up, as well as getting him back up to altitude and safety quicker. But the afterburners sucked a lot of fuel. They also gave off a huge heat signature. So intense that they rendered the decoy flares about useless and made the jet a very easily acquired target for heat-seeking missiles. I didn't use afterburners after pulling off target. This saved gas and made me a less significant heat target; but it also left me lower, slower, and more vulnerable. Life's a huge series of tradeoffs.

Reviewing my FLIR video with Intel after the mission, I was rewarded with an outstanding sequence of one of my bombs making a direct hit on an MRL. The launcher was revetted a few yards from a light armored vehicle. Both are very clearly visible on the tape prior to impact. Because of its clarity, and the accuracy of the hit, this tape was forwarded up the chain of command. A week or so later, I was lucky enough to be lounging around in front of the TV when it was shown on national news. I have since seen this sequence, along with a couple others of mine, and many of my squadron mates', on videos which feature bombing from the Gulf War.

The FLIR video of the gun runs came out kind of neat, too, though the targets weren't too detailed. The rounds coming out of the gun looked like spray from a water hose, or a big swarm of angry bees. The impact of the rounds on target caused what appeared to be big plumes of black smoke to erupt, though much of that was actually heat from the rounds themselves exploding.

Right about this time, there was a great deal of activity on the political front. Saddam was making noise as if he might pull out of Kuwait. It seemed that our side, wanting to forego what were then projected to be huge losses on the battlefield, was willing to listen. The pilots in our squadron saw this as a threat to their mission count and were even more anxious to scam sorties. Me included. However, as events would have it, Saddam was lying.

The Marine Corps and the navy weren't fielding the only Hornets participating in the conflict. F/A-18s from the Canadian armed forces were continuing to man the CAPs that we (and they) had manned in Desert Shield. Not allowed by their government to participate in the actual strikes until late in the war, the Canadian pilots aggressively intercepted unidentified contacts as they headed south out of the battlefield. It was not an easy job sorting through the confusing stream of aircraft continuously cycling through the area.

The next morning, I flew again as a D escort. It was an early morning mission that put us over the target just at sunrise. This was the first mission I flew where smoke from the battlefield had an impact on our ability to find and hit the enemy. The Iraqis had not yet started to blow the oil wells on a wholesale basis, but there were already a few oil fires burning. The smoke we encountered on this day was nothing compared to what we would run into ten days later, but combined with the early morning fog, airborne dust, and the low sun angle, it was enough of a factor to frustrate us and cause problems.

We were working an area east of the Crotch. There was a military compound of some sort that was shaped like two large squares, arranged side by side. The Iraqis had occupied this, and in and around it had arrayed all manner of neat stuff. Tanks, armored vehicles, artillery, MRLs, support vehicles, and troops. A veritable smorgasbord of attractive ground targets. There was even a huge parking lot filled with civilian autos.

But the poor visibility was making it extremely difficult for us. The battlefield smog, and the low sun angle made it very difficult to see a target from any distance. It was easy enough to see a target while looking straight down. But as we offset ourselves for our runs, we would lose the target in the haze. The FAC(A) was absolutely miserable as he tried to mark targets for four separate sections of Harriers. Bombs were flying all over the place. Not much was getting hit, and because of that, tempers were wearing thin. The FAC(A) was yelling at the Harriers, the Harriers were yelling back at the FAC(A), and at each other. During the whole mess, the two-seater and I went to the tanker twice in between sections of Harriers. Finally it became obvious that we were wasting our time. The bombing aircraft were largely unsuccessful and were running themselves low on fuel while they groped around in the murk looking for something to hit.

After we had handled all of our assigned aircraft, the D crew and I tried our own hands at working in the gunk. I had a couple of Rockeye cluster bombs and my gun, while he had a couple rockets and his gun. We didn't have much more success. I slung my Rockeye at some vehicles revetted near the entrance to the compound but couldn't even tell where they had hit. With my cannon, I put several long bursts out toward the camp in general, and I am sure that I didn't hit anything important. The FAC(A) didn't do any better. We had been up there for nearly three hours, and worked with eight other aircraft, yet the day had been little more than a total bust. Not much good for morale.

We landed at base uneventfully. Our recoveries back at Bahrain were rarely complicated by weather. Generally the only problem we had was limited visibility due to haze, and even then, it normally wasn't that bad. Which was fortunate for us. Though just about every plane built since the mid-1960s, including Mooneys and Bonanzas, was equipped with an instrument landing system (ILS) our Hornets were not. The ILS enables the pilot to follow a very precise glide path down to touchdown by tracking a radio signal. This type of system is invaluable for landing in bad weather. It is simple, cheap, and very effective. No air force in the world would dream of buying modern aircraft without equipping them with an ILS. Except the navy and the Marine Corps.

To be fair, our Hornets do have an ILS that is compatible only with aircraft carriers. But there are just fourteen or fifteen aircraft carriers, while there are probably over a thousand airfields which have the type of ILS our system can't use. It's probably a case of penny wise and dollar foolish. We probably could have equipped every Hornet in the fleet with a solid gold ILS with the money that was wasted on the navy's failed AX bomber program, or the aborted airborne self-protection jammer.

The marines and the air force were not the only folks waging war out of Shaikh Isa. After a good deal of time, probably wrestling with the sensitivities of a tiny nation striking out against a stronger Arab "brother," the Emirate's air force finally mounted strikes against Iraqi forces in Kuwait.

The Bahrainis operated F-5s and F-16s. The F-16 is by far a better bomber. It's faster, longer legged, more accurate, and can carry a bigger bombload. It's also a better fighter—more maneuverable, better radar, more endurance, and so on. Well, for whatever reason, prior to the war, the Bahrainis had decided that their F-16 pilots would train to the air-to-air role exclusively, and that the F-5 folks would handle the dirty business of dropping bombs on people's heads. So when it came time to dance, the relatively outdated F-5s got to go to the ball, while the Fighting Falcons stayed home and flew CAP (about the fifteenth layer of defense against an enemy who could barely get airborne with any competence, much less penetrate allied air defenses and strike a target over three hundred miles away).

The F-5s seemed game. We could see them on occasion, blasting off ready to wreak destruction on their Islamic brethren. Their standard load seemed to be five MK 82 general purpose, five-hundred-pound bombs and external fuel. Not bad for such a small airframe, especially considering the distance involved. Just because of the nature of the beast though, I'm certain that they really didn't have much of an effect. They flew too few sorties and just weren't capable of the required accuracy. Chats with their American advisors confirmed this.

But whether they were inflicting real damage on the Iraqis wasn't really the point. For all the effect the Bahraini aircraft had on the outcome of the war, they might just as well have been dropping cantaloupes. The real point of the strikes was that they were a demonstration of the Emirate's solidarity with the coalition, and anger at Iraqi actions. For the Bahrainis to do what they did, particularly the provision of bases from which U.S. forces could launch strikes against Saddam, was no small thing. Islamic nations do not take aggression against each other lightly. The individual Bahraini pilots were a curious bunch to us. Overall, and I think that this is true of about every air force in the world, I am sure that they weren't as well trained as us. For one thing, they didn't have much of an experience base, or the tactical or technical expertise to give their training direction. They certainly did not have access to the latest and greatest in weapons employment, or much beyond the most rudimentary air-to-air tactics. How could they?

Early on, before the war, I flew a one-versus-two mission against one of their F-16 youngsters and his USAF instructor exchange pilot. The young pilot performed passably, and the flight turned out to be a good training evolution for all concerned. The USAF pilot told me later that the young pilot had been chosen for the mission because of demonstrated ability and, more important, because he was open to, and actually responded to and learned from, criticism. Not a foregone conclusion in the very proud world of the Arab male.

I heard a gem of wisdom several years ago relative to the subject that I think is very true. That is that nearly every nation in the world, no matter how small, can field a "starting lineup" of pilots that is every bit the match of any other nation's "starters" in terms of raw talent. This is probably true no matter what the profession. For example, Norway's top five prostitutes are probably as equally talented as the United States' top five prostitutes. But because of the smaller population of the Nordic country, it doesn't have the tremendous pool of talent that the United States does. And so Norway's top one thousand hookers probably aren't the match of America's top one thousand. That is, once the starting lineup has left the bench, there's not much talent left to back them up in a smaller country.

The point is this: During war, once the best pilots have been lost or attrited, the smaller countries are unable to field replacements of the same caliber. However, countries such as the United States have an enormous pool of expertise to draw from. This can influence greatly the outcome of a conflict. The same thing probably can't be said about prostitutes . . . but who knows?

Anyway (I got lost, where was I?), back to the Bahraini pilots. Some of them had talent to be sure. But as a whole their actions, background, and trappings almost suggested a yacht club more than anything else. Or maybe what you would picture a polo club to be like. They all appeared to be fairly wealthy (I know that several of them were from well-placed families) and used to being treated like it. In their ready room they were waited on by what we called a "tea-boy." He was an older servant who prepared tea or other treats and saw to it that everyone was comfortable.

It wasn't as if they were unpleasant or snobbish. Almost to a man, the Bahraini pilots were very cordial, even deferential, to us. But they didn't exhibit any eagerness or ambition to "pick our brains" or learn anything from us. To us it felt as if they saw us as the useful, but still unclean, intruders from beyond Islamdom. Perhaps they were just overwhelmed by our sheer numbers, which made them shy. I don't know. To us they fulfilled the classic cousin-marrying, rich and pompous, Arab elite stereotype that emerged from the oil embargo days of the 1970s. They almost completely ignored, or perhaps misinterpreted, any type of friendly overture we made. Perhaps it was a cultural or religious misunderstanding. Perhaps not.

And their religious practices struck us as unusual, to say the least. Well, perhaps we weren't the most worldly or understanding bunch in the world. Several times a day it seemed, at the mosque near the chow hall, the Islamic faithful would be called to prayer. The problem was that the vocal summons, and the prayers that followed, were, to us, the worst, most ear-splitting caterwauling in the world. Particularly when we were trying to sleep in between missions. The prayers seemed to be half-shrieked and half-sung by a thirteen-year-old. Though always respectful to the Bahrainis, among ourselves we called it "cat-skinning music." For it sounded exactly as one might imagine the noise a tabby might make if he were being skinned alive.

At any rate, there was plenty of mutual respect all the way around. They suffered our intrusion well. After all, we *were* helping to protect their country. And though they may have thought ill of us at times (who wouldn't?), they never gave voice to those thoughts. Mutually, our own boys were very guarded against offending them.

Chapter Eighteen

A Hornet Pilot's Thoughts on the Harrier

B y the time this book is published, I will probably already have left the Marine Corps. If not, then I fully expect the Harrier Mafia within the Corps to exercise enough influence to punish me professionally. What follows are my thoughts on what I believe is one of the greatest propaganda successes in aviation history.

I like Harrier pilots. They're just like Hornet pilots except that they fly a different airplane. We enjoy a good-natured rivalry and tremendous mutual respect. I don't like the Harrier. Despite claims as to its safety, many pilots have died in this airplane. Many of my friends. Relative to a "normal" jet, it is not easy to fly. It is mechanically complex and not as forgiving as other tactical aircraft. There are people who have flown the jet, had bad experiences, and have refused to fly it again. There are very few knowledgeable people who would say their fears are unfounded.

The Harrier is not nearly so capable as its more conventional contemporaries. The F/A-18 Hornet can fly farther, faster, and higher and carry a larger payload. Its radar can fire the AIM-7 and AIM-120 missiles, while the AV-8B Harrier can fire its limited air-to-air weaponry only within visual range (some Harriers, at great expense, are only just now being fitted with a radar; it is nearly identical to the Hornet's). The F/A-18 radar also gives it bombing capabilities the AV-8B does not possess.

Some people have written of the Harrier's supposed unrivaled prowess in air-to-air combat, a prowess lent to them by their supposed ability to vector in forward flight, or VIFF. That is, they can adjust their nozzles, much as they would in hovering flight, to get an opponent to overshoot. These people are idiots. An AV-8B that does this simply slows down to a point where it sacrifices its already inferior maneuverability (relative to fourth-generation fighters). Never in my experience, in Phantoms or Hornets, have I seen a Harrier do this effectively. The aircraft simply isn't in the fourth-generation class in terms of maneuverability. I have never even *heard of* a Harrier beating a Hornet, or an F-16 or F-15, in a dogfight. Perhaps more telling, I have never heard a Harrier pilot boast that he could do it.

The only thing the Harrier can do better than a Hornet is take off and land in a shorter distance. And hover. But to take off vertically the Harrier is limited in the payload it can carry, thus reducing its usefulness.

I'm not being parochial. The F-16, F-15, Mirage 2000, and latest Russian designs, except that they lack VSTOL/STOL capabilities, are all much more capable than the AV-8B. Derived from British design, the AV-8B is a product of two aerospace giants: McDonnell Douglas, an American company, and British Aerospace (BAe) in Britain. The engine is manufactured by Rolls Royce, another British concern. Ironically, McDonnell Douglas also builds and sells the F/A-18.

One of the primary justifications for having the Harrier is that it can be forward-deployed near the battlefield. The "gee-whiz" bunch has an image of the Harrier rising stealthily out of a small jungle clearing, zipping to the battlefield, where it rains death and destruction upon the enemy, then racing back to its jungle lair, where after hovering for a moment, it slips vertically back into its hideaway.

Well, maybe; but I have my doubts. First, if it is deployed too close to the battlefield, it becomes vulnerable to the enemy it is supposed to destroy. If it is located too far away, it can't carry a very large payload, or perhaps even get there. If it has to take off vertically, its payload is also significantly reduced.

The logistical aspects of supporting an operation of this type are nightmarish at best. Large quantities of fuel would have to be made available to the dispersed jets. Water as well. The Harrier engine requires large amounts of distilled water to support the aircraft in a hover. Don't forget the heavy bombs that the Harrier needs to destroy the enemy. Communications are another consideration. How is the pilot going to know when to take off and land? How is he going to know where he is supposed to go and who he is supposed to hit? How about the troops to maintain and repair the jets? There has to be enough men, with the right skills and adequately provisioned with food, water, shelter, and other necessities. There also needs to be a system to deliver parts to the maintenance troops when the aircraft needs repair.

And repairing the jet isn't easy. Just to change the engine, the entire wing needs to be lifted clear of the rest of the airframe. Essentially, the aircraft gets pulled into two large pieces when the engine is changed. The equipment needed to support this evolution is large and cumbersome. The task itself is time consuming.

Security for the dispersed sites needs to be considered as well. They would appear to be perfect targets for saboteurs or enemy special forces. The marines who are maintaining the jets can't be counted upon to provide all of the security. It is difficult to turn a wrench and handle a machine gun at the same time (though marines could pull it off if anyone could). Even then, these types of dispersed sites are still difficult to defend.

So while this type of scenario might technically be possible, in real life it would be very difficult to successfully pull off. Particularly if it had to be sustained for any length of time. A more realistic scenario might have the jets clustered together at a site which has some sort of access for ground transport. And an area for storage of equipment and supplies. With access to communications gear, provisions for the troops, and facilities for maintaining aircraft. And hopefully enough open area for the jets to be able to execute at least a short takeoff roll, which would enable them to carry a larger payload. A site sort of like . . . an airfield! I concede, though, that the Harrier is the only tactical jet we have that is capable of operating out of an unimproved site—should that requirement ever arise.

That requirement never arose during the Gulf War. The Harriers were moved closer to Kuwait than the Hornets for the simple reason that they had a shorter range than the F/A-18s and needed to be closer. Even then, Hornets would often step aside from a bombing mission they had already been working so that a newly arrived group of Harriers could dump their bombs and hurry home before they ran out of gas. Once the AV-8Bs had departed, the F/A-18s would return to their business.

Most of the Harriers were not working dispersed out of a remote site but operating out of a permanent airfield. To their credit, there was absolutely no need for them to operate from dispersed forward sites. Why bleed if you don't have to? They were enjoying all the amenities of a fixed base yet flying a jet that was not as capable as others that could have used that site. More Hornet squadrons in the States, for instance, that were chomping at the bit to get involved.

There were Harriers, however, that were operating out of an environment that no other fixed-wing aircraft could have used. Harriers operating off amphibious helicopter carriers were generating a significant number of sorties. That the AV-8B is the only fixed-wing aircraft capable of providing support for our marines from this type of platform is indisputable. In fact, working off the same sorts of ships in the Falklands War, the Brit Harriers were hailed as saviors of the fleet. My hat is off.

But my impression is that airframes other than the Harrier would have served pilots better in the Persian Gulf. Five of them were lost to enemy action. No marine Hornets were lost. They were certainly no more daring than we were. They were slower. Also, their engine exhaust, the primary target for a heat-seeking missile, is located in the center of the underside of the jet. This is a very dangerous place for a missile to impact. Additionally, the fact that they have only a single engine makes them less survivable for obvious reasons.

There are a lot of folks who would argue that the Marine Corps could have saved itself a bundle of money by buying modernized A-4 Skyhawks (which the Harrier replaced), and would have lost little in terms of employability while perhaps realizing some gains in performance. It's a touchy subject to a lot of people. Watch what happens to me.

Chapter Nineteen
Kuwait on Fire

By now our squadron had been equipped with more FLIR pods. These had come at the expense of the Hornet squadrons that had come from Hawaii. They had newer C model aircraft, which had the capability to employ the infrared Maverick weapon. We weren't able to use this weapon with our older A models, so the decision was made to give our unit some of their FLIRs while they would spend more of their sorties using the Maverick. We got the better end of the deal. The IR Maverick wasn't very well liked. For us it was not a reliable weapon, often failing before the aircraft arrived over the battlefield. The video wasn't so hot either, significantly less clear than the video from the FLIR pod. Additionally, the magnification was not as good, which made it difficult to identify and lock onto targets. When launched it would miss the target as often as it hit. I never heard any of our F/A-18 pilots praise the IR Maverick with much conviction, though I know the air force A-10s used them with some success.

On the evening of 16 February, Z-Man and I made our way north on a killing box mission. We were both carrying FLIR pods and so were able to work independently. That we both had "eyes in the dark" obviated the need for the awkward and difficult buddy-bombing tactics Dip and I had used earlier. Once in our designated area, we split up and went hunting as singles.

Deconflicting for midair avoidance by altitude, I trolled about at an altitude two thousand feet higher than Z-Man. Prior to rolling in for a bomb delivery, I would give my approximate position and heading to Z-Man, who, if he wasn't in the vicinity, would clear me in. He, of course, operating at a lower altitude, was able to operate freely without conflicting with me.

The last several days of the war our squadron came into its own as far as night hunting/killing sorties were concerned. By now we were all fairly familiar with operating the FLIR pod (prior to leaving the States, most of us had never used one), the pods had been fine tuned, and we had developed decent tactics. An additional development, though, which surely didn't hurt our effectiveness, was that it seemed that now there were more targets than even the week prior.

On this night, I found a set of W-shaped trenches similar to the ones I had bombed a week or two earlier with Kato. Because we were not scheduled for aerial refueling on this mission, we had only about twenty minutes or so to find our targets and kill them. I decided, then, to drop my bombs in three runs, rather than make five runs of one bomb apiece.

I set my bombs up to come off in pairs, each bomb spaced one hundred feet apart. This would leave just one bomb on my third and last run. With this program, I could aim at the middle of the trench and be assured that my bombs would hit some portion of it. My first run started out beautifully, with an excellent FLIR track and delivery. An instant before impact, however, the FLIR broke track and started looking off toward Oregon or somewhere. My shouts of frustration are quite audible on the video tape. I wasn't concerned that my hits wouldn't be good; the bombs had already been dropped and didn't need in-flight guidance. I was mad because I had been robbed of the ability to watch my bombs pulverizing the target. The next two deliveries went well, with good FLIR video down to impact.

The enemy was helpless during these missions. With their radars taken out of service, and no way to pick us up visually, they were basically blind to any airborne threat. After bomb impact, there would be a great sparkling on the ground from muzzle flashes as they blindly fired their guns skyward.

Several of us had our wits sorely tested on these night missions. The U.S. Army had multiple rocket launchers deployed just south of the border. These were surface-to-surface rockets designed to be employed in a fashion similar to artillery. They posed no threat to aircraft. However, when they launched a salvo of rockets at positions in Kuwait, it looked like the biggest SAM launch in the world—lots of rockets with all the attendant smoke and flames. More than one of us had to shake our trousers out after we recognized the rockets for what they were.

The big navy battleships were also bombarding targets during this time. It was impressive to see a huge blast of fire from the gulf, followed moments later by the shells exploding on the battlefield. It was ironic that these big, old bruisers were almost literally museum relics and yet were operating side by side with the latest technology that could be fielded. That the battleships were able to operate so close to the coast was a testament to the success of the air campaign up to this point. Obviously, the naval commanders felt that the Iraqi air force was not a threat. Kudos to the U.S. Air Force. The same could be said for any ground-based weapon that might have been able to damage the battleships. And don't forget the minesweeping work.

The battleships' presence also indicated that the coalition was pulling out all the stops to prepare the battlefield for the upcoming invasion. The navy had moved the aircraft carrier *America* from the Red Sea into the gulf. The shorter distance to the battlefield increased the effectiveness of the ships by enabling them to launch more sorties. About this time as well (21 February), the navy pulled the USS

Nassau and USS *Tarawa* close enough to the coast so that its embarked Harriers could be brought into the fray.

The marine Hornets kept up a "'round-the-clock presence." Despite all the destruction that had already been wrought, the Iraqis were far from finished. Though the battlefield was littered with bombed-out hulks and destroyed equipment, new enemy formations continued to appear. The enemy was also becoming more clever in the manner in which he dispersed his equipment. It was becoming common to find perfectly operable vehicles and equipment dispersed in old bomb craters. Surrounded by the wreckage of the old equipment and the blackened earth, the new gear was very easy to overlook or dismiss as already destroyed.

There was also intelligence that described deceptive tactics that the Iraqis were supposedly employing. One of these was the ignition of decoy fires as smoke screens. Supposedly, after Iraqi positions had come under attack, the enemy was lighting fires around the attacked equipment (assuming it had not already been destroyed) to deceive us into thinking that the target had been destroyed. I have trouble with this idea. First, one has to assume that the Iraqis had flammable material readily stored near their weapons. Though I don't believe the Iraqis even vaguely resembled military wizards, I don't think they would have endangered their gear this way. I may be wrong.

Second, somebody had to leave cover in the middle of an attack and ignite these fires. So imagine this: An Iraqi tank has just been attacked, but the bomb missed. Now somebody has to make the decision to leave their protected position and set a fire near that tank. Meanwhile, that someone has no idea if the missed tank is going to be attacked again in five seconds, or sixty seconds, or at all. That someone would have to be very brave. Or stupid. I don't think it's a practical idea, and I did not, during any of my missions, see anything which indicated this type of activity.

Another tactic of deception the Iraqis may have practiced seems more plausible. That was the construction and employment of decoys, particularly those that imitated armor and artillery. This idea has been around for awhile and was used very effectively in World

War II. In fact, we had decoys (F-16s) in place on the edge of the runway at Shaikh Isa Air Base. From altitude it was very difficult to tell these from the real thing.

The same would have been true of enemy decoys on the battlefield. Even at five hundred feet, it is difficult to tell one type of tank from another. A reasonably well constructed decoy would have been difficult to recognize as well. I do not recall seeing anything that I identified as a decoy. Though, with my eyes, I have trouble identifying myself in a mirror. I very well may have attacked decoys that I considered to be real targets. There is no way for me to know. During discussions with people who had toured the battlefield immediately after the ceasefire, however, I met no one who saw any indication of this practice. I'm guessing that if this tactic was employed, it was on a very limited basis.

As the date for the ground war approached, more and more emphasis was put on the destruction of enemy battlefield assets, particularly the artillery, which was in many cases superior to our own. At a "sand table" conference near the front, a pair of marine division commanders cornered a couple of young marine Hornet pilots. In a straightforward fashion, true concern in their eyes, almost fear, they spoke with the pilots man to man. Marine to marine. The upcoming invasion wasn't an exercise. Men were going to die. The Marine Corps was not at risk of just losing a battle. The Marine Corps's entire existence was at stake. Fully one-third of the Corps's ground assets were going into this campaign. If the marines met with disaster, the service would *never* recover. Marine aviators must ensure that their brothers on the ground did not meet with disaster! Those young captains left that meeting with a sense of responsibility, of mission, that they would never, ever forget.

On 18 February I led a division into central Kuwait to work targets deployed around Ahmed Al Jaber airfield. They were the same sorts of targets again, artillery and armor. With Z-Man on my wing and controlled by the FAC(A), I was pretty pleased with the results. In my journal I called it a "duck shoot," and remarked on a particularly outstanding set of secondary explosions from one vehicle I hit. The place was a madhouse, though, Hornets and Harriers everywhere.

There was no way that the Iraqis were going to be able to sustain that kind of beating.

They were not impotent, however. During this last portion of the war we had three Hornets sustain damage from hand-held SAMs. Two F/A-18s from VMFA-314 were hit while on virtually the same bombing run. Both were struck in the aft portion of the aircraft, the afterburner cans (or engine nozzles). Though the damage to both jets looked absolutely terrible, they made it safely back to Shaikh Isa, foregoing landings at other fields along the way. The jets were made flyable a relatively short time later.

The third jet struck was a two-seat FAC(A) from VMFA(AW)-121. This one, too, was hit in the same place and made it safely back to base. That the Hornet was a jet capable of taking battle damage and still surviving to bring its crew home was quickly being established.

As for the AAA, the Iraqis were becoming more cagey. At times they would put up a significant response. At other times they were completely silent. They were fearful that their muzzle flashes would give their positions away and bring swift retaliation. That fear was not unfounded. By now, we were launching aircraft loaded with HARMs and bombs to provide a roving umbrella over the battlefield. If the crews could find a target for their HARM, they would launch it. If they could visually pick up AAA positions (particularly from their muzzle flashes), they would bomb them.

On 19 February I led another four-ship up to an area about ten miles north of Ahmed Al Jaber Air Base. More artillery and vehicles. This time after dropping our bombs, the area was so crowded with aircraft that I was afraid that if we stayed to strafe, we'd have a midair or get bombed.

Lurch was my wingman. I grabbed him and flew a little farther north, where we could have some quality time alone together (this was the 1990s). We found some revetted artillery tubes and other equipment and quickly went to work. We got immediate results. I strafed a couple of positions and obviously hit some ammo. These were some of the best secondary explosions I saw throughout the whole war. Hair, teeth, and eyeballs everywhere.

Moving to another position, I hit a target (I don't know what it was, just revetted stuff) that didn't so much explode as just emit huge clouds of gray-white smoke. This stuff became a huge cloud that was visible for miles. I loved the twenty-millimeter cannon. It was accurate, easy to use, and deadly.

We were still using the Rockeye cluster bombs. Now that we were dropping at the lower altitudes that they were intended to be employed from, we were having great success with the accuracy. If we could see a target, and if the cluster bomb worked right, then we could kill it. But we were still suffering from a horrific dud rate. The Rockeye was flimsier and a little more complicated than a general purpose bomb. Sometimes they just didn't come off, or if they did, they didn't open up. Even if they did open up as designed, there was still the dud rate of the bomblets themselves to contend with. After the war I talked with marines who had been on the ground as part of the invasion. They had tales of many, many MK 20 Rockeye canisters lying smashed but unopened on the desert floor, and of unexploded bomblets strewn over large areas. Because of these problems, I think that most of us preferred to have our jets loaded with the MK 83 general purpose one-thousand-pound bombs.

The Iraqis hated the Rockeyes, though. They called them "shower bombs," referring to the manner in which the bomblets showered down on their positions. On top of that, once their position was hit, it was almost as good as mined. Because of these unexploded bomblets, they had to be very careful when they moved about the area. This must have added difficulty to normal operations, particularly at night.

By now our forces had custody of quite a few captured Iraqis, or Iraqis who had just walked across the border and surrendered. Most of them were a mess. Filthy and unkempt, the only way to tell they were soldiers was from their uniforms. One overriding theme during their interrogations was that the never-ceasing air attacks were taking an incredible toll on equipment, personnel, and morale. We heard stories of POWs reduced to blithering idiots; sitting detached from the rest of the group, they would literally shit themselves every time they heard a jet. Regardless of whether or not they were a well-disciplined force, what they had experienced was enough to unnerve even the most professional army.

Weather was still causing problems. Most of our sorties on 20 February were canceled. As luck would have it, I was able to sneak out on a D escort mission to the same area we had worked on the sixteenth. The FAC(A) ran several Harriers through the target, and finally we used up what we had loaded on our jets. I was able to destroy a truck with a MK 83, and he did some good work with his rockets. We strafed a little as well, but I didn't see anything I shot catch fire.

That evening I hitched a ride back to my barracks with an Intel officer from one of the higher headquarters. He was very excited about an impending invasion of Failaka Island. This was the largest island off the coast of Kuwait. The invasion was supposed to take place that night, and he was full of details, which he shared readily with me. He didn't actually share them with me, so much as he overwhelmed me with them.

I was dumbfounded. I couldn't believe that he was openly talking about what was surely a secret operation. Perhaps it was deliberate disinformation. But why did he pick me? Maybe it was my beady eyes and traitorous disposition. I actually debated with myself about whether or not to tell someone about this idiot. Perhaps turn him in. But I had more important things to do. I went and ate chow instead.

As it turned out, Failaka Island was never invaded.

The twenty-first was another tough weather day. We ended up losing most of our morning sorties. I was scheduled with Lurch for the usual FAC(A) controlled work. By now the marines had established a "turn-around" detachment at Jubail, about ninety miles up the Saudi Arabian coast from Shaikh Isa. Closer to Kuwait. The idea was to launch sorties out of Bahrain and have them recover into Jubail after completing their mission. Once on deck at Jubail, the ordnance and turn-around crews could have the jets rearmed, refueled, and airborne again inside of half an hour. This increased our sortie rate and thus our effectiveness.

It was a pair of sorties like this that Lurch and I were scheduled to fly. About fifteen minutes after getting airborne, however, one of the mission computers in my aircraft failed. This meant that I would have to drop my bombs manually, calculating my dive angle, altitude, airspeed, winds aloft, and pipper placement. This was standard in the F-4 Phantom I had flown years before but was never practiced in the Hornet. To do this effectively took a great deal of practice. I would have been lucky to get my bombs to drop within the borders of Kuwait. Rather than waste two sets of bombs, Lurch went ahead on his own and I reversed course and bustered back to Bahrain.

Our plan was for Lurch to press on and fly the first mission with the FAC(A). I would return to base, refuel, and get my mission computer quickly swapped out. Lurch would turn through Jubail. I would launch at a predetermined time and call Lurch on the ground in Jubail when I was twenty miles out. He would launch, and we would effect a rendezvous for the second mission.

And that's exactly what happened. Once I touched down, I went through the fuel pits, quickly gassed up, and taxied back to our squadron flight line. The maintenance troops scrambled over the jet, changed out the computer, and had me stuffed back into my jet, started up, and ready to launch. Once airborne, I gave Lurch a "heads up" and we effected a perfect running rendezvous. Like clockwork. That we were able to pull this off was a tribute to the training and teamwork that everyone involved practiced as a matter of routine. That and a lot of luck.

Anyway, once we got over the battlefield, we worked with the FAC(A) north of Ahmed Al Jaber airfield. It was a circus. Besides us, there were other flights of Hornets, the FAC(A) and his escort, and flights of Harriers, all concentrated over artillery positions, support vehicles, and tanks. I was really pleased with my work, hitting an artillery piece, a truck, and a tank.

As soon as we had dropped our big stuff, we cleared the area to the north and found a complex of what I initially thought were revetted "big-rig" trucks. Lurch and I started strafing them, and as we got lower and overflew them, we saw that they weren't trucks but modular buildings. They looked just like double-wide trailers. How tacky! We wondered if their dates had "big hair" and wore too much blue eye shadow. Anyway, we worked them over thoroughly. I could see my rounds going right through the doors. Knock, knock!

Iraqi emplacements in central Kuwait. Note the revetted positions and equipment scattered about. These types of positions were numerous and easily seen from the air. More difficult was identifying what the positions held. The oil fires are faintly visible in the background. *(Photo by Patrick Greene)*

That was the way that a lot of the targets we worked, especially in Kuwait, were. The Iraqis would set up their positions, artillery, armor, or whatever, then use civilian equipment they had stolen from the Kuwaitis right alongside. Like those mobile homes. It wasn't unusual to see a commercial truck in a convoy with a bunch of military vehicles. What had been delivering melons before the war was now hauling mortar rounds. Or to see a well-entrenched, carefully camouflaged artillery position belied by a couple of luxury vehicles parked right in their midst. Who in their right mind would double park a Mercedes against a T-72? But it happened. The major needs his staff car.

Of course, during the great exodus on what was to become the Highway of Death a week later, all manner of vehicles, military and civilian alike, were shanghaied by the fleeing Iraqis. They were all bombed indiscriminately. It was a curious war.

Early on the morning of 22 February the base received a rude surprise. I was sound asleep until I awoke ten feet above the floor with my fingernails and toenails embedded in the ceiling. We had been abruptly wakened by a tremendous explosion that had rocked the entire airfield. We had no idea what had happened. For all we knew, it had been a terrorist bomb, or an accident on the flight line.

One of the NBC Nazis came running down the hall screaming for everyone to put their gas masks on. The order was ignored. We'd been fooled a hundred times before. If any gas came seeping in, we'd bury our faces in our pillows. After recovering our wits, and shaking out our bed linen, most of us went back to sleep.

The next day we learned what had happened. Evidently the Iraqis had hurled three Scuds our way. One of them appeared to be a threat and was engaged. The other two were left alone and flew harmlessly into the gulf. The engaged Scud was targeted by a Patriot missile launched from the base. The intercept was successful, and the Scud fell harmlessly in the desert close to the base. It had left an impressive crater. These explosions are what had rocked us out of bed. Though we had been subjected to a number of Scud alerts, this was the only time that a missile had actually come close. We were bored with the whole Scud thing and almost always gaffed the alerts.

Well, not exactly gaffed. Here's a story about conditioning. Let's go to Alaska. Kodiak Island. Home of the great Alaskan brown (some would say grizzly) bear. It is also home to a large population of black-tail deer. The deer are hunted very vigorously. Not the bears. They haven't been for a long time. Well, after a deer is shot, it is usually gutted and field dressed. The offal (guts) left behind are a special treat for scavenging bears. So the bears have started making a connection: gunshot equals dead deer, which equals dead deer guts, which equals dinner. Instead of cowering at the sound of a rifle shot, the bears have been seen to take off running and salivating in the direction of gunfire, hoping for dinner on the cheap. Some have gotten so bold, or rude, as to make a practice out of convincing hunters off of their trophies prematurely. Even armed men don't take on the great beasts (and the Fish and Game Department) without a good deal more provocation. Anyway, this isn't the smartest thing in the world that a bear can do. But they've been conditioned.

So had we. During time off at the barracks, if there was a Scud alert, many of the officers would race up the maintenance access ladder to the rooftop, chairs and liquor in tow. Scud watching was cheap, spontaneous, and exciting entertainment. Something the whole community could get involved in. It was exhilarating. We were like a pack of naughty school boys doing something we weren't supposed to and feeling all the more excited because of it. Actually, we never got to see much, as nearly all the alarms were false, but it was nice to sit up on the roof and chat, drink, and tell the same old stories in different surroundings. We came to look forward to these ad hoc social gatherings.

Not so the low-paid Pakistani laborers, and those of other Islamic nations brought into the country as cheap labor. Poorly educated and pitifully compensated, these workers were petrified of the Scud threat. With no access to any sort of gas masks, they came up with some ingenious, though probably ineffective, facsimiles. One of the most elaborate contraptions I saw consisted of a couple of soda cans fastened together, filled with cotton, and connected to a network of tubes and goggles. One of the most pitiable sights I saw was a Pakistani worker who, during the middle of a Scud alert, dropped his shovel, grabbed a garbage bag, and pulled it over his head. I'm not sure he was familiar with the principles of respiration. As it turned out, however, neither he nor anyone on base ever had to test our masks for real. It appeared that the chemical/biological warfare capability of Iraq was overstated.

Things were still being muddled on the political front. The Russians were getting involved, and President Bush gave the Iraqis until noon on the twenty-third to begin leaving Kuwait. For our part, we didn't understand whose noon he was talking about. Baghdad's? Eastern standard time? We received the news very badly. We felt that they should either surrender or be destroyed. If they were given any other option, they would turn it into a propaganda victory of some sort. That would be hard to stomach and would serve very little purpose.

We continued to batter the enemy. Aircraft from one of our sister squadrons, VMFA-333, were pummeling troops in a couple of trenches when they were directed to halt their attacks. The Iraqis were pouring out, trying to surrender. Evidently this scene was becoming more common. It was a foretaste of the waves of POWs that would almost overwhelm our invading forces a few days later.

On the night of 22 February I took Kato into central Kuwait to hit an artillery position. The flight up through Saudi Arabia was incredible. There was no doubt that the invasion was imminent. Roadways were clogged with vehicles and equipment making their way up to Kuwait. The light from the headlights of those vehicles formed a great illuminated band leading to the border. And there was no doubt where the border was. The entire area was on fire with artillery and rocket fire, illumination rounds, and the resultant fires. From the air it seemed apparent where the breach points were going to be.

On arrival we found the artillery site pretty near to the location our Intelligence folks had briefed. Amazing. They must have gotten the information "real time" from another aircraft that had been working the area. The site was composed of about six artillery guns arrayed in a semicircle, revetted, and covered with some sort of camouflage netting. One of the beauties of the FLIR pod was that it wasn't fooled by camouflage netting. The stuff showed up as a sort of translucent shadow over whatever it was covering.

Kato and I split and set up a cloverleaf pattern, advising each other as to which revetment we were targeting, from what direction, and when we were starting and finishing our runs. He and I had come a long way since our first mission, nearly a month and a half earlier. Inside of ten minutes we had efficiently and precisely destroyed every gun in that site. And we did this on a burning, smoke-filled battlefield in the dead of night. This would have been impossible ten years earlier. The Marine Corps had done well by the Hornet. This mission serves as a tremendous example to wave in the faces of all the naysayers of high tech on the battlefield.

When reviewing our video, we were able to see a few troops scurrying about, but nothing compared to the impressive video Moto and Z-Man brought back. They had been operating near Kuwait City, where Z-Man had cornered a truck carrying three or four troops. They had stopped the truck and bailed out, just barely making it to a roadside ditch as Z-Man's Rockeye destroyed their vehicle.

Moto, meanwhile, had also been busy. On one of his runs he had gotten a radar lock on a truck at range. He closed the distance and started a dive to deliver a Rockeye canister. As he neared the target, the FLIR clearly showed it to be a military truck. Thermal energy from five soldiers riding in the back showed up as five white blobs. The canister was dropped and the FLIR momentarily broke lock as the target passed under the jet, out of the radar's field of view. Z-Man called out, "Did you get him?" The FLIR regained lock and showed the obviously stricken truck careening off the road. Moto replied, "I don't know. I think I *may* have gotten him." And people wondered why we called him Master of the Obvious.

The radar mode which Moto had used to bomb the truck could be quite effective. The FLIR wasn't even needed and served only to give video of the attack, while the radar provided data to the mission computers, which in turn performed the complex computations for the attack. Called ground moving target mode, this capability allows the radar to match the velocity of a truck or other moving target against the background of the earth's surface. This velocity differential allows the radar to lock onto the vehicle. But it is essential that the target keeps moving. If the driver stops for any reason, be it a traffic jam or call of nature, the radar is unable to discriminate the non-moving vehicle against the nonmoving earth and accuracy is greatly degraded. In reality this is not a surefire mode, as the radar can have difficulty with masking from the ground, reflections from other nearby vehicles, and other factors. But we did score some successes with it.

Immediately after debriefing my hop with Kato, I was briefing again with our operations officer, Major "Train" Hull, for another sortie. He would be leading me on a suppression of enemy air defenses, roving CAP, over the whole of Kuwait. Basically, this gave us free rein to roam wherever we chose, looking for indications of enemy anti-air activity, which we then were to target and destroy. But we couldn't find any. Most of the radar-guided anti-air systems had long ago been destroyed or hidden away. These missions normally turned out to be nonevents. In fact, IV Bergstrom would drop down to lower altitudes, turn on all his lights, and plug in his afterburners trying to tempt someone to shoot at him.

And a nonevent is what this mission started out as. We didn't have FLIR pods and weren't able to target any AAA sites. Finally, at daybreak, we were relieved by another section of Hornets and turned loose to find targets for the MK 83s we were carrying.

I had just refueled and was "fat" on gas when I spotted a group of five armored vehicles south of Ali Al Salem Air Base. I circled overhead at altitude for a bit, waiting for the light to improve as I watched. They reminded me of a group of beetles just waking up. One of the beetles drove out of its revetment over to another beetle. And then to another. "Hey, wake up! Time for breakfast sleepy head!"

I called for Train to come over. He was just finishing at the tanker. With Train as high cover, I dove and dropped a single bomb, blowing one of the beetles to Kingdom Come. Train followed with his gun and set another on fire. I dove and dropped again. Missed. No more bombs.

By then the rest of the vehicles had scattered. Train led us over to the coastal highway north of Kuwait City to look for other game. The AAA had become very thick. This was the same area that had given us such a warm response on the thirteenth. This time our reception was even warmer. I spotted a truck zipping north on the highway at very high speed. I rolled in and let loose a long burst of twenty-millimeter cannon. Missed behind him. Not enough lead. Exactly what the AAA gunners were doing with me. Evidently we all could have used a little more practice.

It struck me about this time that our original mission had been to destroy this type of AAA. However, the idea of going head-to-head against multiple AAA sites with only the twenty-millimeter cannon seemed to me to be a bad one.

Train had spotted a big-rig racing north and dropped a pair of bombs. Same problem. Not enough lead, which caused him to miss behind. The truck still raced on. This driver had balls. Train strafed him from head-on and missed behind again. By now, though, the driver had had enough. He stropped and made a run for it. With the truck now an easy target, I hurriedly rolled in and smoked it before Train could get back into firing position. Out of ammo, we climbed out of the flak and made for home.

In my journal during this time, there is an entry noting that "we've held peace off for another day." Between the political opportunities being offered the Iraqis and the trammeled condition of their forces, it was obvious that the war wasn't going to last much longer. Our troops were advancing so quickly that it was difficult to keep track of them.

Our operational tempo was approaching maximum effort. That we were able to sustain it was a tribute to our marines. The word "marine" usually conjures up a rifle-toting, mud-slogging, fearless American Hero. Our marines could shoot a rifle, too, but their primary mission was getting those jets ready and keeping them ready. Working in two twelve-hour shifts, which often overlapped into much longer hours, they expertly made sure that every scheduled sortie was provided with a combat-ready, fully mission-capable jet. We depended on these men utterly for our success. For my part, I didn't even know how to refuel an aircraft.

In an effort to make the allied vehicles more readily identifiable from the air, they were painted with large Vs. This may have been of some help to the helo bubbas; I don't know. But as far as we were concerned, they may as well have been painted with Happy Faces. No marking, short of painting the whole vehicle international orange, would have helped us make positive identification. We relied almost exclusively on geographic location to determine if vehicles were friend or foe.

Later that day, two Hornets from VMFA-314 were nearly knocked out of the sky while hitting rocket positions near Kuwait City. Major Bob "Boomer" Knutzen was the flight lead. His story is a classic study in tactics and lessons learned, as well as a testament to the survivability of the F/A-18:

It was the first day of the ground war, and I had Scott "Coma" Quinlan on my wing. After checking in with the DASC, they gave us a mission right away, and sent us up north. The target was a battery of four multiple rocket launchers, a big potential threat to our ground forces, which were already well into Kuwait. The target had been found and ID'd "real time" as an active threat by an RPV.

We descended from thirty thousand feet down through several

layers of clouds until we got near the target about ten miles north-east of Al Jaber airfield. On the way we got a target brief from the FAC(A), while we ran a radar intercept to join with him so that he could lead us to the target. The overcast now was all the way down to eight thousand feet.

Approaching the MRLs, the FAC(A) rolled in and marked the position with a white phosphorous rocket. We spotted the launchers and were lined up perfectly. There were four of them. Diving down in trail formation, we dropped two bombs apiece and plastered them. Direct hits, with secondaries everywhere. The FAC(A) complimented our nice work, noting that there was nothing left. We were feeling pretty good heading back south, when the two-seater called us back. Not so fast. It turned out that the MRLs we had destroyed were targets that he had freelanced on his own. We still needed to hit the MRL position that the RPV had found. We ended up turning around and joining him about five miles south of the original target.

It was getting darker, even though it was still midmorning. The smoke and the overcast had cut visibility down to about three or four miles. Arriving at the new target, the two-seater needlessly pointed out that the threat was AAA. There was a lot of it. It was easy to see the muzzle flashes because it had gotten so dark. Most of the time during the day it's tough to pick out AAA positions.

Anyway, while we were watching all of this AAA, the FAC(A) was trying to talk our eyes onto the target. There were four MRLs on line along the road. Across the road, there was an AAA position. He marked the spot with a rocket, and I dove in from the north trying to pick it up. No good. As I pulled up, not having dropped anything, I rolled left, and was able to visually acquire the target. The same thing happened to Coma. He pulled up and off to the right, so that we stayed across the circle from each other.

I set up for my next run, and again rolled in from the north. This one went real well. My three bombs hit a couple of the positions with nice secondaries again. The same for Coma. The whole time we were jinking to make it tough for the AAA gunners and putting out flares to defeat hand-helds (SAMs). There was still one launcher left, so I selected my gun and rolled in. I had just put the pipper on the target when I heard Coma call out "I'm hit!"

Looking out at my four o'clock, I pulled up and saw him. Letting him know I was on my way, and getting a radar lock on him, I told him to climb into the clouds away from the AAA. At this time, we all thought he had been hit by anti-aircraft fire. None of us had seen any hand-helds fired. There was no smoke trail that we could see.

Jinking as I climbed to join him, I found myself way too slow, about 320 knots. And out of flares, low, and highlighted against the overcast. That's when I got hit. I felt a big thump. It felt just like I had been rear-ended. I didn't hear anything, though. Looking out the right side, it was obvious that the jet had been badly hit. The whole back end was on fire. At the same time the left engine fire light came on. I pulled the throttle off, punched the fire and extinguisher lights, and dumped my wing tanks. The aircraft was still flying fine.

It's at this point that Boomer points out that he just couldn't believe what was happening to him. He was incredulous that he had gotten hit and was very likely going to end up as a POW. He didn't want to be Abdul's girlfriend. This wasn't supposed to happen to him. Remember, every fighter pilot knows that he is invincible. If something bad is going to happen, it'll be to the other guy.

Soon after executing his emergency procedures, the fire went out. The FAC(A) was trying to chase both Boomer and Coma out over the water, at the same time making a Mayday call. Boomer meanwhile had switched his radio over to Red Crown and told them to launch the SAR (Search and Rescue) helicopters. Things weren't looking good for the home team. Remembering tales from Vietnam, he was certain that if he managed to make it out over the water, he would be rescued by friendly forces.

Well, his trusty F/A-18 wasn't going to let him down. He ended up making it out over the bay north of Kuwait City. He was able to talk to Coma and found that he was still flying as well, though he also was staying aloft on just one engine. Both of them by now had jettisoned all of their external stores to improve handling characteristics as well as fuel consumption. Using their air-to-air TACANs (tactical air navigation systems, which provide range and bearing) and radars, they were able to visually acquire each other and headed for a small divert field just south of the Kuwaiti border. A little later, deciding that in their condition they probably ought to divert to a field that had arresting gear, they proceeded down the Saudi coast toward Jubail. Nearing that field they discovered that the weather there was very poor and so opted to continue all the way back to Shaikh Isa. What a great airplane. Boomer continues his story:

> When we got near the field, we both dropped our landing gear and were relieved to find everything worked as advertised. We made normal landings, and pulled off the runway surrounded by the crash crews. My knees almost buckled when I crawled out of the jet and took a look at what had happened. The entire exhaust nozzle on the left engine had been blown to smithereens. The turkey feathers on the right engine had also been knocked off. Shrapnel had perforated both horizontal stabilators, and my arresting hook tip had been blasted off. Additionally there was a good deal of fire damage forward of the left nozzle.
>
> Coma's aircraft looked much the same, though it looked like the missile had flown right up into the engine nozzle, which absorbed most of the explosion and so saved the rest of the aircraft. The missile which had struck my aircraft impacted from the side. There was no doubt that we had been hit by heat-seeking hand-held missiles. The type of damage and the areas stricken were consistent with this.

So resilient is the aircraft, though, that both jets, after having all engines replaced, as well as multiple flight surfaces and panels, were repaired and ready for test flights the next day.

Strangely enough, Boomer opted out of a scheduled follow-on sortie half an hour after he landed. He said something about needing to do some laundry.

Looking back at that day and that mission, now Lieutenant Colonel Knutzen remembers some of the factors that played a part: "A lot of the things I did were classic mistakes that you learn not to do when you're a first lieutenant. The weather had driven us low. We were carrying a lot of weight and drag and so had gotten slow while jinking to avoid the AAA. We had attacked from the same direction several times, and both of us were out of flares. On top of that, we were easy targets highlighted against the low overcast."

What he doesn't mention was the reason he had knowingly taken such risks. The ground war was under way and marines were within range of those very deadly rocket launchers. They had to be destroyed, and he and Coma had done that.

Where survivability is concerned, this incident is a graphic demonstration that two engines are better than one. Had these two jets been single-engine aircraft, the outcome would have been much different. We would have scratched two very valuable assets from our inventory, and quite possibly lost two pilots.

Scotty took me into the Icetray on the evening of the twenty-fourth. A large complex of stock pens kept by once-nomadic bands who had somewhat settled down, viewed from the air, it looked like an enormous icetray. On this evening, from the time we started our brief until the time we walked to our jets, the briefed forward line of our troops changed two times. Our ground troops were advancing that quickly. It was obvious that at this rate the war was going to be over soon. We were hearing stories that the Iraqis were surrendering in such numbers that our guys on the ground weren't able to handle them all. Basically, the would-be POWs were told, "Hey great, but we don't have time for you. Tell the guys behind us."

The skipper wasted very little time. Within minutes after arriving over our designated area, he had found a formation of vehicles with troops standing idly by. They appeared oblivious to what was going on overhead and what was about to happen. Of course, they had no way of knowing. Their demeanor, or disposition, changed not at all right up to the point when Scotty's bombs hit in their midst.

Because I had no FLIR pod, my task was really a "no brainer." Essentially, I tried to maintain visual contact with the point where his bombs had hit. The night was not even half so clear as the evening I had done the same thing with Dip. Without a visual "anchor point" on the ground, it's very difficult to be certain your eye hasn't wandered. Anyway, I rolled in, designated what I thought was the right point, and dumped my bombs. My bombs didn't show up on the skipper's FLIR video, and I have no idea what they hit. Other than the ground.

Lack of FLIRs notwithstanding, the F/A-18 could have been used more effectively as a night bomber. Like most attack aircraft produced in the last thirty or forty years, the Hornet is capable of carrying illumination flares. The F/A-18 uses a system called the LUU-2, which can be mounted six per weapon station. Producing many, many, millions of candlepower, the flares are dropped from the aircraft in much the same way that a bomb is. The flares can be profiled to deploy their parachutes and ignite at a predetermined altitude, depending on the desired effect. They burn for approximately three minutes, and when dropped as pairs or more, will easily provide enough illumination for three or four aircraft to work a target. Very importantly, attacking aircraft are almost invisible from the ground as they rarely go below the altitude of the flare, and so avoid highlighting themselves. In the absence of target tracking radar, the attackers are, for all intents and purposes, invulnerable to directed fire.

In fact, as part of regular readiness evaluations, marine Hornet units are often tested on their ability to perform this mission. As a tactic designed to be employed in a low-threat environment (which Kuwait was, particularly after the first couple of weeks), a single Hornet will generally lead or meet a flight of three or four over a target and coordinate the attack while illuminating the target area. The same thing could have been done over Kuwait and Iraq with one bird, FLIR equipped, coordinating and illuminating for other aircraft. This generally would have been more effective than the technique Dip and I had used earlier, and what Scotty and I had just tried.

On several nights we observed A-10s working with illumination, I assume with some success. As to why we did not employ this tactic, which we had practiced often enough in peacetime, I can only guess. First, and probably most important, is the perception (probably real based on my own experience) that the LUU-2 isn't the most reliable piece of ordnance we employ. It is most often dropped in at least pairs because of its lower than desired reliability rate. Another factor may have been that the ordnance crews were already being pushed for all they were worth. To have saddled them with one more type of ordnance may have been asking too much. I don't know.

Bombing by flares, while much easier and more effective than bombing blind, is still not the easiest mission in the world. It's similar to bombing at dusk or dawn, with lots of weird shadows and skewed depth perception. Target acquisition is more difficult than during the day, and it is almost impossible to keep track of your playmates, which increased the potential for midair collisions.

Also, once the flares light off over an enemy position, the gig is up. They know that they are being targeted, and although they can't see the attacking aircraft, if they have enough weapons of the right type, they can put up blanket or barrage fire. Though ineffective, an unaimed AAA round is just as deadly as an aimed round if it hits you.

Probably the most overriding reason, though, was the simple fact that we had established a routine with which we were comfortable. It was familiar, we were still killing lots of stuff, and the workload was not necessarily overwhelming. "If it's not broke. . . ."

Well it wasn't broke, but it takes a whole lot more whacks to drive a post with a five-pound sledgehammer than it does with a twenty-pounder. I personally believe that with a bit of close attention to the loading and employment of the flares, the reliability factor could have been overcome. Also, some creative scheduling would have allowed packages of four or five aircraft to effectively work a target that normally may have only received attention from one FLIR-equipped aircraft and his "blind" wingman. With a little experience, and wisdom gained from "lessons learned" in the first couple of sorties, I feel that this tactic could have increased our efficiency (a plug for Total Quality Management).

Finally, this tactic could have been effective in mixed formations. Hornets could have illuminated for Harriers. Perhaps the ideal flare bird, with its great payload, endurance, FLIR, and two-man crew, would have been the venerable A-6E. Hell, I've even bombed off of flares kicked out the back of a KC-130. The Herc possesses a range and payload that's hard to top, though it's not the most diminutive of targets.

After landing and a quick debrief, I was briefing for another hop with Dip. The XO was going to take us north of Ali Al Salem Air Base in north-central Kuwait. The Iraqis were on the run. I was excited, as both of our aircraft were FLIR equipped. The routine was familiar. On arrival we split and worked the area individually. The way the enemy had dug in this evening was unusual. They were staying away from each other. Way, way, away. On the order of a couple of hundred yards. They took the meaning of dispersal to new heights.

It didn't matter. We could find them regardless of how they dispersed themselves. And finding them was almost the same thing as killing them. Almost. I found, and rolled in on an entrenched vehicle. Getting closer, I was able to see the barrel of a tank. The designation and delivery were perfect. Almost. Flying through my release cue, nothing came off of the airplane. I almost punched myself. I had forgotten to select the master armament switch. Like the safety switch on a gun, if the master armament switch isn't in the right position, nothing can be dropped from the jet. It's a safety precaution. And it worked. My goof-up ensured the momentary safety of that Iraqi tank.

Coming back around, I found another emplacement and started my run. As I got closer, I wasn't sure there was anything in it. But there was: another tank. Too late. I had flown through the release cue without dropping a bomb. Damn. I was going to run out of gas before I was done. Dip was almost finished already.

I came around for another run and finally dropped a pair of bombs on an armored vehicle. Good drop. Next run, same thing. Dip was finished and anxious to leave. I could hear a number of other flights checking in and ready to work the area. On my last run, I dropped a single bomb for a direct hit on an emplaced semitrailer rig. Finally, rid of my bombs, I joined Dip and we cleared the area for the next flight. Those Iraqis must have spent a wicked night. Those who lived through it.

I was grounded by weather (surprise) on the twenty-fifth. By now the full effects of the oil fires set by the enemy were being felt. Depending on which way the wind was blowing, entire sections of the country were shrouded by smoke and totally unworkable from the air. The smoke, coupled with dust, rain, and low ceilings, made fixed-wing support over the battlefield a near impossibility.

Chapter Twenty
Highway of Death

A lot has been written about the "Highway of Death" and what a scene of carnage and devastation it was. I'm certainly not going to write anything that differs with that viewpoint. That any great battlefield retreat has ever been so savagely and utterly destroyed in modern times is doubtful. There are still great heaps of debris shoved into the desert, waiting to be carted off as scrap or buried by the sand.

The questions of how and why the retreat started have fairly straightforward answers. The great exodus out of Kuwait City by the Iraqi army occurred for a very simple reason: Saddam's forces were being routed on the battlefield. Kuwait was lost. Had the Iraqis elected to stay and try to hold the city they would have ultimately been defeated, but the coalition would have paid a high price in casualties. House-to-house combat is a hideous and costly form of warfare.

Additionally, the city itself would have been shattered far worse than it had been up to that point. That said, the chief Iraqi motivation was fear. Their rush to escape harm turned retreat into a panicked rout.

I am not mocking or making light of their fear, or their decision to flee. They had good cause to be fearful. I would have been terrified. The majority of them had nothing to gain by staying to fight. They would have lost, and might have been killed. And for a cause that they probably didn't believe in. I do find disgusting, though, the manner in which they fled. In vehicles they had stolen, stuffed full of whatever valuables they could steal from the Kuwaitis. They weren't an army. They were a mob of thieves in uniform.

The retreat began sometime during the evening of 25 February. Who first recognized it for what it was, and who was first to strike, will forever be open to argument. There are various claims that F-15Es, A-6s, F/A-18s, and A-10s, among others, dropped the "magic" bomb or fired the "silver bullet" that turned the rout into chaos.

To be honest, I don't believe anyone can take full credit. For one thing, attacks on and around the highways surrounding and leading out of the city had been continuous for awhile. The routes out of Kuwait City are many, and once clear of town there are two main north-south arteries. More than one strike was needed to create the bottlenecks which eventually stymied the flow. Indeed, few would argue with the idea that once the spigot was opened full, a good deal of the traffic was stopped simply by the enormous congestion created by thousands of vehicles trying to use highways which weren't designed to handle such volume. Not too different from the Santa Ana Freeway in southern California.

One thing is certain. Once the Iraqis were on the run, all stops were pulled in an effort to crush and render the enemy incapable of ever reconstituting and threatening allied forces. Marine Hornets were in the thick of it. A sortie flown by Captain Jim "Snake" Daulton was typical of those involving the marines out of Shaikh Isa. Snake was one of the tactics "gurus" out of MAWTS-1 (Marine Air Weapons and Tactics Squadron One). He had made it into theater just before the war had kicked off, and was assigned to work with the wing out of Jubail. On occasion he was able to make it down to Bahrain, where his old squadronmates, the Black Knights of VMFA-314, would throw a few missions his way.

Beggars can't be choosers, so he was especially excited on 26 February when he found himself northbound to join the fracas. Though less than a day old, the great savaging was already being billed as the greatest turkey shoot of the century. As luck would have it, foul weather was a factor again. Though he had originally launched as Dash 3 in a four-ship, the flight had split into two two-ships. Smaller flights are much easier to manage in heavy weather. The clouds were solid from seven thousand feet all the way up to thirty thousand. Approaching the border, they were directed to hold at a control point until the FAC(A) could use them.

The airborne command and control circus in the clouds was nearly as chaotic as the mayhem on the battlefield below. There were aircraft everywhere. Everyone was holding in the thick clag, visually blind, but doing their best to deconflict with radios and radars. Again, it is a wonderment that no aircraft were lost to midair collisions. The radios were a mess as communication discipline began to break down. Everyone was eager to get in on the attack. Tempers were running short. Fuel too.

The two-seat Hornets of VMFA(AW)-121 were doing a fantastic job marking targets and coordinating attacks as aircraft reported on station. They worked whatever flavor aircraft arrived on the scene, air force, navy, and marines. All different shapes and sizes. Their biggest problem was that there were more players than they could use. "Put me in coach!" They worked who they could and sent the rest to killing boxes. Snake remembers:

Finally we got the nod, and my wingman, "Toss" Wright, and I made our way down through the weather. The scariest part of that whole mission was deconflicting as we descended through other flights of aircraft while they were climbing to egress the area. We were totally blind to each other except for the SA [situational awareness] we could get on the radar.

We broke out at seven or eight thousand feet. The scene was incredible. Eerie and shocking. The highway below was unbelievably jammed with vehicles "butt-to-nut." Not just the highway, but also along the sides of the highway where they had tried to get around the mess and gotten stuck in the sand. It was a wide band of burning, stranded, and abandoned vehicles, twenty or thirty across. The whole thing stretched for miles in both directions.

The overcast and the smoke from the burning oil made everything seem darker and gloomier than it should have been for that time of day. Brightly burning fires were everywhere. Aircraft were darting and diving over the entire area. Sharks in a feeding frenzy. I remember "Bull" Pratt was in the Delta (F/A-18D). They put a mark down on a stretch of the road and told me and Toss to work that point and stay east of the highway. They had another two-ship work the same point, except that they stayed west of the highway.

It was like a dream come true. When you're flying in the States you look around and imagine that everything is a target, fuel tankers, trucks, tanks, whatever. Well now it was all laid out right in front of us. Kids in a candy store.

They made their contribution to the carnage. Each of them dropped two and a half tons of bombs on whatever target caught their fancy. And if they missed a particular vehicle, it didn't matter much. Everything was packed together so tightly that the bomb would hit something else (Snake insists he never misses, though). After the bombs were gone, they emptied their guns into the whole mess.

The aerial onslaught was continuous. Captain Daulton goes on: "We were being rushed. Just like me before, there were other flights waiting upstairs. Guys were coming up on the radio telling us to hurry up and get our asses out of there. It was their turn!" Finally done, Snake and his wingman made their way back through the gauntlet of marshaling aircraft. Behind them the scene was being repeated many, many, more times. The retreat was crushed. If there was any lingering doubt anywhere about the outcome of the campaign, it was being held by fools.

Wreckage along the Highway of Death, north of Kuwait City. Note the preponderance of civilian vehicles stolen by fleeing Iraqi soldiers.
(Photo by Patrick Greene)

Not every Iraqi was stopped though. Some slipped away from the deadly logjams and were making their way north toward Basra. Intent on destroying every bit of the enemy's potential to make war, the commanders who ran the aerial campaign ensured that the Iraqis would be harried every inch of the way. Aircraft were sent to attack them.

At the same time Snake and Toss were working the highways around Kuwait City, Vector and I were holding at a control point farther north. All hell was breaking loose with the enemy in full retreat. The DASC was overwhelmed again. No one knew for sure how far U.S. troops had advanced, much less any of the Arab contingents. People were losing patience on the radio, and everyone was trying to bully their way into a mission.

I was getting pissed off at Vector. The control point was supposed to be over land, but we were over water. After pimping him about it, he told me to look outside again, and look close. I did. We weren't over the water. What I had thought was the gulf was actually a thick blanket of bluish black smoke. It looked like it covered half the country. This, as well, was adding to the confusion.

Finally, getting low on fuel, they cleared us to work the highway north of Kuwait City. After descending through the gunk, we found a mass of vehicles but couldn't get a positive ID, and no one would clear us to attack. We moved farther north and found another stream of vehicles moving toward Iraq. We couldn't get clearance to attack these either. But they wouldn't tell us no. Good positive control.

We knew these guys couldn't be ours. Too far north, and well past the briefed forward advance of our troops. We split up and attacked them. The visibility was still somewhat poor, so we had to be careful not to run into each other. We were fairly low and easily visible and so were taking small-arms fire from the troops on the road below. Getting low on fuel, I set my aircraft up so that I'd finish in two passes, two bombs on the first and three bombs on the second.

I offset to the north and targeted a line of trucks that had pulled off to the side of the road. The run was perfect. Shit! The bombs didn't come off. The master armament switch again! I had a disease or something. Earlier I had taken radar locks on Vector so as not to lose him in the fog and gloom. I had left the switch off so that I couldn't shoot him by accident. That had happened once or twice already in our MAG, though fortunately no one had been hit. This also meant that I had been trolling around over the top of the enemy without the capability to employ chaff or flares. Pretty stupid. The master arm switch needs to be on to do so.

I was lucky. There was no harm done other than the fact that I had wasted time and gas. I armed up this time as I rolled in and dropped. I was furious when I saw my bombs hit. Duds! This wasn't my day. There was no reason why those bombs should have dudded.

Not wanting to press my luck by staying in the same area anymore, I flew north a couple of miles to where Vector was working. I came upon a road junction where there was somewhat of a traffic jam. There were quite a few vehicles and troops crammed up against some sort of supply depot ("stuff under camouflage netting"). I offset once more, and this time made doubly sure that everything in the cockpit was perfectly set up. I knew for a fact that I wasn't the only one in this war who had forgotten to arm up (I'm sure that most of us did it at least once), but I seemed to be starting a trend lately. This time my run was perfect. The three bombs impacted dead in their midst and set off some good secondary explosions. Third time was a charm.

I had a hard time getting Vector to take us home. He was on a tear. Having dropped his bombs, he was working a column over with his gun. And he was doing some tremendous work (my gun hadn't been reloaded prior to the sortie; because of the tempo, this wasn't unusual). Just like the Hollywood movies, people were scattering everywhere. Finally, with his gun emptied, and our fuel very low, we left for home.

Reviewing Vector's tape after the flight (he had had a FLIR pod on board), we found what I consider to be the best FLIR-recorded hit of the war. From any aircraft type. He had targeted a moving truck pulling a loaded trailer of some sort. As he pulled off after dropping his bomb, the video recorded his bombs impacting directly into the trailer. The hit and explosion were spectacular. I have since seen this particular run shown in at least a couple of different "war videos."

While cheering Vector's hits, we had a scare which sobered us up quickly. One of the officers from the MAG stopped by and asked where we had worked. He'd had news that there had been some Egyptian units north of Kuwait City and was concerned that they may have gotten mixed up or confused with Iraqi units and been targeted. Fortunately, as it turned out, the formations we had hit were indeed the enemy.

The problems I had been having with my master armament switch (all my own fault) were not unique to me or to the Hornet, or to any other aircraft. The F-16s had been having a problem with inadvertent launches of AIM-9 Sidewinders. The switchology in their cockpit was set up so that the same button was used to both drop bombs and launch missiles. If the aircraft was in the air-to-ground (bombing) mode, the button released bombs. If the aircraft was in the air-to-air mode, the button launched missiles. What happened more than a few times was that a Falcon pilot would release his bombs and pull up away from the target and start looking for enemy threats. In the intensity of the moment he often was still holding down the bomb-release button. When he switched back to the air-to-air mode to use his radar to look for enemy fighters, if he was still holding down the bomb-release button (now the missile-firing button), then *whoosh!* Mr. Sidewinder was on his way. Fortunately, there were no accidental shootdowns because of this. Just a few more prematurely gray Viper pilots.

That evening (still the twenty-sixth) I flew on Moto's wing on a killing box mission. For a number of reasons, this was one of the most memorable missions I flew. When we arrived over Kuwait it was dusk. And it was eerie. There were isolated thunderclouds, with lightning flashing to the ground and from cloud to cloud. The horizon was still orangey, darkening through red and purple, and finally dark blue high above. Above the smoke and clouds the air was crystalline clear, with the stars just beginning to show. The moon was a huge yellow ball, as bright as any I had ever seen. Accenting the dark sky were our own jets' formation and strip lighting. Below, the battlefield was black, punctuated by fires from the oil wells and flashes from all manner of weaponry. Fighter pilots don't usually get sentimentally goopy over the scenery, but this truly was the most extraordinary aerial panorama I had ever seen.

After splitting up and deconflicting by altitude, Moto and I went to work. The area we were working was again the main north-south highway, but farther up in northern Kuwait and southern Iraq. Immediately, I found a convoy of light armored vehicles headed north. I got a tremendous FLIR lock on one of the middle vehicles. With everything looking great, I dropped an MK 83 and waited for the explosion that would be my target. Passing over the top, I could see it was a six-wheeled armored vehicle.

And it stayed a six-wheeled armored vehicle. The bomb had missed. I could see debris from the explosion passing over the top of the vehicle from behind. Whether or not it hit one of the trailing vehicles, I don't know.

By the time I got turned around and set up again, the convoy was gone. Or more correctly, I couldn't find it. While the FLIR was a great piece of gear, it still required some amount of expertise to operate well. Not that I didn't have a great deal of expertise, but I still couldn't find the damned convoy.

The FLIR can, in fact, be dangerous, particularly at night. Gyro stabilized, the FLIR always presents a picture that's oriented upright, regardless of the attitude of the aircraft. Many are the pilots who have spent too much time staring at the FLIR video and have stopped flying the aircraft to find themselves nearly upside down, too close to the ground.

After chasing my tail for a circuit or two, I found a truck parked off the road. One pass, one bomb, and the truck went tumbling.

By now, both Moto and I were low on fuel. We tagged up and made our way to the tanker. It was still spookily beautiful at altitude. I could have made money with a picture of it all. It was incredibly clear above the clouds, dark purple, not yet black, with that big beautiful moon and lightning, manmade and natural, flashing below.

Fat on fuel, we dropped back down into the "battle-soup." Trolling up and down the highway, I found a tank situated in the middle of the northbound side. I don't know if it was there as a rear guard or to stem the flow of retreating Iraqis, but there it was. The dive and delivery were again flawless. I was excited, waiting for the explosion.

"Oooohhaaughhh!" An anguished me. The bomb flew right over the top of the tank, probably missing by no more than five or ten feet.

"What? Did you just miss?" Moto answered. He knew. He'd been there before.

"Yeah, I just missed a tank. Went right over the top."

"Ahh . . . I hate it when that happens."

We may as well have been playing pinball.

And that is very close to what we were doing. Playing a high-tech video game. Black as coal outside, yet technology put the whole battlefield literally at our fingertips.

After setting up for a second run, I tried a different mode of FLIR delivery. I wished that I hadn't. The hit was way off the mark. That was the first and last time I ever tried that mode. Finally, offsetting and bringing myself back around, I dove to drop my final bomb. Halfway down the chute, I realized that I wasn't targeting the same tank, but his buddy on the opposite side of the highway. No matter. In this situation one was as good as the other. Getting closer, I could see the dark exhaust from his running engine. I dropped the bomb and waited. Direct hit. The tank disappeared.

"Bull's-eye."

"Roger."

Moto and I joined and went home.

The next day, 27 February, was the last day in the war for marine Hornets. Vector and I were scheduled for a quick-turn, two sortie mission through Jubail. The war was going too well. Our first mission got canceled. We didn't wait around to find out if the second was going to get canned as well. What we did was almost akin to taking Dad's keys and sneaking off with the car. Except that the car had five MK 20 Rockeyes and a twenty-millimeter cannon. Actually, we didn't technically sneak off, but we didn't linger anywhere very long either.

Once airborne, we passed through all the controlling agencies without getting canceled but had to wait at a control point again. There just about literally was nowhere left to work. They were feeding most of us into the Bubiyan Island vicinity. On the border of Kuwait, Iraq, and Iran, the marshy island was uninhabited, but a significant number of enemy troops, with their equipment, had retreated through the area.

We teamed up with a FAC(A) over the island. The place was a graveyard of enemy equipment, most of it abandoned and undamaged. I dropped a pair of Rockeye on an artillery piece trailered to a truck. The Rockeye worked and the equipment was destroyed. A second run on a tank was more typical. The two canisters failed to open and dudded into the ground. To add insult to injury, the last Rockeye failed to even come off of my jet.

I don't remember that Vector had much better luck with his Rock-eye. So we switched over to the gun. There had been no enemy AAA or reaction of any kind. In fact, we saw no indication whatsoever that there was even anyone down there. This being the case, and with plenty of stuff for us to shoot at, the FAC(A) left us on our own.

With his gun, Vector set a tank smoking and then moved on to another. I worked two tanks over but wasn't able to set anything afire. I switched over to another truck and started it burning. Once we had emptied our guns, we joined, climbed, and headed for home. We had just left what was essentially the world's most realistic target training complex. Full of lucrative and varied targets and no one to shoot back.

Fifteen minutes after we landed, the skipper and his wingman touched down, and VMFA-451 was finished with the war.

Chapter Twenty-One
Awkward DFC

F or marine F/A-18 aviation, the war was almost over. There were, however, still a few missions to complete on 27 February before we could call it a game.

Late that afternoon Captain Bryant (his real name's Newell, but he doesn't use it) "Otis" Day and his wingman Captain Paul "Knife" Demers of VMFA-314 were northbound for a battlefield area interdiction (BAI) mission when they were informed by the DASC that an F-16 had been shot down. Their mission had now changed. They were needed to help with the Search and Rescue (SAR) effort to recover the downed pilot.

The procedures for coordinating and recovering a downed pilot are reviewed during every flight brief. It's done as a matter of course without much thought. Most of the time, thankfully, an SAR effort isn't required, and as each situation is different, only the very basics are covered during the brief. Pilots tend to hide behind the "it won't happen to me" curtain.

But it had happened, and now Otis and Knife, hearts in their throats, were busy rearranging their cockpits, kneeboard data, and mindset for the new mission. Otis takes it from here: "There was another section of aircraft airborne from a sister squadron, and I coordinated with them to come with us. Typical of a situation like this, it seemed that every agency or controller we talked to had a little bit of information on the situation, but nobody had the whole story. After about six frequency changes I was finally talking to 'Pointer,' an F-16 pilot who was airborne overhead the area of the crash serving as the on-scene commander."

The on-scene commander is the pilot of an aircraft who is generally at or near the site of the downed aircraft. His job is to help coordinate the rescue effort by controlling other aircraft at the scene, describing the enemy's disposition and ability to interdict the mission (for example, if the enemy is covering the area with too much fire), talking with the downed aircrew if he can, and coordinating with command and control authorities to get a rescue effort under way, among many other tasks. As the link in the chain with eyes on the scene, and the best real-time picture of what is happening, his job is crucial and extremely busy.

Otis continues:

Pointer passed the coordinates of the downed aircraft's location. It was near Basra, the last stronghold of the retreating Iraqi Republican Guard. Pointer also passed that the threat in the area was intense hand-held SAM activity and AAA, an SA-6, and perhaps SA-2s and SA-3s. The weather in the area was briefed as thunderstorms with extremely limited horizontal and vertical visibility due to smoke from the burning oil fields. The crummy weather became obvious as we neared the crash site.

As we approached, Pointer told us that he'd like us to concentrate our ordnance on the AAA along the rescue helo's proposed flight path. The idea was that we would help clear a AAA-free lane through which the helicopters could ingress and egress.

The weather was abysmal, with Mr. Murphy's thunderstorm right over the wreckage. As the clouds and smoke kept us from seeing anything yet, I asked Pointer for a visual description of the area. He replied that there was a main road running basically north to south. Not much of a description. In the desert there isn't a lot of terrain relief to work with. I decided we would come in from the north and use the road to help orient us. This would hopefully help us with the visibility as well, as it seemed there was less smoke to the north.

Because of how far north we were, close to three hundred miles from base, we were all low on gas before we even started down to attack. The section from our sister squadron had just enough fuel to make one run and leave, so they went down first. We orbited overhead at twenty-five thousand feet. Pointer was above us at thirty thousand feet.

Prior to commencing our descent through the weather I directed Knife to pick up a close parade position off of my aircraft. I didn't want him to lose sight of me on the way down and then have to worry about us running into each other. We flew to the north then commenced a spiral descent. The lower we got, the more the aural tones from our radar warning gear confirmed Pointer's threat brief. We were "lit up like Christmas trees." Finally the constant harangue from the warning gear was so bad that I couldn't stand it any longer and just turned the volume down.

Passing through eight thousand feet we finally cleared the clouds. While that was good, the visibility was still awful. Because of the smoke, weather, and overcast, and the fact that it was now late afternoon, it was nearly as dark as night. We couldn't even see the ground yet. I asked Pointer how low we needed to go before we would be able to see the ground. His answer surprised me. He didn't know. He hadn't been down to take a look yet. Evidently he had relieved the previous on-scene commander at altitude and hadn't had the opportunity to go down and see for himself yet. Helpfully, though, he again pointed out that the reported anti-aircraft fire was very heavy and that we should be careful. I radioed the other section that we had sent down earlier, and they relayed that we should be able to start seeing well enough to operate at about two thousand feet, though they hadn't been able to find any wreckage. They had struck the first reasonable target they found and departed.

Right after this conversation, AAA tracers ripped literally right between Knife and me. Unbelievably, neither one of us was hit. Knife immediately pulled away.

A wingman in close formation has most of his attention directed at his lead and is unable to look around for threats or to operate his own weapons. Additionally, the lead is unable to execute any hard maneuvers for fear of running into his wingman.

Otis goes on:

I told Knife to go into a "fighter-wing" position so that he could maneuver and keep a lookout while we looked for the crash site. Several minutes went by as we jinked all over the place avoiding AAA and hand-held SAMs while we looked for the crash. I was scared to death. Sometime during all of this Knife and I lost sight of each other. It was very dark and disorienting down there.

Finally I found the road, and soon after, the wreckage. Pointer called us and said that the helos were going to be coming from the west. Under normal conditions, Knife and I would have executed coordinated attacks with one aircraft providing lookout and cover as the other attacked. These weren't normal conditions. Our mutual support was limited to encouragement over the radio.

My game plan was fairly simple now. I directed Knife to attack anything he could find from the area of the target extending west. I did the same. Making several attacks, I dropped some Rockeye on a AAA site which finally stopped firing. Knife had a more difficult time as he was loaded with MK 83s and needed to get more altitude to ensure his bombs would fuse and explode. He made it work, though, and silenced and got good secondaries off of another AAA site.

During this time the anti-aircraft fire had intensified. I had called Knife several times over the radio and gotten no response. Either we were getting jammed or in his excitement he wasn't hearing and answering me. I started to get panicky. "Great," I thought, "now I've gotten my wingman killed." Finally, though, he answered. His voice sounded just like I'm sure mine did. Squeaky. He relayed that "shit was coming up from everywhere" and that "he was getting the fuck out of here . . . now!" I couldn't agree fast enough. We both made one more run, dropped the last of our ordnance and started a climb for home.

I radioed Pointer that we were out of gas and headed home. Actually, we didn't have enough gas to get back to Shaikh Isa. We would have to stop in Jubail. I also told him that the crash site was way too "hot" and told him to direct AWACS not to send the helicopters in. There was no way that they were going to be able to get in and out of there safely.

Knife and I were able to rejoin somewhere in between thunderstorms. As we made our way to Jubail we were told that the helos had been shot down. It was sunset and raining when we touched down. We had less than five minutes of fuel remaining.

One of the survivors from one of the helicopters was Major Rhonda L. Cornum, a female flight surgeon who had jumped aboard in case medical assistance was required during the rescue. Both of her arms were broken in the crash, and she was subsequently captured and brutalized by the Iraqis before she was repatriated at the cessation of hostilities. Interestingly, Otis met her after the war while he was serving in an air force unit as an exchange pilot at Eglin Air Force Base. They were seated together at a dinner when the conversation drifted to the war and the connection was made. She had written a book about her experience and confirmed Otis's warning about the "hot" crash site.

Otis also had the opportunity to talk with the downed F-16 pilot after the war. He had actually been captured fairly soon after ejecting from his aircraft. During the evolution Otis describes, the Iraqis were literally holding a gun to his head. Evidently the exploding bombs, anti-aircraft fire, and noise from the jets, along with everything else that was going on, made for a very unnerving spectacle. Indeed, with the unlucky pilot already captured, it would seem that the entire SAR effort was a futile exercise unless the plan was to wrest him away from the enemy (doubtful).

There were less than ten Distinguished Flying Crosses (DFCs) awarded to the marine pilots out of Shaikh Isa. Otis was awarded one for this mission. In his own words he feels "awkward wearing the award because I know that there are others who should have one as well, who do not." His wingman Knife, he feels, certainly deserves it as much as he. Otis, like most of us, realizes that there was heroic work during the war that went unrecognized. And there is probably an instance or two where unwarranted awards were given. Awards were a touchy subject, as the process appeared to be inconsistent and seemingly took forever. But that is hardly an observation unique to this conflict.

Additionally, a great deal of the "awkwardness" stems from the fact that the mission was not a success. Not only was the pilot not rescued, but additional lives were lost during the SAR effort. It was a bitter, hard loss. Indeed, a medal for his heroics was the farthest thing from his mind. At the time, he thought he was going to be reprimanded for recklessly endangering his flight. However, his part of the effort was recognized for what it was: a selfless act carried out at great risk with little concern for his own safety, so that a fellow countryman might be saved. The award was made only after an exhaustive review, including statements from a number of officers from both services, confirmed his worthiness.

He should wear it with pride.

Chapter Twenty-Two
Let's Go Home

We were done, though at the time we didn't know it for sure. To a man, I believe, we wanted to pursue Saddam's army all the way to Baghdad. But that wasn't going to happen. Having achieved our objective, President Bush was going to make good on his promise to bring U.S. troops home as quickly as possible. Within ten days, I was chest deep in preparations to get the unit packed and ready to go home.

There wasn't much for us to do after the cessation of hostilities. A few days after the war the MAG lost two Hornets from VMFA-212, one of the Hawaii squadrons, in a training accident. They had been flying air-to-air intercepts as part of a four-ship evolution. Two of them had collided and gone down.

There are training rules designed to prevent this type of accident, but occasionally situational awareness just breaks down and the odds work against you. Nearly every one of us could picture ourselves falling victim to the same sort of accident on a bad day. It was just such a tremendous shame that we had gotten so far—all the way from the United States, through five months of CAPs and training and a month and a half of war—only to end up losing two perfectly good aircraft in a very unfortunate yet preventable accident. This was the worst day we spent in Bahrain.

Thankfully, both pilots ejected safely and were recovered relatively unscathed. After the accident, flying, for all practical purposes, was stopped, and we only got airborne once before we went home. Much like when we had left Beaufort, the jets were again being groomed. This time for the trip home. We were to get them airborne and exercised and ensure that they were free of maintenance problems.

This exercise flight provided us with a unique opportunity. We were going to fly up to Kuwait for an aerial sightseeing tour. Most of us were anxious to take a leisurely look at the battlefield without having to worry about all the risks associated with combat.

In Bahrain, 250 miles south of the burning oil fields, the smoke had been bad. But airborne now, approaching the border, we encountered a weather phenomenon completely foreign to all of us. A huge, ill-defined black cloud lay before our jets. We tucked tightly together to punch through it, turning our formation lights on full bright to help our wingmen keep sight. It was eerie. The darkness was blacker than any thunderstorm, yet the turbulence and violence associated with storm clouds was missing. Smooth, dark, and vertigo-inducing, with the only illumination coming from our formation lights and a thin glow from the sun trying to power through the sludge from above.

In a short time we came out the other side. There were other oil clouds downwind from other burning oil fields, but there was enough wind that large areas of the country were clear and we were able to drop down for a good look. Yes, there was a lot of damage. The oil-well fires in particular. Burned hulks and battlefield debris were everywhere. But already, in only a couple of weeks, some of the evidence of the conflict was starting to fade. The trenches were

Over an oil storage facility in Kuwait after the Gulf War. Notice the haze from the oil fires. *[Photo by Michael Garrison]*

no longer sharp-lined and well maintained; ever constant blowing sand had already softened the edges and started to fill them in. Many of the bomb craters were no longer black and ugly sores but were also starting to fade and fill. Some were no more than shallow depressions, or dimples, in the desert floor. (I was deployed to Kuwait for two weeks in 1994. Virtually all evidence of the war was invisible from above. Except for scattered "dumps" where debris had been collected, there was very little to indicate the carnage of three years earlier.)

One very striking sight was the enormous quantities of shattered glass. Particularly along the hard-hit highways. As we flew along and our position changed relative to the sun, we were dazzled by the sparkling reflections of millions of tiny shards of glass, all of which had come from the blown-out windows of destroyed vehicles.

We made several low-formation passes over encampments of our own cheering troops. Anxious to go home, many of them were living in abysmal conditions. Still living out in the field, but this time under the acrid clouds of burning oil. The smoke from the burned petroleum left a grungy soot over bodies, clothes, everything. There was no escape. Now, four years later, many point to this smoke as a contributor, or perhaps even source, of the poorly understood Persian Gulf syndrome.

Finally, "mission complete," we formed up and made our way through the smoke and back to Bahrain. Once on deck, the jets were parked until we left for home. My only regret concerning this flight was that none of us had thought to bring along a camera and so missed an opportunity we would never be presented again.

Mostly we sat around and waited to go home. There was a lot of frustration as we waited for word on when we would depart. Much like the trip over, we were passed a dozen different versions of our itinerary home. To alleviate the boredom, we spent a good deal of time in town shopping for gold, rugs, and other souvenirs. The Bahraini rug merchants proved to be nearly as worthy an adversary as the Iraqis had been. Certainly more savvy.

Bull Durham's wife had sent him a little thirteen-inch color television with a built-in VCR. The bunkhouse instantly turned into a movie house. At any one time, there were at least twenty of us crouched around that damned little TV, glassy-eyed, spit drooling out of half-open mouths, adrift in the movie, and wishing ourselves thousands of miles away. Since there was virtually no flying, there was little to keep us occupied. I saw more movies in that three-week period than I had seen in the previous ten years. Some of them over and over again. How may times can a man watch *The Terminator* before the process ceases to be entertainment and instead becomes masochism?

As the day of our departure neared, I was excited that I would be flying a jet home rather than riding back in a "tube," as we called the commercial air transports. But that excitement soon turned into mixed emotions. The boys going home on the chartered airliners were going to go home three days earlier. I couldn't stand it. Just my luck. Well, at least I was going to look like a hero when I crawled out of that fighter, rather than a travel-weary businessman stepping out of an airliner.

The last few days in Bahrain were miserable. Except for me, the

Bunkhouse was empty. The rest of the boys had gone home on the military charter. No Z-Man to paw through my chow or steal my blankets. Hatch wasn't there to pick on. And I missed startling Lurch out of his blissful slumbers. Everyone was gone. Even Bull and his little TV. I almost got teary eyed as I shuffled around the room, straightening the furniture and sweeping the dust bunnies out from under everyone's bed (those things *really do* reproduce). We had lived and warred together for so long that I felt very lonely without them. But thankfully everyone was still alive. Of course, I had been invited to room with some of the other remaining pilots, but the idea seemed traitorous to me. A Bunkhouse Boy to the end. That and of course I was way too lazy to pack my gear up and move it to another room.

Finally the big day arrived. April Fool's Day. It may have been, and we may have been, but at least we were April Fools on our way home. With our jets stuffed with all sorts of goodies we would never declare through U.S. Customs, we blasted off from the tiny island. So anxious were we to go home that we didn't even make the customary circuit around the field before heading for Spain. I remember making a conscious effort to turn almost all the way around in my seat for a last long look at our desert home.

The initial portion of the trip went smoothly, with aerial refuelings from KC-135s all the way across the Arabian Peninsula, the Red Sea, Egypt, and the Mediterranean.

We were about one hundred miles west of Sicily when it happened. Vector came up on the radio.

"Skipper, Vector."

"Go ahead." Scotty sounded like he'd just woke up.

"Yes sir, I've got a left engine oil pressure caution. Everything looks okay. I think it's just a bad transmitter."

"Hmmm . . . maybe, but I want you to divert into Sig [Sigonella Naval Air Station in Sicily]." Better safe than sorry was what he was thinking. It wouldn't look too good to have gotten twelve jets and eighteen pilots through the war and then lose one to simple mechanical failure.

Here it came. I knew it was coming. I could feel it in every cell of my body.

"Guinness." It was the skipper. "I want you to follow him back."

Damn! My heart sank. Even though Vector was the CO's wingman, it wouldn't do for the commanding officer to separate from his squadron. I was the logical choice to escort Vector back. And I was crushed. It could take days to get parts and people to fix his jet. And who knew when another tanker would be available to drag our two sorry asses home? I could picture my wife and children now. Standing on the flight line in Beaufort looking for Daddy. But Daddy wouldn't be there.

I was resigned to the task and followed Vector into Sigonella. If nothing else, we got to see some Italian F-104s when we landed (antiques by our standards—relics of the 1950s).

After parking our jets, we scrambled around the flight line looking for anyone with expertise on Hornet engines and the parts to put that expertise to work. No go. The best of them knew which end was the front and which was the back. And if they had parts they weren't admitting it. Finally, with no other recourse, we decided to try the "magic" Hornet maintenance fix.

The F/A-18 is reliant on electronics to an extent that few other aircraft even approach. Sometimes the system hiccups, burps, or otherwise gets clogged (I know that this isn't what happens in technical terms) and one or more components will stop working. The electrons zig when they should be zagging. Many times the problem can be cleared by removing and reapplying electrical power. Or better, shutting the jet down, then starting it up.

We had already shut the jet down. After checking his engine to make certain he really was not experiencing any oil pressure problems, Vector climbed back in to try his magic touch. He started it, cycled the generators once or twice, and . . . voila! His oil pressure gauge was working like a champ. I almost kissed him, but boys don't touch boys.

After arranging to get our jets refueled, we dashed over to base operations to file a flight plan. We wanted to make it to Rota before dark. Checking the charts, we decided that the distance was close to the limits of our range, but that we'd be able to manage it if nothing went wrong. We grabbed an international flight plan with which we were only vaguely familiar, and after a whole lot of head scratching, finally had it filled out well enough that the flight planning clerk would accept it.

While we were messing with the paperwork a navy commander in some sort of official capacity cornered us.

"I know you boys have been having jet problems," he said, "and I'm not going to let you out of here unless I have your total assurance that your birds are in good shape. I'm not going to let a little 'get-home-itis' get the best of you. We can't afford to lose you or your jets."

It was a nice sentiment, but it was wasted on us. At that point we would have told him we wanted to join the navy if that's what he'd wanted to hear. He settled, however, for some half-truths and white lies, and soon we were back at our aircraft.

Not good. A young seaman was wrestling with a fifty-gallon drum, nearly full, that had been placed under the tail of my jet. During refueling a valve had stuck open and dumped fuel all over the place. I hurried him out of the way, assuring him that the valve would close just as soon as I started my engines and that, no, the fuel in the drum wouldn't explode sitting so close to my engine exhaust. I had to get out of there before the commander saw what was going on. "Get-home-itis," hell. That sounded like itchy skin or something. What I had was a full-blown plague.

In record time Vector and I were strapped in, engines on line, jets ready to go. The valve really did shut. We made our way to the runway and were soon airborne.

The trip to Rota went fairly well, aside from a little difficulty dealing with a bunch of controllers with really fake sounding accents (Italian, French, and Spanish). They needed to watch more movies. I did get a little concerned about the fuel. Even though we were carrying three external tanks, they didn't give us as much an improvement in range as one might expect. The tanks are heavy and create a lot of drag. The jet burns a lot of fuel just carrying them around. The more you carry, the more you need. Kind of a law of diminishing returns. Of course, the best way to use them is to jettison them when they are empty, but expense and other concerns preclude that in peacetime. Ever during the war we didn't have the luxury of an endless supply of fuel tanks.

Anyway, we finally arrived safely in Rota and were quickly reunited with the rest of the fighting Warlords. For some reason, Train insisted that it was an ironclad tradition that when in Rota, you drank White Russians. Well, we traditioned ourselves halfway into a coma, celebrating for all the obvious reasons.

Two days later, we were on our way again. This trip went as smooth as silk. We were traveling west with the sun, so unlike the trip over, we didn't need to take off in the middle of the night to ensure that it would still be daylight when we landed. As we approached the U.S. coastline and made contact with American air traffic controllers, we received treatment I had never had before or since. They asked us if we were coming home from the war. Learning that we were, they literally cleared the skies ahead, informing each passing airliner that if they looked out their left (or right) side, they could see a flight of "true American Heroes" just coming back from the desert. It was like being on a celebrity home tour. I think we all sat a little taller in the cockpit.

Finally reaching Beaufort, we did a formation Victory flyby, then broke up into three flights to land. A welcome celebration with guest speakers, bleachers, banners, and so on, had been prepared. It was nice, but all we really wanted was to rush into the crowd to find our families. We weren't allowed. We waited about an hour until our sister squadron, VMFA-333, landed, then started and taxied our jets in close formation almost right up to the bleachers. After crawling out we took our parts in a gathering that included all the Gulf War veterans from the air station.

The speakers were merciful. The ceremony lasted less than half an hour. At the dismissal of the formation there was a crushing scramble as loved ones sought each other, one crowd stumbling out of the stands, the other running from the flight line.

It's hard to describe a reunion like this. And it's probably different for each person. For me it was probably the most wonderful single moment of my life. Monica, I, and our girls embraced in one big, awkward, lovely hug. The release of tension, worry, and anxiety I felt was almost physical. I didn't realize until that instant that I had been carrying such an emotional burden. It had been so long. For no reason, and for many reasons, everyone started to cry. We were together, and safe. And happy. Finally.

Tragically, many families, enemy and allied alike, would never share such a joyful reunion.

Chapter Twenty-Three
After the Ball Lessons Learned

The Iraqi army had been utterly routed, crushed, and embarrassed. Like us, I'm sure that at the cessation of hostilities, many of our ground counterparts had been straining at the tether, anxious to finish off the retreating Iraqi army. Few would argue that we could not have continued into Iraq and taken it as well; though admittedly, it would probably have come at a dearer price than Kuwait.

But technically, we had achieved all of our objectives. Saddam was out of Kuwait. We had succeeded beyond anyone's wildest dreams. We had no mandate to proceed any further. So we "got" while the "gittin'" was good.

There was also the "balance of power" argument. Some said that a too badly weakened Iraq would cause instability in the region, particularly with regard to Iran. I'm no political science expert, but the place doesn't seem particularly stable now, and it certainly wasn't stable prior to the conflict. It seems to me that had we removed Saddam from power and put someone else in his place, the region would be no less stable than it is now. Certainly there would be no embargo on the country, as there is now, with all the suffering it has caused. But again, I'm no diplomatic guru with a fifty-pound head. I have trouble negotiating the TV remote away from my wife. Additionally, over five years later, I'm writing with the benefit of hindsight.

I've not made much of a secret of my contempt for the Iraqi military. The maintenance and employment of their weaponry was abysmal. Their training was wholly inadequate, and their motivation, if it existed at all, was certainly not up to the task. They certainly had the equipment they needed to put up a fierce resistance. Huge caches of ammo and supplies, and a great deal of serviceable equipment, were found abandoned. Had those weapons been manned by troops from any of a number of different countries, our task would have been much more difficult. General Schwarzkopf had gone so far as to say that we could have swapped weapons with them and still have won. Their war-fighting capability against a well-trained adversary was nil.

How badly did we maul them? How much equipment was destroyed? How many of the enemy did we kill? Pick a number. Between the stuff we passed as our own battle damage assessment, what was passed by the FAC(A)s, what was confirmed or discounted by satellite imagery, and what was fired upon again by invading ground forces and double counted, it is impossible to tell with any precision. There are numbers out there, but having seen our Intelligence effort in action, I question their exactness. The bottom line was that the air war crushed much of the enemy's ability and will to resist, making the task for our ground brethren easier and saving a good many lives. In short, our air power did what was required of it, and more.

For the first time in history, air power came close to fulfilling Douhet's prediction that future wars would be won or lost almost wholly in the air. Iraqi forces were so shattered and demoralized by the weeks of aerial bombardment that their resistance to the ground assault, when it finally came, was far short of what it would have been had they not been so badly mauled from the air. Had allied leaders been ruthless and subjected the major population centers to wholesale bombardment, including civilian targets, I am certain that the withdrawal of Iraqi forces from Kuwait would have been quickly negotiated. Air power alone could have achieved the strategic objective, though at a moral price. Imagine the awful carnage of a carpet-bombed Baghdad. Or better yet, read about the horror of firebombed Japanese and German cities during World War II.

Having said that, it still needs to be remembered that a strong army (and Marine Corps!) is an absolute requirement. Aircraft can smash the enemy, but they can't physically take his territory.

When I was a young lieutenant, all of our combat expertise resided in that fast-dwindling group of pilots who had flown in Vietnam. Many of the lessons brought home from that conflict influenced, and still influence, the way we make war now.

Big picture, we learned what a demoralizing and debilitating effect political meddling in the day-to-day business of warfare can have. In Vietnam, so many restrictions and rules of engagement were placed on our military that the enemy was able to wage the war on his own terms—when and where he wanted, with safe haven into which he could retreat. For instance, U.S. warplanes were forbidden to bomb dikes in North Vietnam. The resultant flooding would have displaced and ravaged the civilian populace. Consequently, the North Vietnamese moved anti-aircraft artillery atop the dikes. The military leaders in the Persian Gulf did not have their hands tied nearly so much. There is no doubt that this was a major contributing factor to our success.

On a tactical level, the boys in Vietnam learned a long list of lessons. For instance, they learned that massed AAA is a far greater threat than radar-guided SAMs. That truth held out during the Gulf War. Additionally, they found out the hard way that a jet engine that smokes is going to allow the enemy pilot to visually acquire friendly fighters from a very long range. With this comes a tremendous situational awareness advantage for the foe. None of the U.S. fighters in the gulf had engines that smoked. These are but a couple of items on a very long list of lessons that still influence combat aviation today.

What did *we* learn in *this* conflict? First, the investment of billions
of dollars in sophisticated weapons systems paid off in spades. Never
again should anyone seriously raise the quality over quantity argument. The superiority of our systems over the Iraqi gear, much of it
Russian made, was unquestioned. There is little doubt that even had
they been outnumbered two, or even three, to one, the U.S. fighters
would have prevailed. This should quiet the naysayers who used to
point with alarm to the numerical superiority of Warsaw Pact nations
relative to NATO's air forces.

Also, the value of the Maritime Prepositioned Force, until the war
an unproven concept, was validated. Though it hadn't functioned
perfectly, the bottom line was that equipment and troops were married up and ready for combat in an acceptable period of time.

The immense demand for troops and equipment to be moved
quickly and in strength from the United States and other theaters highlighted the shortcomings in our nation's maritime lift assets. Many
times we were told that our badly needed parts, bombs, Archie comics,
or whatever were dead in the water somewhere between Southwest
Asia and the States, aboard a broken-down freighter or container ship.
The shortage of bombs due to such ships had gotten very serious at
times. Allowed to deteriorate badly following World War II, this facet
of our strategic capability has since been reinvigorated by increased
funding and attention. Still, for all the shortfalls, it must be noted that
nearly 95 percent of all the material moved into theater was sealifted.

The air force's ability to airlift men and material was stretched
to the limit and also highlighted the need for more, and more modern, transport aircraft. The C-141s used then, and still the backbone
of the service's heavy lift capability, are operating under restrictions
as they continue to age. The giant C-5s aren't getting any newer
either. Currently, the C-17 program designed to lead the way for
heavy lift into the next century is just starting to make an operational
impact. Accusations of shoddy accounting, poor design, ever-increas-
ing costs, and questionable performance nearly kept this aircraft
from reaching operational status and have put further acquisition on

slippery footing. It's interesting to note that the C-17, like the F/A-18, is also a McDonnell Douglas product.

Tactical lessons learned were many. Our lack of jet photo recon capability, for prestrike intelligence and poststrike BDA as close to a "must" as it gets, was a serious handicap. The photo recon pallet for the Hornet has been promised, repromised, and diddled about for so long that its mere mention elicits a snort of contempt from those who have been around for any length of time. This capability is only just now reaching the fleet five years after the war.

Previously suspected, but never validated on a large scale, was the effectiveness of small, man-portable SAMs: they were numerous and deadly. There was the difficulty in employing Rockeye at high altitude, and there was the effectiveness of the twenty-millimeter cannon. Many novel and successful methods of employing the FLIR were developed. The list goes on and on.

All of these factors and more relate to marine aviation in a broad way, but the most important lesson we brought back from the war was the undeniable fact that marine aviation works. Outstandingly maintained and capable aircraft were airborne in the numbers required, on time, and were delivering bombs on target, or fulfilling other missions as directed, in a professional fashion. The marines were providing sorties in quantities disproportionate (far greater) to their presence in theater. On top of that, those missions were delivered at a cost significantly below that of both the air force and navy. Our bases aren't pretty, and our troops don't receive a lot of the frills, but we deliver the goods and we're inexpensive (not "cheap," as that word intimates low in quality as well as in price).

In fact, where the Hornet was concerned, though one would have never guessed it from the media coverage, marine units flew more bombing sorties than the navy. And marine tactical aviation delivered more tonnage per aircraft than any other service, including the air force. This is amazing when one considers that most of the population doesn't even realize that the Marine Corps operates jets.

On a personal level, I don't know that the war caused many of us lingering problems. Certainly I've not heard of anyone suffering from any sort of post-traumatic stress syndrome. Not many of us have been waking up in terror during the middle of the night. Our experience generally wasn't like the horrors of earlier conflicts. Likewise, I've no knowledge of any marines from Shaikh Isa suffering from the still mysterious (if it exists at all) Persian Gulf syndrome.

Marriages, though, did suffer. There were a lot of divorces across the board. Officers, enlisted men and women, pilots, mechanics—it didn't matter. Marital strife is no stranger to the military. It's part and parcel of a lifestyle that takes husbands and wives away from home for half a year or more at a time. It's an ugly part of military life and it never gets any easier. Perhaps the hardest and most emotionally wrenching part of military service involves dealing with just the normal day-to-day problems of married life. Not easy from thousands of miles away. Throw in some bigger problems (everyone has them sooner or later), and performance and morale will start to sag. Imagine hearing secondhand that your wife is sleeping with the next-door neighbor. You're six thousand miles away and won't be able to even get to a phone for three weeks. Not to worry. You can sort it out when you get home in six months. And there's always the mail. Some guys get physically sick. The problem will only worsen as the United States continues to cut forces while it extends commitments abroad.

Professionally, those of us who went to the war probably have an edge on those who didn't. Though the Marine Corps made a special effort to assure those who didn't participate that they wouldn't be discriminated against in terms of promotions or selection to choice billets, I don't think it was very convincing. It's a very tough nut to crack, and frustrating for those who didn't go. For instance, there are idiots who went to the war. They are still idiots. But on paper, because of the war, they look better than some folks who are actually much more capable but are not Gulf War veterans. I believe that this is a chief reason, among many others, that people left or are leaving the service. Though now, five years later, most of the fallout has already occurred.

A more superficial but still sensitive issue was the bag full of ribbons and medals that the typical pilot ended up with. Prior to the war, an average fourteen-year major might have been authorized to wear four or five ribbons. Yet after the war, there were four-year first lieutenants who looked like medal-bedecked Third World generals. Small potatoes in the big scheme of things, but enough to start an itch of resentment. Everywhere, one could find a certain professional envy toward those who went from those who didn't. I'm proud to say, however, that I never saw it manifested in an ugly fashion.

Finally, what about the jet? No one could argue that the Hornet hadn't performed marvelously. Its sortie rates, maintainability, accuracy, and versatility were truly outstanding. Yes, F/A-18s had gotten hit, and the navy had even lost one—officially to a SAM, unofficially to an AA-6 fired from an Iraqi MIG-25 (two more navy F/A-18s were lost not in combat but due to pilot error). But of all the major fighter and attack types participating in the conflict, few flew as many sorties and had a lower loss rate due to enemy action. The other U.S. aircraft with a similar mission and performance, the F-16, had a much higher loss rate (remember, the F-16 has only a single engine). And they weren't even used down low to strafe.

So why did the F/A-18 have such a low loss rate? A big chunk of credit goes to the tactics and protective measures discussed earlier. But another big chunk should go to the airframe itself. After all, the jet was flown into some of the deadliest anti-air barrages of the war. First, the airframe is fast and not overly large. Second, the jet was designed with survivability in mind. The two hydraulic systems, which power just about everything, are independently driven, multiredundant, and widely separated. The flight control system is also multiredundant, being four-channeled and operated by two different computers. One of the biggest saving graces, as evidenced by three separate heat-seeking SAM hits, is the far aft location of the engine exhaust, well back from most of the jet's other systems. A shot in the "turkey feathers" was not enough to bring the jet down. Finally, the cockpit was designed so that the pilot could operate the aircraft as required and still look out the window. That window being a super canopy design that permitted good visibility in all directions. For all of this, Hornet drivers everywhere owe a hearty thank-you to the design teams of McDonnell Douglas and Northrop.

Afterword

wrote this book from a soda-straw perspective (me, me, me). Actually, I concentrated generally on my own squadron's activities with particular (and selfish) emphasis on my own. My participation was neither more nor less spectacular than that of the majority of the other Hornet drivers on the base. Over five thousand F/A-18 missions were flown out of Shaikh Isa, and I'm sure that there are many more great stories. (Having said that, I would never hold our achievements up to the heroic exploits of those who in earlier conflicts fought much more deadly adversaries.)

I am not an expert on the other aspects of the air war, but I believe I have written the first treatment of marine Hornet action in the conflict. Our activities, particularly after the first week or so, were confined mostly to the skies over Kuwait and southern Iraq. Though I didn't make much mention of their participation, the navy and air force also did a great amount of work in the area.

I have been critical of much that I saw. Many will say that I don't understand the intricacies and machinations germane to the problems I noted. I don't deny that. Still, the shortcomings were there.

But the problems were only a very small part of an overwhelming success. This conflict was an affirmation of the course our leaders, military and civilian, charted for us in terms of training, equipment, and structure. An affirmation as well of our most important asset: our people. I am proud of what we did, and who and what we are.

Appendix
Shaikh Isa Murfeez Laws (Abridged)

1. If you walk late for your CAP mission, you will have aircraft problems on start up.
2. The longer your CAP period is, the less fuel you'll have.
3. If there is an attractive woman on base (there isn't), she will be your wife's sister.
4. If you actually have to eat an MRE, someone will have already rat-fucked (stolen) the chocolate nutcake out of it.
5. The longest distance between two points is the distance from you to the tanker.
6. The tanker is capable of supersonic flight when he is headed away from you.
7. The tanker is always off-station as scheduled.
8. The tanker is never on-station as scheduled.
9. The tanker is always flown by the load master.
10. The tanker always seeks, and finds, the rough air.
11. The tanker will always maneuver so as to put the sun directly in your eyes.

12. Everyone will always have more flight time and better sorties than you.
13. You will always have more nighttime and tower ODO watches than everyone else.
14. The group CO can be recognized by his logbook. His monthly flight time will be double that of the next highest man.
15. The individual with the brown spot in his flight suit and the panicked expression on his face has misplaced his nine-millimeter pistol and can't find it.
16. You never leave shit stains in the slit trench/toilet. Everybody else does.
17. Everyone has imagined themselves downing seven MIGs in the FEZ and everyone has forgotten to enable their AIM-9 coolant.
18. You will remember to check if your missiles tuned when you are recovering from Point India to the field.
19. If you spend thirty minutes copying the day's code words, you won't need them.
20. If you do not copy the day's code words, you will need them, and the general will be on your wing.
21. If the general is on your wing, something will go wrong.
22. If there is a guard shack within five miles of the general, he will run into it.
23. If you carry your gas mask with you nine days out of ten, you will be gassed on the tenth.
24. Everyone, even you, has imagined himself deftly dispatching rabid terrorists with his trusty nine-millimeter pistol.
25. Everyone, even you, has masturbated since they've gotten here.
26. Everyone, even you, will deny that they've masturbated since they've gotten here.
27. Behind every meal served with chicken, there is a man with a chain saw covered with feathers.
28. The dollar-dinar rate of exchange is whatever they hand you. You'll never figure it out anyway.
29. The ATO will disappear when you most need to see it. No matter; when you find it you won't be able to read or understand it.
30. No squadron is as good as yours and no other squadron gets as many raw deals. No matter what squadron you're in.

About the Author

An Indiana native, Jay Stout was born in 1959. After graduating from Purdue University in 1981, he was commissioned a second lieutenant in the Marine Corps and soon after earned his naval aviator's wings. In a career that has included assignments in both the F-4 Phantom and the F/A-18 Hornet, he has amassed more than 4,300 flight hours.

Major Stout resides in San Diego, California, with his wife, Monica, and his daughters, Kristen and Katherine.

The **Naval Institute Press** is the book-publishing arm of the U.S. Naval Institute, a private, nonprofit, membership society for sea service professionals and others who share an interest in naval and maritime affairs. Established in 1873 at the U.S. Naval Academy in Annapolis, Maryland, where its offices remain today, the Naval Institute has members worldwide.

Members of the Naval Institute support the education programs of the society and receive the influential monthly magazine *Proceedings* and discounts on fine nautical prints and on ship and aircraft photos. They also have access to the transcripts of the Institute's Oral History Program and get discounted admission to any of the Institute-sponsored seminars offered around the country.

The Naval Institute also publishes *Naval History* magazine. This colorful bimonthly is filled with entertaining and thought-provoking articles, first-person reminiscences, and dramatic art and photography. Members receive a discount on *Naval History* subscriptions.

The Naval Institute's book-publishing program, begun in 1898 with basic guides to naval practices, has broadened its scope in recent years to include books of more general interest. Now the Naval Institute Press publishes about 100 titles each year, ranging from how-to books on boating and navigation to battle histories, biographies, ship and aircraft guides, and novels. Institute members receive discounts of 20 to 50 percent on the Press's nearly 600 books in print.

Full-time students are eligible for special half-price membership rates. Life memberships are also available.

For a free catalog describing Naval Institute Press books currently available, and for further information about subscribing to *Naval History* magazine or about joining the U.S. Naval Institute, please write to:

Membership Department
U.S. Naval Institute
118 Maryland Avenue
Annapolis, MD 21402-5035
Telephone: (800) 233-8764
Fax: (410) 269-7940
Web address: www.usni.org